What [illegible]

"My response is overwh[illegible]*can be used for small group studies,* [illegible] *nd seminars or even 10-week semina*[illegible]

—A.C., Australia

"If we had the SSTS materials in my time we would have had help to exist as persecuted Christians."

—A seventy-six-year-old pastor, interred for ten years, Soviet Gulag, Russia

"I had tears in my eyes as I read the SSTS manual. Please convey my appreciation to Open Doors for writing this material...."

—Z.M., Dagestan

"Thanks to Open Doors for the privilege of working on SSTS...the group process, the discussions and dynamics have been particularly enjoyable and stimulating. Persecution of Christians is relevant and real for us today in Australia. The entire process of evaluating the material was submitted to God in prayer.... We sincerely pray for the book's success."

—Anne Horton, leader of women's Bible study group, Australia

"If I had the SSTS material earlier, I would have been better prepared for the persecution in the past. Now the problem we face in this area is that Christians are very old or very young. The middle-aged members left for America chasing the green dollars...."

—Pastor "Alexander," Russia. [For security reasons, in some instances we have used pseudonyms or initials of people's names.]

"The world is changing rapidly. We need to do more preventive work like teaching SSTS, rather than stepping in after the crisis begins—or is over.... The Persecuted Church needs to 'share its blessings' with the free church, and send missionaries to other countries to help them prepare by evangelism and training."

—Rev. Carlin Weinhauer, Canada

"This has been timely and most encouraging. I was feeling defeated in my ministry, but the Holy Spirit used the SSTS seminar to lift my spirit!"

—Pastor B., Uzbekistan

"Remove the fear of dying and you become fearless as an evangelist. The fear of death is the root of all fear. Everybody wants to go to Heaven but nobody wants to die."

—Comment during a discussion at a SSTS seminar in Central Asia

"The hardest passage for me to exercise in all of Scripture is when our Lord said: 'Father, forgive them, for they do not know what they are doing.' The radical fundamentalists who torched my church and burned my home and killed my children did know what they were doing. But the teaching on forgiveness has helped me. Please tell Christians in free societies not to say, 'It will never happen here!'"

—Pastor at SSTS seminar in Ambon, Indonesia

"Thank you for teaching us how to stand strong. God spoke to me a lot through this seminar. I was afraid to die but not any more.... I have peace to go and spread God's Word."

—SSTS translator, Uzbekistan

"The SSTS teaching provided us with lessons that will last the rest of our lives."

—Pastor, Caucasus region

STANDING STRONG THROUGH THE STORM

Compiled by Paul Estabrooks and Jim Cunningham

Open*Doors*
Serving persecuted **Christians** worldwide

P.O. Box 27001
Santa Ana, CA 92799
U.S.A.

Telephone: 1-949-752-6600
Fax: 1-949-752-6536
E: odidev@od.org
I: www.od.org

ISBN: 0-901644-20-X

Other Scripture quotations taken from:

KJV *King James Version*
LB *Living Bible* (Wheaton, IL: Tyndale House Publishers, 1979).
Msg *The Message* (Colorado Springs: Navpress, 1993).
NCV *New Century Version* (Dallas: Word Bibles, 1991).
NKJV *New King James Version* (Nashville: Thomas Nelson, Inc., 1983).
NLT *New Living Translation* (Wheaton, IL: Tyndale House Publishers, 1996).
TEV *Today's English Version* also called *Good News Translation* (New York: American Bible Society, 1992).

Cover photo © stevebloom.com
Typeset and Printed in the United States of America

Contents

SECTION TWO: PROVISIONS FOR VICTORY

The Bible, Prayer and the Holy Spirit

Acknowledgments

Standing Strong Through the Storm (SSTS) is "a-work-in-progress"—the result of years of research done by Open Doors personnel in both restricted and free societies of the world. As the materials were gathered and compiled, it became apparent that the keys to victorious Christian living identified in restricted countries could also be valuable in any context.

This text is a compilation of several previous major productions as well as additional new material. The first study was produced by Open Doors-Asia and written by Dr. Everett Boyce. Alice Smith of the U.S. Prayer Center wrote some of the material used in Chapter Four.

The current text was analyzed and evaluated from a theological point of view by several people. Special thanks go to a long-time friend, Dr. Terrance Tiessen, author of *Providence and Prayer* and *Who Can Be Saved?* His recommended changes and additions are much appreciated.

All known sources of material have been footnoted where possible. All Scripture quotes are in italics and are from the *New International Version of the Holy Bible,* unless otherwise noted.

Together we wrestled with issues presented here, as well as field tested this material in several hot-spot "*restricted*" and "*threatened*" countries and "*free societies.*" More than two hundred friends of Open Doors International from eleven countries invested time to help us evaluate the content. Many of their recommended changes are incorporated in this edition.

Thanks to everyone who contributed in any way, large or small! Special thanks are in order to the evaluators whose contributions went "over-the-meter": Ed and Aretta Loving, Bible translators (USA), Anne Horton's women's group (Australia), Professor Daniela

Malheiro (Brazil), Ethel Dueck's women's group (Canada), and Dennis Schlecker and Roger Neill (Canada). And we extend our gratitude to all who prayed for the development of this material *"to the praise of His glorious grace."*

—Paul Estabrooks, minister-at-large, Open Doors International

—Jim Cunningham, SSTS coordinator, Open Doors International

September, 2004

Introduction

THE COMING STORMS

He replied, "When evening comes, you say, 'It will be fair weather, for the sky is red,' and in the morning, 'Today it will be stormy, for the sky is red and overcast.' You know how to interpret the appearance of the sky, but you cannot interpret the signs of the times."

MATTHEW 16:2-3

George and his wife, Carol, along with Sanjit and his wife, Yvonne, sat around the table enjoying their Sunday afternoon lunch together. They soon settled into serious discussion because their church friend Sam joined them. He had just returned from a business trip to East Africa.

"Have things improved for our brothers and sisters over there, Sam?" Yvonne asked.

"Not at all. While I was there, police jailed three prominent pastors and a popular Christian singer. They really need our prayers."

"But Sam," Yvonne continued, "didn't you tell us the same story last trip?"

"Sure did. But this is new. Now there are an estimated three hundred or more Christians in prison—some of them held in stifling hot shipping containers. The government crackdown has been going on against evangelical Christians for a number of years. But this seems to be an escalation."

Sanjit interjected, "But what's the problem there, Sam?"

"As best I can understand," Sam said, "the traditional church has put pressure on the strong-handed ruling government to stop the growth of the evangelical church. They're accusing the evangelicals of being a dividing force, undermining national unity, not wanting to defend their country and being spies for intelligence agencies."

"Is that true?" Carol queried.

"Of course not, but disinformation is difficult to counter when you're an unprotected minority group."

"Tell us about it! You don't have to go overseas to be targeted by disinformation," Yvonne retorted. "Did you see the paper this morning? Our pastor was maligned as 'intolerant' for his view that Jesus is the 'only way' to God."

"Your pastor didn't originate that; Jesus did in John 14. If they have a problem, it's with Jesus, not your pastor!" George responded.

There was silence for a moment. Sam slowly took a sip of coffee and then quietly added, "That's exactly right, George. But isn't that the crux of the issue? All persecution is targeted at Jesus—Jesus in us. As Jesus said, 'No servant is greater than his master. If they persecuted me, they will persecute you also.' "

Sanjit quickly chimed in, "Yeah, I thought I was leaving intolerance and persecution behind when I emigrated, but I think it's just as bad for us evangelical Christians in this country. I can be anything and believe anything I want but don't try and tell anyone else about it. Just keep it to yourself."

"That's because our society has completely adopted the philosophy of secular humanism, believing man begins with himself as the center reference point of life and meaning," added Sam.

"But how does this affect us as evangelical Christians?" Yvonne asked.

"It all begins with disinformation and discrediting, especially by academic and media types," Sam said. "They are determined to marginalize Christian belief."

Carol had been quiet for some time—just listening. Suddenly, she blurted out, "You mean like the criticism this past week of our prime minister because he used God's name in a public statement—not as a swear word, but rather when he was really talking about Him?"

"Sure," Sam responded. "It almost seems many secularists are happier when a government leader tells a bold lie than when he admits a faith in Jesus Christ. Their catch word is *tolerance.* The irony is that we who believe Jesus' own claim to uniqueness are branded as the 'intolerant' of society—even though Jesus' teaching and lifestyle modeled tolerance for others."

Yvonne was eager to continue the discussion. "Isn't it the Bible that is under attack more than just our being people of faith?"

"It sure is," Sam quipped. "It's the source book of the absolute truths we believe and practice. But in a postmodern world, no truths are considered absolute truths. That's why there are repeated accusations now in the media branding the Bible as *hate literature.* It won't be long before we will only be able to read the Bible at home or in church—definitely not in public."

George picked up on the last sentence. "You've hit a soft spot with me, Sam, 'cause I'm a Gideon. Our organization used to be able to give a free New Testament to every fifth grade student. Then it was only possible if the students brought a note of approval from their parents. We even gave New Testaments to graduating police officers. Now we can't give them out to either group in—or on—public property. Why, just yesterday, I got a call from a fellow Gideon who was stopped by the police from handing out free New Testaments to students on the sidewalk—off the school campus.

The police couldn't tell him what he was doing wrong nor did they charge him with an illegal act. They just insisted he stop. Ironically, the government still lets us give New Testaments to prisoners in our bulging penitentiary system."

"I can see the attack on the Bible," interrupted Sanjit. "But I think our mission—evangelism—presents a bigger challenge and concern to the world. In my birth country, a number of states have actually legislated anti-conversion laws. There is tremendous fear of proselytizing—especially from Christians."

"What's the difference between evangelism and proselytizing?" asked Yvonne.

There was a short pause and Sam responded again. "Evangelism is a process of invitation and persuasion while proselytizing has implications of force or incentives or trickery. God never forces Himself or His will on anyone and neither should we."

"So why is there so much antagonism to true evangelism in our country?" Yvonne queried again.

"Sam, drink your coffee and let me respond to this one," Carol said. "This is my interest area since we run the *Discovering Jesus* program at our church. Sanjit, you're a good example of our multiculturalism! Every person from every kind of ethnic background has equal opportunities and rights in this country while still keeping their ethnic identity. The problem for evangelism is when multicultural values are mixed with religious pluralism and syncretism."

"What's *sinkretism*?" queried Yvonne. "Sounds like a disease from hand-washing dishes too long!"

Carol laughed then responded, "I've dealt with a lot of diseases—but never that one. Syncretism is literally a blending of things or philosophies—a belief that absolute truth no longer exists. A natural extension of this lack of absolutes is the widely held view that there is equal truth in every religion. More important, this belief leads to the conclusion that all roads lead to heaven. Therefore individuals can pick and choose the elements they wish from whatever belief system and mix them all together. One writer called this 'salad-bar Christianity.'"

Sam joined the discussion again. "The key words of syncretism are *tolerance* and *dialogue.* Tolerance now means you must not insist on anything. And it is really wrong to encourage anyone on 'their own valid path' to change to yours."

"But it's not a matter of taste or choice; it's a matter of life and death!" Yvonne blurted out.

Sanjit had been sipping a cup of tea and was amazed to see his wife so animated. "Good for you, my love. We can't afford to be indifferent or passive about this. Reminds me of the book I just finished reading about Chinese Christians titled *Back to Jerusalem.* In it the house church network leaders in China essentially say that if we in free societies would boldly preach the truth of God's Word to sinners inside and outside our churches, we would soon face persecution just like they do in China."

In Brother Andrew's fifty years of experience with the Persecuted Church, he reports that he has heard only two comments about persecution: "It will never happen here!" and then later, "We thought it would never happen here!"

"I think that's right," Sam responded. "Ultimately Satan, our real enemy, wants to destroy the Church of Jesus Christ, wherever it's located. And Jesus Himself is the stumbling block to those who don't believe. When we say He is the only way—George, you're right, Jesus actually said it first—we are labeled as exclusivists and on this basis we are then considered intolerant."

"I heard a program host on the radio the other day," broke in Yvonne, "and he was obviously upset by this. When someone told him Jesus is the only way to God, he shouted that we evangelicals are the scum of the earth!"

"Whoa," Sanjit responded. "That's a little heavy, isn't it?"

Yvonne continued, "Well, he went on to say it wasn't the belief to which he objected so much but he objected to the arrogance of any person claiming 'my way allows no other way' and writing off the rest of the human race to eternal damnation."

"All of this discussion clearly points out," Sam concluded, "we are facing—and will face even more—attacks because of Jesus in us. Persecution may not be just for those brothers and sisters across the seas in places like East Africa, but perhaps even for us."

There was a long silence.

Again Yvonne asked the obvious, "How can we prepare?"

Consider what happened on Ambon Island, in the South Moluccans of Indonesia. Christians and Muslims lived peacefully side by side for more than three hundred years. In 1998, a team from Open Doors International went to Ambon to teach a course to prepare pastors and church leaders for coming persecution. The team was told the course was not relevant because "even though there is violence against Christians in other parts of our country, *it will never happen here!"* Within twelve months violent attacks began which over the next three years claimed the lives of many thousands—both Christians and Muslims.

Christians who live godly in Christ Jesus will be persecuted and share in the suffering of Jesus. 2 Timothy 3:12; 1 Peter 2:21-25; Acts 14:22

Two months after the infamous September 11, 2001, attack on the World Trade Center towers and Pentagon, the authors visited Ambon and found a significant openness among the church leaders to study biblical principles of persecution. After this second seminar the pastors appealed to us to tell Christians in free societies, *"Don't say, 'It will never happen here!'"*

In the Upper Room Discourse, just days before His crucifixion, Jesus told His disciples, *"If the world hates you, keep in mind that it hated me first."* (John 15:18) Hatred of Jesus Christ is foundational to the persecution, however intense, of Christians.

Today, evangelical Christians in free societies are hated by many because of their faith in the supernatural Jesus—even though *Jesus* in the form of jewellery worn around the neck, movies, music and even tattoos has become somewhat trendy.

As well as attacks against our faith in Jesus, there are also attacks against the Bible, the church and its mission—evangelism. The winds of these storms are beginning to gust.

How then do Christians living in free societies *respond* to these storms?

- Do we cower in paralyzing fear and lose energy for doing good works to help others before, during and after the storm?
- Do we flee the coming storm and try to hide?
- Do we become verbally and physically aggressive, lashing out in righteous indignation to change a system that is out of control?
- Do we complacently smile and say, "Things have to get worse before our Lord Jesus Christ returns to earth as *King of Kings* and *Lord of Lords.* Therefore, persecution is good because it separates the sheep from the goats and allows the church to grow, so 'Don't worry, be happy, everything will be OK!' "?

These options are neither biblical nor realistic. Based on our observations of other countries that have endured—or are currently experiencing—persecution, we must prepare ourselves intellectually, practically and spiritually for the coming storms.

After Vietnam's reunification, an Open Doors co-worker visited a pastor who leads the fastest-growing house church network. It was reported that the authorities were threatening him with imprisonment. He told our colleague, "I know it is coming. I have prepared my people for my imprisonment. I am ready for prison." The pastor's answer reveals his preparation in three areas:

- Intellectually—"I know it is coming."

- Practically—"I have prepared my people for my imprisonment."
- Spiritually—"I am ready for prison."

Compare this brother's humble response to our own, and then ask these questions:

- Is it possible to obey Jesus and fight with those who hate you?
- Is it possible to love Jesus and argue with those who think differently?
- Is it possible to follow Jesus and abuse those *made in His image?*
- Is it possible to serve Jesus and kill your enemies?

After fifty years of ministry among Christians persecuted for their faith (primarily providing Bibles, training and encouragement), Open Doors staff members observe that many of the persecuted believers have far more to teach us about the application of biblical truth to everyday living than we can contribute to them.

> *[God] comforts us in all our troubles, so that we can comfort those in any trouble with the comfort we ourselves have received from God. (2 Corinthians 1:4)*

The lessons of this text are the living testimonies that Christians, in countries or regions we define as the Persecuted Church, share with brothers and sisters in the gradually shrinking "free world." We believe the biblical principles in their testimonies are the seeds of spiritual renewal for every society and culture.

"Christians are like tea leaves. You have to put us in hot water to know how strong we are!"

We want to present Jesus Christ as the central figure of our study. He is the absolute Word, God incarnate, and has defeated Satan on the cross.

In this book we will closely examine persecution and the result of persecution—suffering. Satan wants to dishearten us and create hopelessness through persecution and suffering. We will expose Satan's lies and show what God does to restore our "hope"—the oxygen of the human spirit. We will study and discuss these areas intellectually, practically and spiritually.

Let's begin by looking at who our enemy is.

We keep our eyes fixed on Jesus Christ, the Living God, not demons or distractions, for victory is assured in Him.

See Hebrews 12:2

SECTION ONE

Who Is Our Enemy?

Satan's Strategies Against Believers

1

KNOWING OUR ENEMY

He who does what is sinful is of the devil, because the devil has been sinning from the beginning. The reason the Son of God appeared was to destroy the devil's work.
1 John 3:8

China's house church leaders, representing more than ten million members, met a few years ago for a conference to discuss the main problems facing their churches. They ranked their top three problems, and came up with strategies to solve them.

At the top of the list was *gossip*. Leader after leader told stories of how their ministries had been compromised by this subtle sin. Problem two was *materialism* and problem three was *heresy*. One house church leader from Henan Province shared the following experience.

"I went into an area to lead Bible studies for coworkers and they wouldn't let me into the house where we were to hold the seminar. I asked them through the closed door what the problem was, but they wouldn't tell me. They just told me to go away. It was winter and I went a little ways outside the town, knowing I must start a fire to sleep beside or I would freeze to death. I wondered what on earth could have made those brothers and sisters turn me away on such a cold night without a word of explanation.

"But a brother took pity on me and brought me secretly to his home. I eventually pried the truth out of him. The leaders in the area had received an anonymous letter denouncing me as a 'lover of many women.' Try as hard as I might, I could not get them to listen to me or let me see the letter.

"Later in another part of the country, I learned the letter had been sent by a brother I had disciplined for moral laxity, and he had sent it out of spite.

One of the reasons Christians face persecution and suffering is because of the cosmic clash of two warring kingdoms: the kingdom of light and the kingdom of darkness.

"I went to him and he repented. He sent another letter, but because the first one was unsigned, they didn't believe him. Both of us offered to go there, but we weren't welcomed. The testimony of the church was ruined. I still have to explain myself wherever I go. It's a victory for the devil.

"I went with the offending brother out to the countryside and told him to pluck a chicken. We walked along while he did; the wind blew the feathers far over the fields. When he was finished, he asked, 'What now?' I told him, 'Pick up every feather, and put it back on the chicken.' He said, 'That's impossible.' I replied, 'You are right. It is impossible, just as the damage your words have done cannot be repaired.'"

The house church leaders pledged to be more loving, and to hold more face-to-face meetings with each other to minimize the sin of gossip.

In any battle, there is an enemy and victory is determined by how well you know the enemy, how well you know his tactics, and how well you fight against him strategically.

The Bible teaches that conflict in the Christian life comes from four sources: the *flesh,* or sinful nature (Mark 7:20-23); *life circumstances* (John 16:33); the *world system* (James 4:4; 1 John 2:15-17); and the *devil* (Ephesians 6:10-12; 1 Peter 5:8). When challenges come, it is not always easy to identify the source of the conflict. We need discernment to identify which of our trials and problems are a result of a spiritual attack, because we are not to be ignorant of the enemy's devices (2 Corinthians 2:11). We need to know when we are at war and when it is time to stand!

Suffering in the will of God has meaning and purpose: God's ultimate goal (whether by persecution or freedom) is for us to be conformed to the image of His Son. 1 Peter 1:6-7; 2 Corinthians 12:7-10; Hebrews 12:3-10; Philippians 1:14; 1 Corinthians 3:12; John 17:23; Acts 8:1-4; and Romans 8:29

A. OUR ENEMY'S IDENTITY

The devil, Satan, is the enemy of God and His church. The word "Satan," in both Hebrew and Greek, means *adversary*—one who is an enemy, one who opposes another. In his desire to be like God, he sought to usurp the position that can only belong to the one true God.

In a most effective way, C. S. Lewis tries to bring this point across in his renowned book *The Screwtape Letters.* It would please Satan if we only consider him to be an evil influence underlying human nature or recognize him to be nothing more than ancient people's ignorant explanation for wickedness surrounding them.

On the other hand, Satan has deceived those who acknowledge him into believing he is God's equal, God's opposite. He cannot be God's counterpart because he himself was created by God. Satan as a fallen angel can be understood better as the opposite of Michael the Archangel. He is **not** omnipresent and has only limited power.

At the same time, we should not identify "the enemy" as one particular government or person or other religion. While we are to

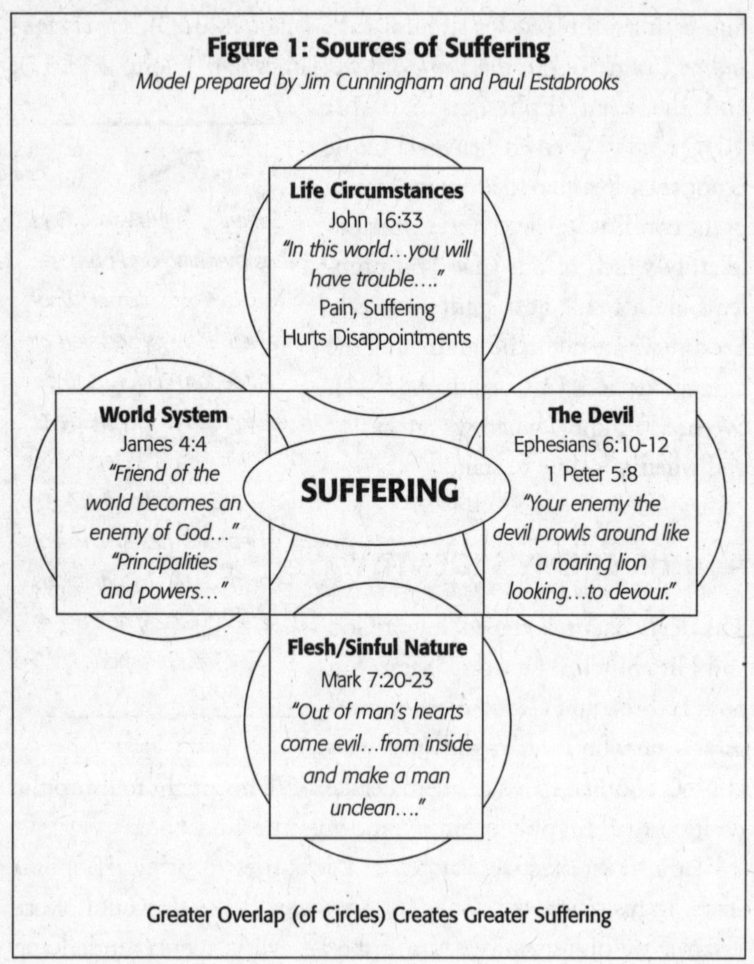

pray for protection from wicked and evil men who do not have faith (2 Thessalonians 3:2), we also must be aware that wicked and evil men are not our greatest enemy. They are merely human pawns of the supreme enemy, Satan, himself. We thus recognize there is a power beyond human institutions that fights against God and His plans for the world through His church. (Ephesians 6:12)

The Bible speaks often about our enemy Satan. Seven books in the Old Testament and every writer in the New Testament refer to him. Of the 29 references in the New Testament, Jesus is speaking in 25 of them. We need to know for sure what the Bible teaches about this enemy whom the Bible calls "a sinner from the beginning" (1 John 3:8). Paul wrote that we should not let Satan take advantage of us by being ignorant of his devices (2 Corinthians 2:11). A list of his names gives us some of his chief characteristics. (Figure 2)

An important scheme of Satan is that he does not want us to recognize the reality of his existence.

B. OUR ENEMY'S ORIGIN

Sometimes Christians ask where Satan came from. Isn't God the creator of everything? The Lord says: *"I am the LORD, and there is no other. I form the light and create darkness. I bring prosperity and create disaster. I, the LORD, do all these things."* (Isaiah 45:6b-7) From these verses we see that although God is not evil, darkness and disaster have their source in God. Ten times in Isaiah 45, the Lord says, *"I am the LORD, and there is no other."*

Once we establish that God is sovereign and we follow His revealed will, even to our death, we are increasingly able to put evil in perspective. One Chinese brother told a group: "Persecutors persecute because they are afraid, not because they are strong." In a strange twist of events, persecutors and the evil they perpetrate can help others come to know God. In 1949 there were more than 8,000 missionaries from the West in China, and an estimated 800,000 evangelical Christians. Communist government officials in an attempt to control the people expelled all "foreigners." It appeared that Satan had won. But today, the church in China consists of more than eighty million people and it is growing by thousands of new believers a day! Persecution can help others come to know God.

Why would God create Satan? The Bible does not tell us very much about events before the creation of the world described in

Figure 2: Our Enemy Has a Name

1. Disobedient ruler	
• ruler of the kingdom of the air	Ephesians 2:2
• prince of this world	John 14:30
• god of this world	2 Corinthians 4:4
• prince of demons	Matthew 12:24
• the hinderer	1 Thessalonians 2:18
2. Deceiver	
• the accuser	Revelation 12:9-11
• liar and father of lies	John 8:44
• angel of light	2 Corinthians 11:14-15—his servants masquerade as servants of righteousness
• the tempter	1 Thessalonians 3:5
3. Destroyer	
• roaring lion	1 Peter 5:8-9
• a murderer	John 8:44

Genesis chapter one. However, it is possible to piece together certain information about that period. It seems Satan was created as a member of a high order of angels who disobeyed God. Satan became very proud and attempted to assume an even more exalted position (1 Timothy 3:6; 2 Peter 2:4; Jude 6). As a result, he was cast down from his favored position, and he was judged along with other angels who joined his rebellion. Their eternal doom has already been determined. But while they await the execution of God's judgment, they try in every way they can to destroy God's church. God allows this so His church can gain strength only available through disciplined struggle.

The world today is under Satan's authority. He is called *"the ruler of the kingdom of the air"* (Ephesians 2:2) and *"prince of this world"* (John 14:30). He boasted to Christ that he controlled all the kingdoms of the world, and Christ did not dispute that claim (Luke 4:6). He is even called *"the god of this age."* (2 Corinthians 4:4)

God created the world and gave it to those "created in His image" to oversee (Genesis 1:3-30), but people turned it over to Satan by submitting to him (Genesis 3:1-6). People still do not seem to understand the principle that is clearly taught in Romans 6:16: *"Don't you know that when you offer yourselves to someone to obey him as slaves, you are slaves to the one whom you obey…?"* Satan has used his power to continually deceive people as he did in the beginning. And people still think serving Satan can give them a good, enjoyable and prosperous life.

Satan has no power to create life–he can only destroy.

God offers life *"to the full"* (John 10:10). Satan can only give *"the pleasures of sin for a short time"* (Hebrews 11:25). While God loves us and gave Himself for us (Romans 5:8), Satan's only goal is hatred and destruction. He still hopes to destroy God's plan of a new heaven and a new earth populated with redeemed people who love God of their own free will.

When we face tragedy and seemingly senseless pain in this world, we must remember this is Satan's world and it is operating just the way he likes it (Revelation 17:17). But our God will still intervene on behalf of His redeemed children. We can still call on His power and then Satan must flee. (James 4:7)

C. OUR ENEMY'S ACTIVITIES

As an enemy of God, how does Satan carry on subversive activities?

1. Satan as a disobedient ruler

First, Satan opposes God by usurping the authority that belongs to God alone. He is called the prince of the power of the air, the ruler of the world, the god of this world, and the prince of devils.

We see a very good example of how Satan works in his

attempts to make Jesus sin (Luke 4:1-13). He waits for a time of weakness. Persecution may be such a time. He then promises instant gratification of sinful desires. Satan first suggested that Jesus use His divine power to meet His normal human needs. Then he tried to appeal to Jesus' desire to be accepted as a leader. And finally he offered Him the whole world—which was Jesus' true heritage anyway, but He had to gain it God's way. Satan was trying to find any weakness in Jesus, even quoting Scripture in his attempts to lead Him astray. Note how effectively Jesus used the Word of God to refute the devil.

2. Satan as a deceiver

Another biblical description of Satan is the Greek word *diabolos,* which means slanderer. Jesus clearly says that Satan is a liar and father of lies (John 8:44). We can see this characteristic demonstrated in several ways:

a. He lies about the words of God.

One of the ways in which Satan seeks to oppose God is by distorting the words of God. For example, when God created Adam and Eve, God said to them: *"You are free to eat from any tree in the garden; but you must not eat from the tree of the knowledge of good and evil, for when you eat of it you will surely die."* (Genesis 2:16-17)

But when Satan talked with Eve, he said, "Did God really say, 'You must not eat of any tree in the garden?'" This was a clear distortion of God's word. This kind of "playing" with God's Word causes us to try and defend God's Word and then fall into a trap in our attempt to prove something. But in this exchange Satan articulates The Great Lie that he has repeatedly told through the centuries: *"When you eat of it your eyes will be opened, and you will be like God...."* (Genesis 3:5)

The Bible tells us that Satan himself masquerades as an angel of light (2 Corinthians 11:14) and those who are his followers also masquerade as servants of righteousness.

b. He lies about believers.

When Satan came to God in the book of Job, we hear him accusing Job, God's servant. Revelation 12:10 also tells us that Satan is *"the accuser of our brothers, who accuses them before our God day and night...."*

It's no surprise then to see that in a time of persecution one of his most frequent attacks on the church is through false accusations. Rather than to deal with the truth, believers are pressured to bear false witness against each other. Consequently the love and trust among believers is broken and destruction of the church takes root right in the core of the body. Perhaps one of the most tragic experiences of the church is in this area. Believers need to learn to recognize Satan's wicked devices as he tempts us to be like him and accuse our brothers and sisters. The believer must build relationships that will withstand these kinds of pressures.

When asked what made a certain type of Chinese house church stronger during persecution, one answer was that the members of that group had stronger emotional ties with each other. They truly experienced the oneness of the Body of Christ in that fellowship. Thus in spite of false accusations, they remained strong.

c. He lies to believers.

In the English language, Satan could easily be referred to as the D-man. His *modus operandi* tends to start with the letter "D": disagree, dispute, deny, debate, discourage, depress, deceive, defraud, divide, deviate, demolish, destroy, defeat and death. Our Lord's response to Peter was, *"Get behind me Satan! You are a stumbling block to me; you do not have in mind the things of God, but the things of men.... If anyone would come after me, he must deny himself and take up his cross and follow me."* (Matthew 16:23-24)

3. Satan as a destroyer

The Bible tells us that Satan is also a murderer (John 8:44). He opposes God in the way he attempts to kill. The successful temptation of Adam and Eve led to their spiritual and physical death. Now, as then, his desire is to see that no one comes to know Jesus Christ as Lord and Savior and thus be saved from the coming death.

When Jesus told the parable of the seed sown in four different types of soil, He said that some seed fell on the path and the birds came and ate it. He was referring to those who receive the message about the Kingdom of God but do not understand it. The Evil One, Satan, came and snatched away what was sown in their hearts. (Matthew 13:19)

Satan may openly attack the church as a *roaring lion* or attempt to deceive from within through his evil messengers. In the days of the New Testament church he used threats, imprisonment, beatings, mobs, and even murder in his open, direct attacks against the church.

But he also tried to work from within through Judas and the Jewish legalists who claimed to follow Jesus but actually wanted to change the Gospel. The Bible tells us about all these ways Satan attacked the church so we would know how to deal with him, no matter how he attacks.

We must face the fact that, as the destroyer, Satan will use every means and excuse to stop believers from evangelism and discipleship training. Gratefully, as we read the history of persecution, we can see that persecution has not kept believers from witnessing. In fact, persecution can be used by God to bring more people into His kingdom. As people see how believers faced persecution, it has also led them to consider more seriously the claims of Christ.

Thus we must evaluate the effective forms of evangelism in a time of persecution and pressure. One may not be able to preach on street corners, but there are indeed many other ways to consider. Christians who have been imprisoned and led dozens—sometimes even hundreds—of people to Christ inside the prison present us with one of the more challenging models.

D. CONCLUSION

While it is important to know our enemy, it can be depressing to let our minds dwell on his power. Jesus saw Satan fall as lightning from heaven when the disciples ministered in divine strength (Luke 10:17-20). Jesus has promised us the same victory (John 16:33). The Apostle Paul experienced this and wrote to the church at Rome about it (Romans 8:28). The Apostle John promised Satan's final defeat (1 John 3:8). Although the churches of John's day were suffering at the hands of the enemy, torn by false doctrine, plagued by the unholy living of some of its members and the complacency of others, still Satan could not prevail. (Revelation 3:8-10; 12:10-11; 20:10)

Victory is always obtained by faith. Faith keeps us from being defeated at the hands of suffering. 1 Peter 4:19

The enemy is cruel and strong. We must recognize him as such. But we can still be victorious, for the Bible says, *"Thanks be to God! He gives us the victory through our Lord Jesus Christ"* (1 Corinthians 15:57). Eugene Peterson's paraphrase of John 1:5 in *The Message* reads: *"The Life light blazed out in the darkness; the darkness couldn't put it out."* Yes! We can be victorious no matter how dark the times become.

STUDY GUIDE/DISCUSSION QUESTIONS

PASTOR FOCUS

1. What would you rank as the top three problems facing the church in **your** area?

1.
2.
3.

At the top of the Chinese list was *Gossip,* second was *Materialism* and third was *Heresy.*

WOMEN'S FOCUS

1. As an enemy of God, how does Satan carry on his subversive activities within the Christian church and the Christian family?

YOUTH FOCUS

1. *"The mind controlled by the Spirit is life"* (Romans 8:6). *"Daniel resolved not to defile himself with the royal food and wine…"* (Daniel 1:8). If life is a matter of "choice" and "control," how can you choose to respond biblically to things that appear to be "beyond my control"?

MEN'S FOCUS

1. Tell how the following would help us understand who Satan really is.

   "the ruler of the kingdom of the air"—Ephesians 2:2

"the prince of this world"—John 14:30

"the god of this age"—2 Corinthians 4:4

2. If Satan can only imitate God and cannot create anything, what are our adversary's long-term goals?

3. Sometimes people act as if Satan is just an evil influence. How do we know he is a real being? Why does this distinction matter?

4. How do we answer people who say, "If there is a God, why does He allow innocent people to die in earthquakes (or floods, or other natural disasters)?"

5. What are ways in which evil is masked as good, but in the end it destroys?

6. People have said, "Satan cannot harm a Christian." Do you agree? What does the book of Hebrews teach about this? (Hebrews 11:32-39)

7. How does our adversary try to use fellow Christians against us?

2

THE BATTLE WITHIN

Submit yourselves, then, to God. Resist the devil, and he will flee from you.

JAMES 4:7

An anonymous writer, who perhaps was inspired by C. S. Lewis's *The Screwtape Letters*, visualized the following scenario:

Satan called a worldwide convention. In his opening address to his evil angels, he said, "We can't keep them from reading their Bibles and knowing the truth. We can't even keep them from family values. But we can do something else. We can keep them from forming an intimate, abiding experience in Christ.

"If they gain that connection with Jesus, our power over them is broken. So let them go to church, let them have their conservative lifestyles, but steal their time so they can't gain that experience in Jesus Christ.

"This is what I want you to do, angels. Distract them from gaining hold of their Savior and maintaining that vital connection throughout their day."

"How shall we do this?" shouted the evil angels.

"Keep them busy in the non-essentials of life and invent unnumbered schemes to occupy their minds," he answered.

"Tempt them to spend, spend, spend, then borrow, borrow, borrow. Persuade the wives to go to work and the husbands to work 6 or 7 days a week, 10-12 hours a day, so they can afford their lifestyles. Keep them from spending time with their children. As their family fragments, soon their homes will offer no escape from the pressures of work.

"Overstimulate their minds so that they cannot hear that still, small voice. Entice them to play the radio or cassette whenever they drive, to keep the TV, the VCR, and their CDs going constantly in their homes. Tempt them to spend more time on their computers, especially watching Internet pornography.

"And see to it that every store and restaurant in the world plays music constantly. This will jam their minds and break that union with Christ.

"Fill their coffee tables with magazines and newspapers. Pound their minds with the news 24 hours a day. Invade their driving moments with billboards. Flood their mailboxes with junk mail, sweepstakes, mail order catalogues, and every kind of newsletter and promotional offering, free products, services and false hopes.

The internal weapons our enemy Satan uses are often very subtle and effective for his cause.

"Even in their recreation, let them be excessive. Have them return from their recreation exhausted, disquieted and unprepared for the coming week. Don't let them go out in nature. Send them to amusement parks, sporting events, concerts and movies instead. And when they meet for spiritual fellowship, involve them in gossip and small talk so that they leave with troubled consciences and unsettled emotions.

"Let them be involved in soul-winning. But crowd their lives with so many good causes they have no time to seek power from

Christ. Soon they will be working in their own strength, sacrificing their health and family unity for the good of the cause."

It was quite a convention in the end. And the evil angels went eagerly to their assignments causing Christians everywhere to get busy, busy, busy and rush here and there and spend, spend, spend![1]

A. INTERNAL TACTICS OF THE ENEMY

In this section we are not dealing with all of Satan's tactics, nor even those he most often uses. Rather, we are limiting our focus to those tactics that persecuted Christians have alerted us to as ones they struggle with the most.

Some teachers describe these internal tactics as "the enemy wearing socks." He quietly sneaks up on us and we're often not aware he's right behind us. Also, when he isolates us from the encouragement and assistance of the local body of Christ, he feels he has us right where he can more easily attack us. He achieves this by pointing out our personal sins or weaknesses and playing on every selfish motivation with which he can tempt us.

1. Pride

We each have to come to terms with Satan's deadliest tactic, which the Bible calls *pride.* Ever since the Garden of Eden, Satan has promulgated The Great Lie: *"You will be like God"* (Genesis 3:5b). We all must learn to overcome pride, which was Satan's own initial sin and which is his pervasive and repetitive tactic against us.

In Proverbs 6:17, *"haughty eyes"* are first on the list of the seven things that are an "abomination" to God. Proverbs 27:2 adds, *"Let another praise you, and not your own mouth."* Christ spoke of pride in Luke 18:14 when He instructs, *"Everyone who exalts himself will be humbled, and he who humbles himself will be exalted."* Over and over again, we are reminded in the Bible of God's utter disdain for a prideful spirit:

Why does God have so much to say about this issue? Because, ultimately, a prideful person is saying, "I don't need God. I can do it on my own." As our Creator and Sustainer, God has the perfect plan laid out before us. Attempting to "go it alone" will only lead us down a path of self-destruction. No one knows that better than God—He has seen pride destroy the lives of His creations throughout eternity.

In the Old Testament we see an example of this in the life of King Nebuchadnezzar (Daniel 4:28-37) until he acknowledged the Most High God. We also see it in the life of King Belshazzar, who saw the handwriting on the wall and received judgment because of his pride. (Daniel 5:22-31)

In the New Testament, the Pharisees, filled with self-righteousness, denied the work of Christ, even as He stood before them. The Apostle Paul warned the Corinthians to *"not take pride in one man over against another"* (1 Corinthians 4:6). Peter repeats the warning from Proverbs 3:34 that *"God opposes the proud but gives grace to the humble."* (1 Peter 5:5)

Pride is so devastating because of its deceptiveness. C. S. Lewis said, "A proud man is always looking down on things and people; and, of course, as long as you're looking down, you can't see something that's above you."[2] We may easily point out pride in the life of someone else, completely oblivious to the stranglehold that pride may have in our own lives. Pride causes us to focus solely on being "better" than someone else. Don't compare yourself to others; compare yourself to Christ. Remember where you came from, and recall what God has saved you from.

When all else fails, God may allow adversity into our lives. Nothing gets our attention better than going through a difficult time. He allows these experiences in order to filter out pride, causing us to return our focus on Him. As much as our prideful spirit may disagree, we cannot live a fulfilling life without God. Simply put, when God is out, pride is in.[3]

2. Guilt

Satan continually accuses us in our own hearts and heaps feelings of guilt and failure on us. True guilt is that which comes from disobeying God. One reason that this approach is so effective in crushing the witness of a saint is because it is partially true. We all have failed the Lord. None of us has triumphed in power over every circumstance as we could and should have done. So when Satan accuses us, we know in our hearts that there is much truth in his accusations.

But God has provided us with a way to cleanse ourselves of any sin and the guilt that accompanies that sin. When we realize we have failed the Lord, we confess the specific sin and He forgives and cleanses us (1 John 1:9). Once we have confessed our sin it is gone, and our feelings of guilt are relieved.

David's experience shows us God's method of dealing with sin: conviction, acknowledgment, confession, seeking forgiveness, receiving forgiveness, praise and joyful service (Psalm 51; Psalm 32:3-4; 2 Samuel 12:1-13). Once sin is dealt with in this manner, true guilt will disappear.

Paul warned Timothy that in the last days many professing Christians would live wickedly. He teaches that people will be so burdened by the guilt of their sin that they will be unstable and easily led astray (2 Timothy 3:1-7). Unresolved guilt is a serious matter. If a Christian feels confused, unstable and powerless, he should examine his heart and be sure he is not harboring unconfessed sin. If a believer knows his heart is right he can have confidence that any lingering feelings of guilt are simply false guilt and are therefore from Satan.

According to Revelation 12:11, believers counter the accusations of Satan in three ways:

> *"They overcame him by the blood of the Lamb and by the word of their testimony; they did not love their lives so much as to shrink from death."*

- *The blood of the Lamb*

We are made clean by faith in Christ's blood. His saving grace and a willingness to receive us as sinners saved by grace is the key to that cleansing, not our feelings of worthiness.

- *The word of their testimony*

The believers declared Christ's love and forgiveness aloud to themselves, to Satan and to the world. Romans 8:31-43 declares the same.

- *Sacrificial love*

Within those believers was the ultimate secret of victory that destroyed any consideration for reputation, safety, comfort or freedom. Patterned on Christ's own life, they willingly offered themselves and their future completely to God and obeyed Him despite the circumstances.

The revolutionary army told a young Christian in Chad, Africa, that he must submit to old animistic tribal rituals. They wanted to destroy Christianity and stimulate patriotism and loyalty by reviving the ancient pagan customs. The leaders of the churches of the area agreed that Christians must refuse to participate in the animistic rituals.

When the young man refused and was beaten, he stood firm in his faith. But when the authorities stripped him naked and beat him in front of his mother, sisters and other young ladies, his courage failed and he permitted them to perform the pagan rituals.

Then he felt terrible. He had failed the Lord. His guilt was heavy. Satan tried to convince him that the Lord could never again accept him. But he knew the scriptural promises of God, and he confessed his sin. The Lord forgave him and restored his joy.

He began to publicly witness to his neighbors and he was arrested. The authorities demanded that he denounce Christ or be buried alive. This time, his faith was strong and he refused to deny Christ. He was beaten and thrown into prison to await execution, but his faith grew stronger and the Lord delivered him when the oppressive government was overthrown and he was released.

3. False Guilt/Legalism

If true guilt is that which comes from disobeying God, then false guilt comes from the judgments and standards of men. It usually arises out of putting too much confidence in the opinions of men, rather than in what the Word of God teaches. Often these opinions of men are simply another form of legalism.

Mature believers who continually study the Word of God under the leadership of the Holy Spirit are able to discern between true guilt and false guilt. Hebrews 5:14

Satan will often try to continue giving you a burden of guilt for sin that has already been forgiven and thus effectively immobilizes you. Although the failure was real, the guilt was false. But Satan cannot stand against the truth of Scripture and must flee. Of course, he will return again and again, but he can be defeated each time!

a. Facing questions

When believers find themselves facing persecution, with their buildings closed, their programs abolished, and their leaders discredited and suffering, they often wonder, *Why?* Satan is always there with many answers. He wants the believers to feel guilty. He will tell them that they didn't pray enough, or their faith was weak, or their sin demanded God's punishment. This is a burden of false guilt that weighs heavily, drains spiritual energy and accomplishes nothing.

Satan tries to make us concentrate on the past or the future. God wants us to concentrate on the present, claim forgiveness for the sins of the past, commit the future into His hands, and live for Him in the present. The valid question that believers must face is "What would You have me to do now, Lord?"

b. Outward forms of worship

When the pressure of persecution builds and Christians turn to less public patterns, Satan is always there to accuse them of being radicals or cowards. He will claim they are denying Christ if they do not attend a public worship service on Sunday morning.

Some may ask: Can a gathering of two or three under a tree on a weekday be *real* worship? Is it really *Bible study* when someone quotes a Scripture verse and the group discusses it, and no one even has a Bible? Is it really a *prayer meeting* to sit quietly in the dark with two or three other believers and pray silently? Can it really be *witnessing* just to work hard at your job and be pleasant under pressure? Yes. All of these are legitimate ways of serving and living for God. Satan will flood the minds of the believers with such questions and immediately supply the negative answers. And the burden of false guilt grows.

c. Attitude toward the government

When a believer attempts to obey the biblical teaching to be a good citizen of a restrictive country, Satan accuses him of compromising his Christian witness. If he tries to resist the government's oppression, Satan will accuse him of disobeying the Scriptures and refusing to submit to authority. If Christians in a restrictive land love their country, Satan will accuse them of being traitors to the cause of Christ. Jesus taught, *"Give to Caesar what is Caesar's, and to God what is God's"* (Matthew 22:21). Paul teaches in Romans 13:1-7 that no governmental power exists without God's permission. But a secular government does not have all authority (see 1 Peter 2:13-17; 1 Timothy 2:1-4; Titus 3:1-2). We are taught that our responsibility to the government includes:

- being submissive
- obeying the laws
- doing good
- respecting those in authority

- being peaceful and friendly
- praying for those in authority
- not speaking against them
- paying taxes

We noticed in Jesus' response to the Pharisees to *"Give...to God what is God's"* (Matthew 22:21), which teaches us that some areas of authority belong uniquely to God. If human governments attempt to usurp this authority and infringe on those areas reserved to God, the believer must then obey God rather than those in control (Acts 4:19; 5:29). This concept is taught by word and example throughout the Scriptures.

Suffering should never be for evil deeds, but suffering for what is right becomes our joy and honor. 1 Peter 2:20; Matthew 5:11-12

- Shadrach, Meshach and Abednego refused the king's order to worship the golden image.
- Daniel refused to obey the king's order that he could not pray.
- Peter and John refused to obey the ruling council's directive not to preach about Jesus.
- Paul disregarded a city ordinance when he left Damascus in a basket over the wall to escape murderers.
- Paul witnessed to his military guards in Rome although Christianity had been outlawed.

It is important to note that this disobedience came only as rulers moved from the realm of civil authority into the realm of worship and obedience to God. We must be careful of Peter's warning (1 Peter 2:15-16) not to use our Christian freedom to justify evil.

d. Submission and obedience

If the Christian turns against his own country because it has fallen under the control of a political force that is hostile to Christianity,

Satan will try to lay a burden of guilt upon him that will undermine his spiritual life. The Christian can show his good citizenship under a repressive regime by being an unusually good worker, sharing already meager food rations, or helping to share the load being carried by an older person.

Some Christians may seize an opportunity to flee from a repressive country. But, often in these cases, the Christian can expect Satan to viciously attack him with guilt feelings for leaving. This is part of the price a Christian always has to pay for any unpopular stand he may take under the leadership of the Holy Spirit. But we have learned how to deal with this, whether it is true guilt, based on disobedience to God, or false guilt, based on the judgments and traditions of men.

4. Fear

It is natural for people to be afraid. We especially fear the unknown, being hurt and death. There is nothing our adversary would like more than to see us paralyzed with fear—just like King Saul was when he faced the Philistines and Goliath. (see 1 Samuel 17)

Satan uses and plays on one of the basic elements and instincts of our nature—fear.

a. Personal fears

Why do we allow fear to control us? On the one hand, we have past experiences that we don't want to relive, and on the other hand, we are very hesitant about what might lie ahead. But often the events and situations creating the most fear in people have no basis in reality.

All fear is based on perception. Thus **FEAR** has been defined in the English language as an acronym for "**F**alse **E**vidence **A**ppearing **R**eal." If we could consciously remember this, it would help us to allay many of our fears. But that false evidence sometimes is so convincing! However, we must always realize that dread and fear, like other tactics of the enemy, are based on a lie. This is why throughout the Scriptures we are repeatedly commanded to *"fear not."* It is intensely liberating for our witness when we personally overcome the fear of death. This allows us to focus on Christ and His kingdom.

b. Combating fear

The Christian must be solidly anchored on four biblical pillars to combat fear:

- God is in control. He will only allow us to experience what He knows is best for us. We must trust Him as we're encouraged to do in Philippians 4:6-7 and Acts 27:23-25.
- We are only pilgrims and strangers on this earth. Our real home is heaven. Some of us may be called to enter our heavenly home earlier than we expect. We must be ready. (see Hebrews 10:32-39)
- God always brings good from evil as we're told in Romans 8:28. Joseph told his brothers, *"You intended to harm me, but God intended it for good...."* (Genesis 50:20)
- The enemy can only harm our bodies, not our eternal condition (Luke 12:4-5). Jesus advised us to get our priorities straight when He said, *"Do not be afraid of those who kill the body but cannot kill the soul. Rather be afraid of the One who can destroy both soul and body in hell."* (Matthew 10:28)

c. Fear in crisis situations

Satan also delights in causing "panic attacks" in a crisis situation. The Chinese have an interesting lesson in the two characters chosen for their word *"crisis."* One character is *danger* and the other is *opportunity.* The inference is that in every crisis experience, both elements are present. So a crisis is a dangerous situation presenting an opportunity.

When you focus on just the danger, you become paralyzed by fear. Focusing on the opportunity, however, enables you to fly with wings of faith. It is we, ourselves, who choose on which of the two we will focus.

d. Fear of speaking out against injustice and sin

Similar reasons for our personal fears also keep us from being the voice of God in a fallen world on behalf of His church. There is a time for Christians to speak out forcefully against the injustices and sinfulness of our own society and culture. This is especially true in situations where we can help our brothers and sisters who suffer. But fear can keep us tongue-tied. As the church, we must learn to speak out and not be cowed by fear.

But remember, when we are fearful, we can claim the promise of Scripture: *"For God did not give us a spirit of timidity, but a spirit of power, of love and of self-discipline"* (2 Timothy 1:7)..We must always remember who has won the ultimate victory and what Satan's final outcome will be. (Revelation 20:10)

And we must remember that the positive side of fear is what the Bible calls *"the fear of the Lord."* The respectful fear of God dispels all other fears.

e. Fear of death

For many in our world today, our number one fear is public speaking. Our number two fear is death. One comedian commented, "That means that if you are at a funeral, you are better off in the coffin than giving the eulogy."[4]

When Jeremiah was still a child, he was called by the Lord to speak to the spiritual leaders of the nation. It appears he was fearful of the assignment when he said, *"I do not know how to speak; I am only a child."* But the Lord said to him, *"Do not be afraid of them, for I am with you…"* (see Jeremiah 1:6-8). One translation has this wording: *"Be not **afraid of their faces**: for I am with thee to deliver thee, saith the LORD"* (KJV, emphasis added). Looking at the eyes of people while we speak, especially to a group, is for many people an intimidating process. We may wonder whether they like us and agree with our words, or if they are going to turn against us and harm us.

Fear of dying is for many people their number one fear! There is a sense of the unknown ahead. Hamlet's famous "to be or not to be, that is the question" soliloquy echoes this haunting uncertainty of death when he says, "For in that sleep of death what dreams may come, When we have shuffled off this mortal coil, Must give us pause." (Hamlet, Act III, Scene I, line 67)

The primary secret of Standing Strong Through the Storm *is to have no fear of death. Luke 9:23; Galatians 6:14 and Revelation 12:11*

Virtually every fear has a relationship to death and a connection to dying. For example, why are we afraid of flying? The plane may crash and we may die. That is why Christians around the world take great comfort in the words of our Lord when He said, *"Do not be afraid of those who kill the body but cannot kill the soul. Rather be afraid of the One who can destroy both soul and body in hell."* (Matthew 10:28)

At an SSTS seminar in Central Asia, our translator looked at us at the close of our three-day session and commented, "Thank you for teaching us how to stand strong. God spoke to me a lot through this seminar. I was afraid to die but not any more. I have peace to go and spread God's Word." She is now serving the Lord in a strategic mission in her region.

A significant factor in dealing with the fear of dying is realizing that we are *already dead* in Christ (Galatians 2:20). Open Doors colleague Hector Tamez says that this concept is clearly seen in the lives of Christians living in war zones of Latin America. The Christians caught in the civil war between the government and Shining Path guerrillas in Peru are a classic example for us. Here is how Hector expresses their commitment:

They know that they are going to be killed. And they say, "In order to be a Christian here, you have to recognize that you are already dead in Christ. Once you recognize this, then any day that passes by in your life is a gain."

In some countries, surviving one day or one year means that you have one God-given day or year to testify not only with your words but with your deeds. Fear should not control your life! Christ should control your life!

> *If you are a Christian and you are filled with the Holy Spirit and have lost your fear of death, you are unstoppable until God calls you home to heaven!—Paul Estabrooks*

5. Syncretism

Satan has led many quasi-religious groups to unite around a mixture of religious teachings and then brand honest Christian believers as *bigots* for clinging to salvation in Christ alone.

An outgrowth of the postmodern era in which we live is that many people no longer believe in absolute truth. A natural extension of this lack of absolutes is the widely held view that there is good in every religion and all roads lead to heaven. Individuals can then pick and choose the elements they wish from whatever faith and mix them all together. This is true syncretism. Chuck Colson refers to its impact on our faith as "salad-bar Christianity!"[5] Thus the New Age Movement would be classed as syncretistic.

The key words of syncretism are *tolerance* and *dialogue.* Both of these are good words and concepts, but they are used in this context to bring about a compromise of biblical teachings. Josh McDowell has written an entire book explaining how the definition of *tolerance* has been changed by the world to now mean more than respect and acceptance. Now it means you must approve and endorse the other person's beliefs, values and lifestyle.[6]

The biblical character Lot allowed compromise in the form of syncretism to creep into his life. In Genesis 13, we see him living in the Jordan valley near the wicked city of Sodom. By chapter 14, he is living inside the city. And by chapter 19, he is sitting at the gate, a position of leadership in those days. Due to his Uncle Abraham's pleading with God, Lot's life was spared in the destruction of Sodom and Gomorrah.

Satan is delighted when people believe and expound on his lies. He does not want anyone to know the truth and come to a personal relationship with Jesus who is **the** truth, **the** way and **the** life (John 14:6). Jesus is the **only** way.

One man reportedly traveled the world to find one name for God that would be universal and bring all people together. Instantly the word *love* came to his mind. He later wrote, "Give God the universal name of Love and we will create a golden cord to tie together the truths of all the religions of the world."[7] But *love* is not God's name. It is His nature. And God expressed it most fully when He sent His Son to die for our sins (John 3:16). Only when we accept Christ's sacrifice for us will we know the love of the one true God that can bind people together.

A few years ago, an inter-faith group of 10,000 people met at the Vatican in Rome. The group included the Pope, the Dalai Lama and Muslim Imam W. D. Mohammed. An outspoken Hindu woman was quoted as saying, "It was refreshing to note that the idea that all religions have universal truths, and are merely different paths to the same goal was accepted as a given from the outset by all delegates without a single dissenting voice."[8]

"Tolerance" is the Shibboleth (Judges 12:6) of our post-modern society.

The same delegates also endorsed a general condemnation of "aggressive" proselytizing. This is the prevailing thinking of our day and age. Satan will do all he can to cause this thinking to even invade the church and individual Christian thinking and action.

The end result of syncretism in free societies will be anti-conversion laws and a prohibition of Christian witnessing. The euphemism for this law will probably be called "religious freedom." Some free nations (for example, Brazil) already have a federal law declaring it a crime to "practice, induce, or incite discrimination" against members of another religion.

Figure 3: Act for the Protection of Religious Freedom

Key provisions of the legislation proposed in Sri Lanka
(COMPASS DIRECT, 24 June, 2004)

The bill introduces itself as legislation that will strengthen the "mutual trust/unity that exists among religions and with a view to protecting the religious freedom that people have enjoyed in the past. An Act to provide for the prohibition of conversion to another religion forcibly or by use of force or inducement, or by fraud, or by unethical means or in any other manner…."

The key focus of the bill appears to be on the person responsible for the conversion, rather than the person who actually converts, although both are covered by the bill. Section 2 states: "No person shall convert or attempt to convert another person to another religion, and no person shall provide assistance or encouragement towards such conversion to another religion."

Sections 3, 4 and 5 deals with "conversion by force"—persuading someone to attend "prayers or prayer meetings of any religion of which he is not a member." This applies particularly to any employer or person holding a position of trust or responsibility, including teachers, hospital staff and children's caregivers.

Under Section 5(v), if conversion is "committed" by a group of persons, "every director or shareholder...partner, member, employee or officer of that group or company shall be guilty of an offense."

Under Section 5(vi), any non-permanent citizen of Sri Lanka who is found guilty of an offense under this Act may be expelled from the republic and banned from re-entry.

Under Section 6, court action against conversion may be initiated by the police, by any person "affected aggrieved by an offense" or by anyone "interested in the welfare of the public who has reason to believe that the provisions of this Act have been contravened."

6. Materialism

Satan subtly promotes the attitude that says money, property, possessions, physical comforts, as well as worldly fame and honor are the most important things in life.

While God created all things and is the source of all we have, He does not condone our allowing things and money to usurp His first place in our lives. The prosperity that He so freely gives us, and wants us to have, is indeed a blessing until it takes the place of God. Materialism is thus the attitude that says money, property, possessions, physical comforts, as well as worldly fame and honor, are the most important things in life. Not to say, "There is no God," but to say, "We don't have any need for God!"

Materialism is the subtlest trap of Satan. We can have all the Christian externals and yet be complete materialists in our hearts.

For Christians, materialism is much like the frog in a pan of water that is slowly being heated. He boils to death because he does not realize the danger quickly enough to jump out of the pot before it is too late.

A church leader from the country of Romania, which was once a communist-dominated land and is now free, commented, "In my experience, 95% of the believers who face the test of external persecution pass it, while 95% of those who face the test of prosperity fail it!"[9]

In Jesus' day, a rich person was one who had more food than needed for the day and who had more than one set of clothing.

Satan is ecstatic when he succeeds in luring us into this trap. This is the dark side to money and possessions that many Christians are either unaware of, or unwilling to face. As a result, the spiritual vitality of many has been sapped and the church as a whole has been weakened spiritually. Like fire, money is a good servant but a destructive master. If the church is to survive this challenge, there is an urgent need to be aware of the true nature of materialism. Unfortunately, it has become such a vital part of our culture that Christians are often unaware of its control.

By the standard of the people around Jesus, many of today's so-called poor are very rich as well as almost all those in free societies. Being rich is not in itself wrong. Materialism, however, has the following characteristics.

a. Materialism has extremely seductive power.

Riches are dangerous because their seductive power often causes people to reject Christ and His kingdom. The rich young ruler who turned sadly away after being told that he had to part with his riches to inherit salvation prompted Jesus' statement, *"How hard it is for the rich to enter the kingdom of God."* (Luke 18:24; Mark 10:23; Matthew 19:23)

b. Materialism can cause people to do almost anything.

A desire for riches can cause people to do almost anything—even to the extent of selling their souls. The result, Scripture warns, is anguish now and damnation later (1 Timothy 6:9-10). An abundance of possessions can easily lead us to forget that God is the Source of all good. The people of Israel were warned of this before they entered the Promised Land. (Deuteronomy 8:11-17)

There are two opposing masters on Earth: God and Money. You are a slave to the one you obey. Matthew 6:24; Romans 6:16

The pursuit of wealth often results in wars. James 4:1-2 says this clearly and it is amply confirmed from world history. Instead of fostering more compassion toward the poor, riches often harden the hearts of the wealthy. Rich persons are often unconcerned about the poor at their doorstep. (Luke 16:19-31; Isaiah 5:8-10; Amos 6:4-7; James 5:1-5)

c. Materialism is insatiable.

Money is not neutral; it is a power with a life of its own. It is a power that is even demonic in character. When Jesus uses the Aramaic term *mammon,* translated as *money* in the NIV (Matthew 6:24), to refer to wealth, He is giving it a personal and spiritual character as a rival god. Mammon is a power that seeks to dominate us.

Hence, money is an active agent. It is a law unto itself—capable of inspiring devotion. It is tremendously instructive to stand back and observe the frantic scramble of people for money. And this does not occur just among the poor and starving. Even the super rich still seek it furiously. The middle class continue to buy more houses, acquire more cars and purchase more clothes than they need. If money were only a medium of exchange, it would make no sense at all to attach such prestige to it. We value people in relation to their income. We give people status and honor in relation to how much money they have or appear to have.

d. Materialism is powerful, but it can be overcome.

How is the god Mammon conquered? The Bible offers a perspective from which to view all of life's economic decisions. The Holy Spirit is with us; Jesus is our present Teacher. The following are some suggestions.

- *Get in touch with our feelings about money.* Get in touch with our fear, insecurity, guilt, pride or envy. We are afraid to be short of money. And our fears, though irrational, are real. We need to face up to these feelings before we can apply God's promises to our financial situation.
- *Stop denying our wealth.* Instead of seeing the small picture of our situation, let us become world citizens, looking at ourselves in relation to all humanity.

- *Create an atmosphere in which confession is possible.* Much of our preaching about money has been either to condemn it or to praise it but not to help each other relate to it. Many of us feel isolated and alone. How much better if we could confess our fears and temptations by praying, "Forgive me, for I have sinned; money has captured my heart!"
- *Discover one other person who will struggle with you through the money maze.* Together covenant to help each other detect when the seductive power of money is beginning to win. This needs to be done in a spirit of love and graciousness. We need people who will help us, rebuke us, encourage us or prod us.
- *Discover ways to get in touch with the poor.* One of the damaging results of affluence is allowing us to distance ourselves from the poor so that we no longer see their pain. We need to be among the poor, not to preach to them but to learn from them.
- *Give with glad and generous hearts.* Giving has a way of rooting out the tough old miser within us. Even the poor need to know that they too can give. Just the very act of letting go of money, or some other treasure, does something within us. It destroys the sin of greed.

In our struggle against the power of mammon, let us view God as a friend who wants to help us, rather than as an enemy who condemns us. This journey toward a simpler lifestyle begins with prayer, that is, telling the Lord that we want to follow Him all the way. The rest is obedience as He directs and instructs.

Chinese house church leaders recently met together to discuss their problems. They concluded that their number two problem (after gossip) was money and the lure of materialism. There are two main sources of this. One is the rising standard of living in the coastal areas, which is tempting good teachers into commerce, depriving the church of much-needed leaders.

The other is the kind, but often indiscriminate, giving of some wealthier Christians and missions to house church networks. One group of churches from Europe gave a house church leader U.S. $10,000 to start an underground seminary. [Note: This is equivalent to receiving an amount (in cash) equal to *one hundred months* of one's current monthly income!] The house church leader used only a third of it for that purpose, and emigrated with the rest.

His supervisor noted, "Few of us can handle that kind of temptation, especially as we have been very poor all our lives. But he should not have been put into that situation—the money was given privately, without accountability."

Church leaders came up with a number of strategies for ensuring greater accountability among the pastors. They also issued a plea to Christians: "Please pray very carefully before you give money, and try to give it mainly through established missions that have a history of contact with house church movements. Keep private giving to a minimum."

B. CONCLUSION

Our adversary tries to misinform, confuse and deceive believers in every way possible. He also tries to capitalize on our disposition to fear. But the Holy Spirit, who is the Spirit of Truth, can expose all Satan's lies, and give us the courage we need, if we seek His guidance.

Satan uses two familiar tactics—deceit and intimidation—for the ultimate purpose of alienating us from God.

We must be determined to not give Satan any opportunity (Ephesians 4:27). We must arm ourselves against him (Ephesians 6:10-18), and then resist him with our God-given strength (James 4:7). We can call upon our Lord to rebuke him (Jude 9) and have the confidence that by the shed blood of Christ victory can be ours. (Revelation 12:10-11)

STUDY GUIDE/DISCUSSION QUESTIONS

PASTOR FOCUS

1. You are traveling in a restricted nation and money is scarce. Bibles and other spiritual training materials are in short supply. One day you hear that a well-meaning Christian leader has promised a local pastor that if he can plant new churches, there will be much more money available. They come and ask your advice on the offer.
    - What guidelines and safeguards would you offer the local church leaders to ensure proper accountability of resources for both the giver and receiver?
    - To whom should money be given: an individual or a committee?
    - What accountability procedures should be established?

2. If materialism is the "subtlest trap" of Satan (because we can have all the Christian externals and yet be complete materialists in our hearts), and if as one church leader from Romania observed: "95% of the believers who face the test of external persecution pass it, while 95% of those who face the test of

prosperity fail it," how do **you** overcome materialism as a pastor and what do you teach about it without becoming legalistic?

3. Using principles from the lives of the following people, outline how **you** would teach Christians to *"obey God rather than men"* (Acts 4:19; 5:29). What are the biblical guidelines for civil disobedience?
    - Shadrach, Meshach and Abednego
    - Daniel
    - Peter and John
    - Paul

WOMEN'S FOCUS

The Chinese word for "Crisis" is a combination of the characters for "Danger" and "Opportunity."

CRISIS

DANGER 危

OPPORTUNITY 機

What do **you** use as biblical principles to overcome the following?

- Fear in crisis situations

- Fear of speaking out against injustice and sin

YOUTH FOCUS

1. How does Satan use "fear" to increase pressure and persecution in your life today?

   How does *"perfect love cast out fear"?* (see 1 John 4:18)

2. Tell how **you** can use the following biblical defenses against "fear."
   - Philippians 4:6-7 and Acts 27:23-25

- Hebrews 10:32-39

- Romans 8:28

- Luke 12:4-5

- Matthew 10:28

MEN'S FOCUS

1. Why is guilt such an effective weapon?

2. If you confess your sin, what will happen to the true guilt?

   How can you tell true guilt from false guilt?

3. How do **you** deal with unresolved guilt?

4. Explain how the following can counter Satan's accusations. (see Revelation 12:11)
   - The Blood of the Lamb

   - The Word of Testimony

   - Sacrificial Love

5. What kinds of things are outside the authority of a civil government?

6. How might **you** handle those who ask, "Why are you not obeying the government?" (see Romans 13)

7. How might **you** answer the voice of doubt inside that asks, "Can a gathering of two or three under a tree on a weekday be real worship?"

8. Identify what Scripture teaches regarding our attitude toward and responsibility to government.

3

THE BATTLE AROUND US

Be self-controlled and alert. Your enemy the devil prowls around like a roaring lion looking for someone to devour. Resist him, standing firm in the faith, because you know that your brothers throughout the world are undergoing the same kind of sufferings.

1 Peter 5:8-9

Chinese pastor Wang Ming-dao was under tremendous pressure after his first arrest. He was promised release from prison and return to his pulpit if he would just "preach for the government." In his mind this would be lying and he was certain he could not live a hypocritical life.

Pastor Wang was firm in his resolve—until he heard that his beloved wife, Debra, had also been arrested and was in grave danger. He heard that she was not eating properly and was growing critically weak because of the poor food she was receiving in prison. She would not survive if something was not done. This news so disturbed him that he broke and agreed with his persecutors that he would preach a lie and join the government-controlled church.[1]

His plan was to get his wife to safety with her mother and then he would commit suicide. He reportedly wandered the streets murmuring, "I am Peter... I am Peter...," and his heart-sickness began to affect his body.

When the authorities realized that he would not compromise himself by preaching in the government-controlled church, Pastor Wang and his wife were rearrested. She received a fifteen-year sentence, and he life imprisonment.

Early in this second imprisonment, God brought to his mind Micah 7:7-9, a passage he had memorized many years before.

> *But as for me, I keep watch in hope for the Lord, I wait for God my Savior; my God will hear me. Do not gloat over me my enemy! Though I have fallen, I will rise. Though I sit in darkness, the Lord will be my light. Because I have sinned against him, I will bear the Lord's wrath, until he pleads my case and establishes my right. He will bring me out into the light; I will see his righteousness.*

Wang Ming-dao was no longer afraid for himself or his wife. He was finally released in 1980 at eighty years of age—very frail, nearly blind and all-but-deaf. He had served more than twenty-three years in prison. His wife, Debra, had been released three years earlier for health reasons. In the remaining eleven years of his life, he greatly encouraged the church in China as well as the many foreign visitors he and Debra entertained.

A. SATAN'S METHODS

Often in a physical battle, it is the ability of an army to turn defeat into victory that wins the war. This is not a theme foreign to the Scriptures—it is the very heart of the Gospel. Death was overcome by life. (1 Corinthians 15:54-56; Hebrews 2:14-15)

Scripture is realistic about our nature. Battle scars are never grafted over. In heaven itself, Jesus will bare His own scars to remind us of our human limitation and also of the great cost of our redemption.

We may sin and fail, but our failure must turn into repentance and renewal with deeper dependence on the Lord and not into self-condemnation.

Satan has the power to work signs and wonders (2 Thessalonians 2:9), and all his evil power is directed against God and His church. This is why the Bible says that we are not fighting earthly rulers or authorities. (Ephesians 6:11-12)

Christians of the Persecuted Church do not want to be considered as superheroes, never to doubt or falter in their walk with Christ.

Satan's effort to make us sin does not excuse us from being responsible for our own actions and reactions. We are morally responsible before God for our own *bent* to sinning. Yet we must also recognize the enemy's tactics when we are tempted.

Some sin mainly affects the person who sins, but much of our sin influences others in significant ways. For example, Satan has been stirring up racial hatred between groups, and some Christians have been caught up in this sinful hatred. Satan has caused militant religious groups to wage direct and violent acts of aggression, terror and war against Christians. He will even try to cut believers off from contact with those people they can influence and from those who can nurture their faith. He also creates conflict and division between believers who fellowship together.

We must not assume that any one political or religious system is inherently more "satanic," evil or anti-Christian than any other human-generated system of government.

Every totalitarian regime deals with Christians and the church on the basis of control issues. Paranoia is thus a major characteristic of all totalitarian regimes. When confronted with direct and severe violence, Christians are totally dependent on their relationship with the Holy Spirit.

B. SATAN'S EXTERNAL TACTICS IN THE NEW TESTAMENT

In the New Testament, we see Satan using five external tactics against the church: rulers, priests, merchants, mobs and families, and these often occurred in combinations. When the enemies of Jesus Christ see people following Him, these enemies tend to unite. Therefore, unlikely alliances are often formed.

Jesus Himself saw this happen. The Pharisees and the Herodians—two groups of people who usually would not speak to each other—got together to plot His assassination after He healed a man with a withered hand on the Sabbath. (Mark 3:6)

1. Government/"Rulers"

Surprising to some, rulers are not the biggest persecutors of Christians in the New Testament. That dubious honor falls to the Jewish priestly caste. But, there is no doubt that strong opposition came from rulers. For example, Pontius Pilate had a part in the death of Jesus; Herod Agrippa killed the Apostle James in Jerusalem (Acts 12:2); and in AD 64, Nero initiated a terrible persecution against the Christians of Rome, the community to which most scholars think Mark wrote his Gospel to encourage persecuted Christians there.

2. Priests/"Religious" Officials

It is not "politically correct" to say it was Jewish priests who were primarily responsible for putting Jesus on the cross (Matthew 26:3-4). But, on the Day of Pentecost, Peter was very direct when speaking to a Jewish audience about the crucifixion of Jesus. He called Jesus, *"this Jesus, whom you crucified"* (Acts 2:36). Pilate wanted to let Jesus go and tried to accomplish this by arranging to release Him to the crowd (see John 18:31). Though in the end it *was* Pilate's order to prosecute Jesus, the Jewish high priest was the one who pushed Pilate into giving the order for the prosecution. Throughout His ministry, Jesus' bitterest enemies were the priests.

And so it proved for the early church. The first flogging of Christians was done under the auspices of the Sanhedrin (Acts 5:40), and the first martyrdom of a Christian (Stephen) was carried out by enraged clerics (Acts 7:54-59). And so it continued also for Paul, the main character of the early church, ironically a former Pharisee and a witness to the stoning of Stephen.

Yes, it is a sad fact that the classes threatened most by committed Christians are either those with different religious beliefs or those from a rival religion. This is not to say all clerics are persecutors. Many Pharisees became followers of Jesus, and some, like Nicodemus and Simon, were the very model of courtesy and open-mindedness. Nevertheless, in the history of the Church, other "believers" have perpetrated the most violence on Christians.

3. Merchants/"Rich Guys"

Merchants, or businessmen, represent the economic establishment and often oppose Christians purely because Christians are a threat to their business.

The two clearest examples of opposition from businessmen in Scripture are when Paul visits Philippi and later Ephesus (Acts 16, 19). In Philippi, Paul and Silas ended up in jail because of the actions of the owners of a *"slave girl who had a spirit by which she predicted the future."* That is, she was "demon-possessed" (Acts 16:16). Today we would call her a psychic. Paul commanded the evil spirit to come out of this girl, and she was healed! Her owners, knowing their source of income had disappeared, pressed charges against Paul. They had him jailed for *"throwing the city into an uproar,"* that is, for disturbing the peace. The Scripture clearly states that the motive of the girl's owners was economic. It says that *"when the owners of the slave girl realized that their hope of making money was gone, they seized Paul and Silas and dragged them into the marketplace to face the authorities."* (Acts 16:19)

Later when Paul gets to Ephesus, the impact of his preaching that *"man-made gods are no gods at all"* threatened the business of the silversmiths. A silversmith named Demetrius realized that anything that reduced the appeal of the statues of and the shrines to the goddess Artemis would adversely affect their business. He called a meeting of the silversmiths and after talking with them, they stirred up a riot which resulted in Paul having to leave the city.

4. Mobs/"Rowdies"

Mobs play a major role in persecution. When an elite group cannot get the government to do their evil work for them, they may motivate a mob to do it. A mob can be easily swayed by the heady rhetoric of clerics, or by ruffians who are willing to commit bodily harm for the sake of money.

The clearest scriptural example of this is in Acts 17:5: *"But the Jews were jealous; so they rounded up some bad characters from the marketplace, formed a mob and started a riot in the city."* Christians in Pakistan and Indonesia face the constant threat of complete destruction of their property by mobs. A news agency journalist said, "I'm amazed at how quickly a mob can get going in Pakistan. It just takes three phrases from a mullah at Friday prayers, and five minutes later thousands are streaming out into the streets bent on inflicting injury or even killing Christians."

5. Families/"Relatives"

Anyone from a family of unbelievers who has become a Christian can testify to the many ways rejection and even persecution can be experienced. Jesus warned of this in strong language. He said, *"I have come to turn a man against his father, a daughter against her mother, a daughter-in-law against her mother-in-law—a man's enemies will be the members the of his own household."* (Matthew 10:35-36)

Most families in the world are not nuclear in nature, but rather are extended families. Mark 1:29 gives an example of an extended family. We're told that Simon and Andrew and Simon's mother-in-law shared a "home." Most likely others of the family lived there also.

In an extended family, an entire web of kinship relations is strained when someone in the family becomes a Christian. It could be said that it is one's "family culture" that rejects the Christian witness. One reason for this is over-familiarity. Jesus generalizes from His own experience of rejection in Nazareth, saying, *"And they took offense at him. But Jesus said to them, 'Only in his hometown and in his own house is a prophet without honor.'"* (Matthew 13:57)

Rejection of a family member goes right back to the dawn of human history. The first recorded act in Scripture of such—total rejection of a family member—is in Genesis 4:8. Motivated by religious jealousy, Cain killed his brother, Abel.

Rejection and violence within the family continued through the historical section of the Bible. King David's own son Absalom betrayed his father and sought to take his father's life so that he might become king in his father's place. (2 Samuel 15–17)

The prophet Jeremiah is dismayed to find that members of his own family were involved in an assassination plot against him: *"Your brothers, your own family—even they have betrayed you; they have raised a loud cry against you."* (Jeremiah 12:6)

In China today, if a student converts to Christianity, it is the parents who insist that their son or daughter give up the faith. This is usually out of fear that their child will be allotted an inferior work placement and so bring dishonor to the family.

In Buddhist societies in Burma, to become a Christian is looked upon by the rest of the family as that person saying, "I am no longer Burmese." Family misunderstanding and family rejection are extremely difficult to bear since we crave the love of our family. To have that love relationship ruptured is a great trauma to the one who becomes a Christian.

But Jesus knew both misunderstanding and rejection from family members. When just a boy, He was misunderstood by His mother (Luke 2:48). And later in life, *"his own did not receive him"* as their long-awaited Messiah (John 1:11). His crucifixion was the ultimate rejection by His own.

In Pakistan, a father was asked why he murdered his daughter. He answered simply, "I didn't murder my daughter. When she became a Christian, she was no longer my daughter." He will never be charged for his crime. Satan's activity can also be seen when Christian daughters are abducted and married to Muslim men and the family has no legal way to get them back.

C. OTHER EXTERNAL TACTICS OF OUR ENEMY

We must not assume that any one political or religious system is inherently more "satanic" than any other human-generated system of government. Every totalitarian regime deals with Christians and the church on the basis of control issues. Paranoia is thus a major characteristic of all totalitarian regimes, and control is the main factor. Here are some of the significant external methods Satan uses in our own day and age.

1. Isolation and Conflict

One of the enemy's favorite ways to deal with a dynamic Christian witness is isolation. Satan will try to cut a believer off from contact with those whom he can influence, and from those who can nurture his faith. Many believers have found this tactic very hard to fight. Satan often motivates government officials to bring pressure against public meetings of Christians. Next, key members of the fellowship may be killed or driven to other areas.

Meanwhile, propaganda is spread and weak believers wonder where their friends have gone or why all the missionaries have left. No one mentions that the government has forced the missionary exodus and consciously dispersed Christians. If believers, because of fear, cut themselves off from all contact with other Christians, Satan will have won. Christians cannot survive victoriously for long if they choose to spiritually cut themselves off from fellowship and teaching.

If physical isolation is *forced* on believers, they must turn to a deeper spiritual fellowship with Christ. This must be coupled with an increased alertness to look for other Christians. Often an isolated Christian can speak a simple word, hum a few bars of a hymn, or make a Christian symbol and thereby make contact with other secret believers.

On some occasions, believers will be able to have Christian fellowship at least with their own family. This may be their only encouragement, but they should constantly be on the lookout for other possibilities. It may sometimes be necessary for believers to lead someone else to a saving knowledge of Jesus Christ to end their isolation! We have seen this happen many times when believers were committed to maintain a dynamic relationship with their Lord.

Another favorite tactic of the enemy is to create conflict and division relationally between believers who fellowship together. This may arise over disagreement about forms of worship, power struggles for leadership within the church, or political or family differences. The church must be on guard for this and strive to live in unity above all things (Ephesians 4:3). This may mean putting others' needs above our own (Mark 9:35). Our strength against the enemy depends on unity.

But direct and aggressive conflict from other religious groups is becoming disturbingly more commonplace in our day and age. In Indonesia, Christians are frequently confronted by mob rage whipped up by Muslim extremists. In India, militant Hinduism is becoming more involved in direct violence and even murder. And in Sri Lanka, Buddhism, normally a non-violent religion, has its extremists who have destroyed evangelical churches.

Many, many Christians, directed by the Holy Spirit, can testify of miraculous escapes. Others, who may also have been directed by the Holy Spirit as they sought to escape, are martyred. There seems to be little middle ground. But in both extremes, Christ is glorified and the Kingdom of God marches on victoriously.

When confronted with direct and severe violence, Christians are dependent on their relationship with the Holy Spirit for wise guidance on when to flee, when to stay and when to ask for a miracle. Acts 9:23-30; 13:10-11; 16:22-24; 1 Corinthians 9:22

2. Nationalism

Satan has inspired rulers to try to force Christians to return to their former folk religions or the pagan gods of their ancestors—all in the name of patriotism or nationalism.

Religious nationalism is where a particular territory or culture is staked out exclusively in religious terms. Leaders say, "Only Hindus are allowed to stay in India." Or, "You are a true Sri Lankan only if you are a Buddhist." In such cases where religious nationalism reigns, Christians either must accept second-class citizen status, face daily discrimination, or leave.

Research done by Open Doors indicates that to establish a "Religious State" the Religious Nationalists require four elements: *a villain, a lie, a mob,* and *a vacuum.* They need a "villain" who can unite the people with a powerful message; a "lie" (Christians are intolerant); a "mob" to create chaos (media support helps); and a "vacuum" (absence of moderates in power to control the nation).

Some in India and Nepal argue that their country is Hindu hence other religions are foreign and imperialist. State assistance is denied to those who convert to non-Hindu religions.[2]

At one point, the Mongolian State Intelligence Bureau described Christianity as a "foreign religion." And today, Mongolia's new laws imply that Christianity is "against Mongolian customs."

In Mexico, a mayor of a community in the southern state of Chiapas has tried to justify the ongoing persecution of evangelicals with the claim that they "attack...our culture and traditions." In reality, tens of thousands of Christians have been expelled from their homes for not joining in the syncretistic community spiritual activities.

Christians in an area of Swaziland were told by their chief that each Christian would be fined a cow for not attending the annual cultural ceremonies at the king's royal cattle kraal. The chief announced that he had compiled a list of all his subjects who deliberately avoided two yearly ceremonies: the *umhlanga* (reed dance) and the *incwala* (first fruit). Pastors of churches accused of preaching against Swazi culture are among those fined.[3]

In the first ceremony, young girls wear topless, traditional attire and brief bead skirts that expose the buttocks and thighs. Therefore, Christian parents will not allow their daughters to participate in that ceremony.

In the second ceremony, boys are required to slaughter a black bull with their bare hands, a ritual that church leaders describe as "unchristian." Therefore boys in the local Christian community are encouraged to not take part in this ceremony.

Pastors in the area plan to challenge the chief's fines in a court of law.

Christians must avoid the mistake of identifying religion with nation, and nation with religion. To do so severely hinders the growth of the Body of Christ where there is *"neither Jew nor Greek."* (Galatians 3:28)

The above stories illustrate a common ploy of Satan brought to bear on Christians.

3. Secular Humanism

Satan has led in the worldwide growth and acceptance of humanism, which exalts human wisdom above the revelation of God.

In essence secular humanism is a belief that man begins with himself as the center reference point of life and meaning.

Most world leaders in fields such as government, education, and international business have unknowingly accepted this lie of Satan and therefore mock Christian beliefs. In the secular, postmodern free societies of the world, Satan continues to use every means possible to discredit the Christian faith and the Bible—especially in academic and media environments.

Secular humanists are so determined to marginalize Christian belief that they would rather a presidential candidate lie than publicly profess his faith. They create an uproar that sends a clear message: profess Christianity at your peril. The forces that seek to diminish Christianity desire nothing less than to make those who love Christ not speak His name.

Today, this society of secular humanism—particularly its media—takes strong swipes at the church for standing for morality. They see God as marginal and look at Him as a big policeman. But society's view of God is too small.

"If nothing is worth dying for, is anything worth living for?"[4] Chuck Colson

In his book *The Secular Squeeze,*[5] John Alexander argues that the worst thing about secularism is that it trivializes life and renders it boring. He notes that somewhere along the way, we seem to have traded the possibility of heroism for comfort and "modern conveniences." At least those of us with air conditioning don't have to be bothered by the flies rising from the maggot-beds of a culture of death. This philosophy begins with man and ends in chaos.

Figure 4: The New, Secular Ten Commandments

by Paul Estabrooks and Jim Cunningham

(Original 10 Commandments Paraphrased in Bold)

1. **No other gods:** There is no God and there are no moral absolutes.
2. **No idols:** All religions and objects of worship are equal.
3. **Don't misuse the name of God:** Tolerance reigns: Thou shall not be judgmental.
4. **Remember the Sabbath Day to keep it holy:** All days in all ways are equal and fun.
5. **Honor your father and mother:** Me first, marriage is slavery; we must be free from children.
6. **Shall not murder:** It's my body and it's my choice, therefore, abortion and euthanasia are okay.
7. **Shall not commit adultery:** Sex for pleasure without moral consequences is freedom.
8. **Shall not steal:** Society owes it to me to pay for my expressions of self-fulfillment.
9. **Shall not give false witness:** Say whatever it takes to get whatever you want–now!
10. **Shall not covet:** Materialism and greed feed the New World Order.

4. Religious Intolerance

Other religious groups are one of the threatening tactics Satan uses against the Church of Jesus Christ. In the book of Acts we see over and over that the primary opposition to the spread of the Gospel in the early church was from religious groups. We must never view these groups as the enemy. We know who our real enemy is. In some parts of the world, the small percentage of extremists among Hindus, Buddhists and Muslims have encouraged mob violence and other forms of persecution against Christians. Our attitude toward them should be as one acronym for ***ISLAM*** suggests: ***I** Sincerely **L**ove **A**ll **M**uslims.*

Christians are to be known for their agape love for one another. John 13:35; 1 Corinthians 13

The tactic that our enemy uses in

these major religions of the world comes from his character of deceiving and lying. Some people are able to perceive elements of truth within the major religions of the world, but their essential teachings are deceivingly false.

a. Anticonversion laws

Anticonversion laws are one way other religions deal with people becoming Christians. In Nepal, Christians have spent years in prison for converting from Hinduism and for aiding others to convert. Apostasy, as defined by Islam, is punishable by death. Thus Muslim background believers literally risk their lives in following Jesus when their conversion becomes public.

b. Worship centers

In more severely controlled countries such as Saudi Arabia, worship of any kind, except in an approved center, is strictly forbidden. House church worshippers are actively hunted out and severely punished. Comparing this to the limited church attendance in free societies, British barrister (trial lawyer) Paul Diamond says, "At all costs, Americans must resist the tide of secularism. More than 25 million people in Great Britain consider themselves members of the Church of England but only 1.2 million attend church regularly. In Italy, less than 15% of the Catholic population attends Mass every week."[6]

c. Intimidation/Antiblasphemy laws

In countries such as Iran, wherever worship services are held in the mother-tongue language, pastors, elders, and worshippers are constantly observed and questioned about their involvement and the practices of their faith. One church in Tehran claims that questioning of someone from the church is a daily experience. Islamic dominant countries introduce antiblasphemy laws. These laws permit officials to arrest Christians on the word of a Muslim witness who claims the Christian said something against Islam.

d. Economic discrimination

In areas of religious intolerance, Christians are singled out and economic pressure is put on them. They then find it hard to get good jobs. If they already have good jobs, once it is known they are Christians they are either asked to leave or are demoted. In some countries, Christians receive fair treatment and enjoy freedom only if they remain quiet about their faith in Jesus Christ.

e. Martyrdom

Often when extremists become frustrated with an effective Christian leader, and all other methods to control fail, someone will be happy to take the leader's life. That Christian leader becomes a martyr with a premature arrival in heaven, but the spouse and children are left behind to suffer from this heavy-handed control method.

Martyrdom: When Christians experience death rather than deny their faith in allegiance to or identity with our Lord Jesus Christ.

f. Proselytism and enticement

Wherever possible, missionaries of cults and other religions do whatever possible to encourage Christians—usually those who are Christian in name only—to convert to their religion. Unfortunately, in countries such as Egypt, a significant number do convert to a cult or to some other religion. The lure to convert can be marriage, money, employment, social acceptance, and any other similar attraction.

Hardini was born to a devout Muslim family in Indonesia where everyone must go to the mosque every day to pray. Her father had strict rules for everyone in the family. One rule was that Hardini should never associate with Christians. Despite Hardini's devotion to Islam, her heart was heavy and she longed for inner peace. A Christian with a great sense of joy and peace befriended Hardini.

Hardini had the courage to tell her new friend about her spiritual hunger, and the friend offered to pray for her in the name of Jesus. After the Christian girl prayed, peace filled Hardini's heart and her life radically changed.

When Hardini's family discovered she had become a Christian, they spent hours and hours trying to entice her with force to recant her new faith. Hardini remained steadfast. Finally her parents made a painful decision—they totally disowned their daughter. That left Hardini with the choices of either recanting her faith or fleeing from her home and family. She chose to flee.

5. Ideologies

It is interesting to see how government people who held ideologies such as communism treated Christians in countries where they ruled, and in at least five cases still rule: China, Vietnam, Laos, North Korea and Cuba. Currently a quarter of the world's population still lives under these regimes.

The pattern of treatment these people used throughout most of the twentieth century included four key tactics.

a. Neutralization

Marx and Lenin did not plan to fight Christians. They expected the Christian faith to just fade away in a communist state. But when it didn't, they attempted to destroy it.

Some Christians fought the regime and were killed or imprisoned. Others denied Christ and submitted to the authorities. Some fled the country or died in the attempt. But a surprising number learned how to live in that hostile environment.

Christians who were familiar with the way the communists usually work were better prepared. Initially, Christians were often deceived into thinking that they could live peacefully with a communist government. The church was then stripped of its schools, hospitals, orphanages and social programs.

All foreign connections were severed, including receipt of funds.

Religious institutions dependent on foreign funds ceased to exist. Only those Christians who knew how to function as members of the Body of Christ were able to continue to thrive spiritually.

As time went on, the persecution became more open and severe. Individual Christians were singled out and economic pressure was put on them. They lost their jobs or were demoted. Fellowship meetings were forbidden. Travel by known Christians was restricted. Known leaders were more severely persecuted and weak Christians found they had no one to turn to for help.

Harassment became commonplace. Bibles became scarce. All printing presses were controlled by the government and could not be used to print Bibles and Christian literature. Then the collection of "reactionary literature" began. Bibles were prime targets. Soon, very few copies remained, and a serious blow had been struck against the church.

By this time, many church buildings were virtually unused, and the government took them over "for the use of the people." In some countries, a few were allowed to remain open as show places for propaganda purposes. In Laos, the government seized the church records when they took over the buildings, and used the membership rolls to identify "reactionaries." Then pressure against the few remaining Christians mounted. Children were indoctrinated against Christian teaching. Christian children were denied educational opportunities. Christians were given the most menial jobs. Food rations were cut.

Would you be able to stand for Christ in the face of such pressure? The thrilling fact is that millions of Christians have survived victoriously in Russia, Romania, Hungary, China, Vietnam, Ethiopia and other places in spite of persecution!

b. Threats

Totalitarian authorities believe that they can frighten everyone with a few violent acts and the fear those acts generate. They do not consider that a greater power, God, may not permit them to carry out all their threats against His children.

The prophet Isaiah tells a story of a powerful king of the Assyrians who in essence told the people of God, "I have conquered every nation I have attacked, in spite of their gods. Surely you don't think that you and your God can stop me!" But the Jews called upon their God and He destroyed that mighty Assyrian army. (see Isaiah 37:8-38)

Of course we must be realistic enough to realize that sometimes God does permit the abuses of evil men to fall upon His followers. Daniel's three friends revealed a godly attitude when they faced the demand of the king to worship his golden image or be killed. They said, *"If we are thrown into the blazing furnace, the God we serve is able to save us from it, and he will rescue us from your hand, O king. But even if he does not, we want you to know, O king, that we will not serve your gods or worship the image of gold you have set up"* (Daniel 3:17-18). This attitude is echoed in Revelation 12:11. There we are told that those who had overcome the evil one had been able to do so because they did not love their lives so much that they were afraid to die.

Victory is always obtained by faith. Faith keeps us from being defeated at the hands of suffering. 1 Peter 4:9

Those in power often use implied threats. This enables them to avoid taking a public stand that might arouse indignation against them by the rest of the world. Another tactic is to discredit Christians by saying Christianity is a dangerous or reactionary "cult."

c. Re-education

Re-education has been used extensively in China, Vietnam, Laos and North Korea to change the thinking of people with *wrong ideas.*

It usually begins with self-evaluation and self-criticism. Those recognized as leaders were usually sent to special "camps" for intensive re-education. The masses were required to join local self-criticism groups. In those groups they spent hours and hours thinking negatively about themselves and their past actions. Military psychologists noted that a person with strong spiritual convictions was the most likely to be immune to these tactics. In China, many Christians were "re-educated" repeatedly without success. Finally the authorities simply quit trying.

When Laos was taken over by a communist government, a leading pastor, Rev. Sali, was put into a prison camp for three years of "re-education." He referred to it later as his university experience. During that time he led five men in the camp to Christ. He had no Bible so he discipled these new believers on Scriptures he had memorized and internalized. Later those men became leaders in the church.

d. Excuses

In the former Soviet Union, government officials claimed that a well-known pastor, Georgi Vins, was an income tax evader. They frequently used such economic excuses, because the poor masses find it easy to believe that leaders are dishonest in handling money entrusted to them.

The Communists also liked to claim that pastors and Bible teachers were "parasites" because they failed to "produce" anything. They had no regard for their spiritual contribution, so this was an easy way to attack them.

Seminary students in Vietnam tried to comply with government standards by working at production jobs and studying only part-time. But the government kept raising their production quotas until the students had no time left to study.

A Christian is always called to the highest level of integrity and action to withstand the attacks of the enemy.

D. PROCESS OF PERSECUTION

It is important to realize that persecution often is a process. This concept was formulated by Rev. Dr. Johan Candelin, the head of the Religious Liberties Commission for the World Evangelical Alliance. He has traveled the world and studied the process of persecution extensively in a number of countries. He concludes that there is a three-stage process leading to persecution becoming entrenched in any society.

1. The first stage involves spreading *disinformation* (first passive, then active) about the targeted group (Christians or others). It begins more often than not in the media. Through printed articles, radio, television, film and other means, Christians are robbed of their good reputation and their right to answer the accusations made against them. This disinformation results in…

2. the second stage, *discrimination* (first passive, then active). The public opinion that results from stage one proceeds to this stage. It relegates Christians to a second-class citizenship with inferior legal, social, political and economic status to the majority in the country.

3. The third stage, *persecution* (first passive, then active) is the end result. Once the first two steps have been taken, persecution can be practiced without normal protective measures taking place. Persecution (as we will see later) can arise from the state, the police or military, extremist organizations, paramilitary groups, anti-Christian sub-cultures and even representatives of other religious groups. The irony is that in many parts of the world, the accusations of the attackers turn the victims into the villains.

If disinformation about any group, including Christians, is disseminated long enough, no one will help when that group is discriminated against because the country has been brainwashed by disinformation. Once discrimination takes place, no one will intervene when persecution comes. "When the process gets to persecution, no one will do anything because, 'You know they are bad people anyway,'" says Rev. Candelin. He adds, "As soon as we see the very first case of disinformation, we need to act right away...."[7]

When Christians live in a godless society and base their faith and lifestyle on the Bible, they will surely experience and endure persecution (2 Timothy 3:12). But what do we mean by the word *persecution*? Jesus defines the word for us in Luke 6:22 using four verbs. He says, *"Blessed are you when men hate you, when they exclude you and insult you and reject your name as evil, because of the Son of Man."*

Note that it is Jesus in you who is the reason for and the target of persecution. He said to His disciples in John 15:20-21, *"Remember the words I spoke to you: 'No servant is greater than his master.' If they persecuted me, they will persecute you also. If they obeyed my teaching, they will obey yours also. They will treat you this way because of my name, for they do not know the One who sent me."* Persecution comes naturally to the follower of Jesus. Yet He asks nothing of us that He Himself did not already endure.

Jim Cunningham developed The Way of the Cross: "HEIR" Persecution Index Chart to identify our enemy Satan's overall strategy. The four verbs defining persecution in Luke 6:22 (NIV) form the acronym **HEIR**:

H – *hate*
E – *exclude*
I – *insult*
R – *reject*

In Romans 8:17, the Apostle Paul tells us, *"Now if we are children, then we are heirs—heirs of God and co-heirs with Christ, if indeed we share in his sufferings in order that we may also share in his glory."* So when we share in Jesus' sufferings (hatred, exclusion, insults and rejection) we become heirs who will also share in His glory.

The four verbs above can be experienced in varying degrees of intensity. We tend to think of persecution as only the very intense

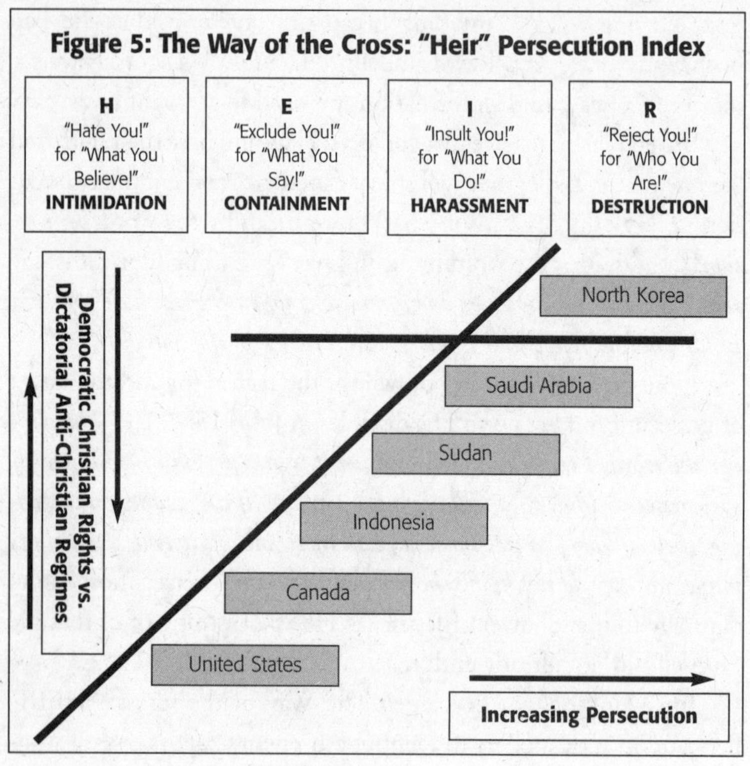

forms. But even when you experience hatred, exclusion, insult and rejection (because of Jesus in you) in a lighter intensity, you are still being persecuted—and therefore an heir.

As one moves to the right on the chart, the scale or intensity of persecution increases. For many years, North Korea and Saudi Arabia have been at the top of the annual World Watch List of Open Doors as deniers of religious freedom for Christians. In these regions, persecution of Christians is reportedly the most severe of any nation on earth. Christians are tortured, killed or imprisoned for being a follower of Jesus Christ. In Indonesia and Sudan there are violent outbreaks between Islamic Jihad warriors and local Christians. It is demoralizing to hear about brutality and deprivation of peaceful, law-abiding Christians. And in free societies there is an increasing body of evidence to suggest that persecution is at the disinformation stage and in some cases the discrimination stage.

The "Way of the Cross" appears to be more severe for Christians worshipping under non-Christian, religiously fanatical, dictatorial governments. The above chart acknowledges that, according to Luke 6:22, each of us faces varying degrees of persecution. The intensity and degree is extremely personal—and regional. Look at the strategy of those influenced by our adversary to persecute Christians:

- **"H" Stage:** *"hate you"*—for what you *"believe"*—to intimidate you, to derail your vision and hope.

  Intimidation is our adversary's greatest weapon to *"Shut us Down."* Just keep quiet, say nothing, do not write letters to the editor, do not speak up in the classroom or in parent-teachers meetings.
- **"E" Stage:** *"exclude you"*—for what you *"say"*—to contain you, to discourage your witness and faith.

  Containment is designed to *"Shut us Up."* After the arrest of Jesus, Peter was accused, and rightly so, of being a Galilean and a disciple of Jesus. That caused him to go into a full denial mode: *"Man, I don't know what you're talking about!"* (Luke 22:60)
- **"I" Stage:** *"insult you"*—for what you *"do"*—to harass you, to defeat your compassion and love.

  Harassment is a common strategy against Christians to *"Shut us Out."* Watch someone try to do something good and be criticized for it. Many Christians lose their sense of good will and compassion and say, "Well, if that's how they feel, I'm out of here." Perseverance and faithfulness to the call of God are necessary traits to resist pressure and persecution.
- **"R" Stage:** *"reject you"*—for who you *"are"*—to remove you, to destroy your being and influence.

  Destruction usually follows the traditional "big three"

forms of persecution—torture, imprisonment and death—to *"Shut us Off."*

The goal of the adversary can be summed up as: "Shut us Down"—"Shut us Up"—"Shut us Out"— "Shut us Off."

STUDY GUIDE/DISCUSSION QUESTIONS

PASTOR FOCUS

1. How do the following examples give evidence of Satan's methods in **your** region?

   - stirring up racial hatred of one group against another

   - waging direct and violent acts of aggression, terror and war against Christians

   - isolating a believer from those whom he can influence and from those who can nurture his faith

- dividing believers who fellowship together

2. Why is *"infiltration"* so difficult for the church to stop? How do you keep unity and trust among Christians? How did the early church handle persecution and division?

3. Pastors in free societies may find it difficult to imagine what it means to belong to a "Registered" or "Unregistered" church. This is not a simple matter of registering for tax purposes, as done in many free societies. To be a registered church group in China, as well as in some other countries, means: "Registered Activities" are permitted only in "Registered Buildings" at "Registered Times" for "Registered Members" of "Registered Groups" led by "Registered Leaders" using "Registered Materials." Under what conditions would you "Register" your church?

4. The government makes a declaration that in one year's time it will enforce a law that all churches without a permit will be closed down. And further, Christians can no longer meet in hotels and other public places. You are pastoring a church without a permit. What strategies or adjustments will you make now to ensure the survival of the church?

WOMEN'S FOCUS

1. Rev. Candelin says, "As soon as we see the very first case of disinformation, we need to act right away. And if we all act together when there is disinformation in any country in the world, we can stop the process which would follow from coming." Tell why you agree or disagree and give an example of how we could respond in a biblical manner to disinformation.

2. Syncretism is the widely held view that there is good in every religion and all roads lead to heaven. Individuals can then pick and choose whatever elements they wish from whatever faith, and then mix them all together. How might you answer someone who expresses the opinion that anyone who seeks to change another person's view is both arrogant and intolerant?

YOUTH FOCUS

1. Roleplay and then discuss each of the six examples of Satan's external tactics. What would you have done? What parallels exist in your own situation? What situations or responses do you need to pray about to be spiritually prepared?

2. Jeremiah 26:24 says, *"Futhermore Ahikam, son of Shaphan supported Jeremiah, and so he was not handed over to the people to be put to death."* Acts 12:2 says, "[Herod] *had James, the brother of John, put to death with the sword."* One Chinese Christian said, "We make too much fuss of those killed by the Herods of this world, and not enough of those spared by the Ahikams. It is no sin to be spared that the Word of God may continue to be preached. Not all of God's words must be written in blood." Do you agree or disagree? Why?

3. How would you respond if someone said, "All religions are equal and lead to the same God"?

"If you are a Christian, you are free to think that all religions, even the queerest ones, contain at least some hint of the truth. When I was an atheist I had to try to persuade myself that most of the human race has always been wrong about the question that mattered to them most; when I became a Christian, I was able to take

a more liberal view. But, of course, being a Christian does mean thinking that where Christianity differs from other religions, Christianity is right and they are wrong. As in arithmetic—there is only one right answer to a sum, and all the other answers are wrong, but some of the wrong answers are much nearer to being right than others." —*C. S. Lewis in* Mere Christianity —*p. 35*

4. One teacher in northern England who teaches English to Muslim asylum seekers, asked her class to write an essay on "If I had twenty-four hours to live, what would I do?" The Muslim boys in her class wrote, "I would go to the mosque, say my prayers, then kill my enemies." What would **you** say to a student who held this view?

5. The map below shows *"New Earth Island"*. It projects what the Earth might look like if the numbers for each category were reduced from a ratio of 6,000,000,000 = 1000 down to a ratio of 6,000,000 = 1. The "Island" would then have a population of 1000 people. Reducing the land mass of the Earth, using the same ratio, gives us an "Island" of some 28 square kilometers on which these 1000 people live. Consider how 500 young people on New Earth Island, who have divergent spiritual backgrounds, would live together in peace?

Figure 6: New Earth Island

© 2003 James D. Cunningham

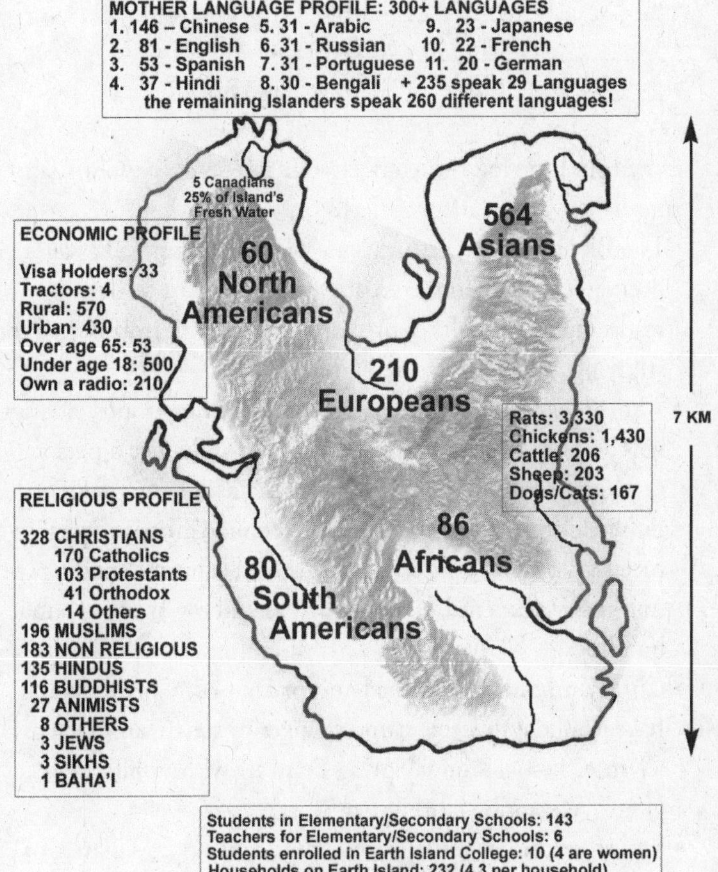

MEN'S FOCUS

1. Identify the five external tactics (groups) Satan used against the New Testament churches. Describe how the parallel group might look or act in your region today.
   - ____________________ Acts 12:2
   - ____________________ Matthew 26:3-4; Acts 2:36; Acts 5:40; Acts 7:54-59
   - ____________________ Acts 16:19 and Acts 19
   - ____________________ Acts 17:5
   - ____________________ Matthew 10:35-36

2. How could the following affect **your** freedom as a Christian currently living in a free society?
   - The Bible becomes regarded as "Hate Literature": Passages deemed contrary to the Charter of Rights not to be read/taught in public. Christians arrested and imprisoned for studying "Hate Literature."
   - Anti-Proselytizing Laws: To protect minority groups, aboriginals and others it will become illegal to influence a person—or attempt to influence a person—to change their religion.
   - Public Christian Services Banned: Public Christian worship meetings only permitted in "Registered" church buildings, not in government buildings such as schools or other public buildings.
   - Christian holidays renamed and/or banned: Christmas and Easter holidays receive name changes to something such as "Winter Festival" and "Spring Festival" with public "religious" celebrations forbidden.
   - Speech on moral issues forbidden if contrary to Charter of Rights: Churches and pastors forbidden to speak out on "biblical moral issues" that run counter to syncretism and multiculturalism.

- Donations to churches/Christian missions no longer receive tax benefits: No tax receipts permitted for donations to "unapproved"/"unregistered" agencies.
- Pastors incarcerated for refusing to marry homosexual or lesbian couples: Pastors go to prison for refusing to marry "couples" not entering a biblically sanctioned union.
- Church banned from performing legal wedding ceremonies: State takes legal right to "marry" from clergy (especially those who do not follow the "guidelines") thereby making marriage a secular institution.

3. How can the following things hinder Christians in their ministry in **your** region?
    - Isolation and conflict
    - Nationalism
    - Secular humanism
    - Religious intolerance
        - Anti-conversion laws
        - Worship centers controlled or registered
        - "Political Correctness"
        - Intimidation—harassment in worship
        - Economic oppression—job inequity

- Family opposition
- Proselytism and enticement

4. "Tolerance" is the *Shibboleth* (Judges 12:6) of our postmodern society. Explain why you agree or disagree.

4

SPIRITUAL WARFARE

The weapons we fight with are not the weapons of the world. On the contrary, they have divine power to demolish strongholds.
2 CORINTHIANS 10:4

A Filipino pastor, a former Muslim, lives on the island of Mindanao in the southern Philippines. He was a notorious gang leader and spent years in prison for robbery and murder. But there in prison he met Jesus Christ.

After his release, he was so effective in leading Muslims to Jesus back home in Mindanao that Muslim extremists in his area kidnapped his fourteen-year-old daughter. They would only return her, he was told, if he stopped preaching about Jesus and returned to Islam.

He and his wife prayed intensely about this and felt they could not give in to this blackmail. He continued to preach faithfully for three years with no definite news about his daughter.

He concludes, "Despite the terrible things they have done to my daughter, I fear no one but God alone! Pray for my daughter and that I will continue to preach Christ."

In early 1995, he received a letter from his daughter. She had been sold into prostitution in neighbouring East Malaysia. But God had helped her escape. She was taken in by a sympathetic Malaysian family and hidden for her safety. And then she fell in love with a young man and married him. She and her parents planned to visit together in a safe place.

"For our struggle is not against flesh and blood, but against the rulers, against the authorities, against the powers of this dark world and against the spiritual forces of evil in the heavenly realms." (Ephesians 6:12)

We have studied the characteristics of the enemy as well as his tactics, and now we examine the characteristics of the battle we wage against him. In a conventional war, a uniform easily identifies the enemy. The enemy's weapons are also clearly marked and battle lines indicate his position.

Vengeance belongs to God. We do not retaliate but overcome evil with good. Deuteronomy 32:35; Romans 12:19-21

However, in guerrilla or terrorist warfare, things are significantly different. It is hard to be sure who the enemy is. He can be anywhere or nowhere. His identification is not clearly marked as friend or foe. The enemy's weapons may be hidden in his house, in his vehicle or on his body. This kind of battle can cause endless frustrations and, many times, make a decisive victory impossible. Or the battle may drag on for a long time at a tremendous cost of money and manpower.

Spiritual warfare more closely resembles guerrilla warfare than conventional fighting. This makes the spiritual battle difficult. Many Christians are not even aware that they are engaged in spiritual warfare. Or they only know about spiritual warfare on a theoretical basis with no reality to it at all. If we do not recognize the unseen forces acting in the visible world we live in and arm ourselves accordingly, we will find ourselves woefully unprepared.

The enemy has done so well that he is practically unrecognizable and his strategies are unknown to the believer. Thus, many are losing the battle without even being aware of it. Yet we were born on a spiritual battlefield. When we were born again, we were dressed in the uniform of righteousness and armed to do battle, a battle led by the Lord of Hosts Himself. He has promised to prepare a table before us even in the presence of our enemies. (Psalm 23:5)

As Christians, engaged in a real battle, it is crucial that we focus not on the demonic but that we focus on the living God.

As a rule, we are to treat the diversions and distractions that the enemy sends our way as gnats along the way. Otherwise Satan and his minions will distract us and cause us to focus on them and the visible world they rule. Our attention should be on the rule of God in the *invisible* world. (Ephesians 2:6; 2 Corinthians 4:18)

A. SPIRITUAL WARFARE DEFINED

Spiritual warfare is the cosmic conflict that rages between the Kingdom of God and the kingdom of Satan. Remember we are not talking about two equal kingdoms battling it out for victory. Satan is only a created being. Christ has all authority and power. Satan's power was broken at the cross. The Apostle Paul records for us in Colossians 2:15, *"And having disarmed the powers and authorities, he made a public spectacle of them, triumphing over them by the cross."* But one power Satan has today is the power to deceive the people of the world—to blind them from seeing the glory of God. (2 Corinthians 4:3-4)

Satan's primary strategy is to divide and conquer. His key tactics include accusation, deception and the interruption of our relationships with the Father and with each other. He is actively leading mankind to defile the land, which belongs to God, in order to keep humanity in darkness. Unity in the body of Christ is critical for the fulfillment of the Great Commission.

Why would someone lost in the chaos of the world want to be part of a fellowship of people that is disorderly, dysfunctional, and even destructive? The Church of Jesus Christ must be ruled by love. We must be a refuge, a place of safety.

We will now investigate three levels on which the spiritual battle rages.

B. PERSONAL-LEVEL SPIRITUAL WARFARE

All humans, male and female, are created in the *"image of God"* (Genesis 1:27) and as a result of the sin of Adam and Eve in the garden all are now involved in a cosmic spiritual battle between God and Satan. Our enemy, known as the Destroyer, has one goal: to destroy God's creation. Satan wants to destroy every human being on earth lest they are restored to a relationship of love and peace with God.

Personal-level spiritual warfare is the initial struggle each of us had as a nonbeliever being delivered from Satan's demonic bondage. Once we accept the forgiveness of Christ's atoning blood we are *"born again"* (John 3:3) into the family of God. From that moment of new birth by the Spirit (see John 3:5) *"the one who is in you is greater than the one who is in the world"* (1 John 4:4). We who are *"born of God"* now have an advocate and a powerful guide in the Holy Spirit to keep us from the Evil One. *"We know that anyone born of God does not continue to sin; the one who was born of God keeps him safe, and the evil one cannot harm him."* (1 John 5:18)

While it is the firm belief of many Christians that once the Holy Spirit lives within a believer, they cannot be "possessed" by Satan, Christians must remember to *"Be self-controlled and alert. Your enemy the devil prowls around like a roaring lion looking for someone to devour."* (1 Peter 5:8)

People may be influenced by demons in the following ways:

- Through willful sin—everyone has turned away from God (Galatians 6:7-8)
- By occult practices or cultic societies (Acts 19:18-19)
- Through traumatic experiences (Mark 9:17-27)
- From inherited or generational iniquity (Numbers 14:18)

In Mark 1:21-28, Jesus gives us an account of a demonized person who was set free from his tormentors.

> *They went to Capernaum, and when the Sabbath came, Jesus went into the synagogue and began to teach. The people were amazed at his teaching, because he taught them as one who had authority, not as the teachers of the law. Just then a man in their synagogue who was possessed by an evil spirit cried out, "What do you want with us, Jesus of Nazareth? Have you come to destroy us? I know who you are–the Holy One of God!"*
>
> *"Be quiet!" said Jesus sternly. "Come out of him!" The evil spirit shook the man violently and came out of him with a shriek.*
>
> *The people were all so amazed that they asked each other, "What is this? A new teaching–and with authority! He even gives orders to evil spirits and they obey him." News about him spread quickly over the whole region of Galilee.*

Observations:

- The man with the evil spirit was in the synagogue with the religious people. We assume he had no difficulty being around those who were seeking after God. Until that day, this demonized man had probably remained relatively quiet and comfortable.
- When the light of God appeared, darkness was dispelled! The man cried out in agony, as the demons knew their judgment had begun.

- Jesus commanded the demons to be quiet and come out. We should not view those in this condition as freaks. Perhaps they are our neighbors, church friends or family. Jesus' intention was to free the man of his tormentors, and to do so in this case without humiliation or embarrassment.
- Jesus did not ignore the situation, but rather He dealt with it quickly. Jesus is compassionate, and He wanted to see this man freed.
- Evil spirits are rebellious. Although Jesus commanded a silent exit, the defiant demon shrieked as it departed.

Rev. Dr. David Cho, Korean pastor of the largest church in the world, tells about a beautiful, well-educated woman married to a famous medical doctor. For ten years she was paralyzed and her doctor husband tried everything to find healing for her. Finally she began coming to Dr. Cho's church.

At one early-morning prayer meeting, she stood up and began to make an eerie sound and then she laughed with a devilish laugh. The Christians ran out of the room.

When Dr. Cho scolded her for her behavior, a masculine, guttural voice came from her mouth and said, "We are going to kill you today!"

Pastor Cho asked, "Who are you?" The guttural voice replied, "We are demons!" And at that point, the lady punched him in the head, knocking him down.

The pastor began to cry out, "Oh Jesus, cover me with your blood!" He then turned to the lady and ordered, "In the name of Jesus Christ, you devil, come out!"

The guttural voice replied, "We are many. We are not coming out! You are defeated today!"

After praying for four hours, Dr. Cho sat down in exhaustion. He continued on for another four hours, commanding the demons to come out in Jesus' name.

It was now dark outside and the pastor was becoming desperate after eight hours of this warfare. He called out to Jesus with a pleading voice and then felt the Holy Spirit rise within him.

Again he commanded, this time in a loud and authoritative voice, "In the name of Jesus Christ I command you to come out!"

The lady began shrieking and vomiting while rolling on the floor and then suddenly lay still as though dead. She opened her eyes and said, "Pastor, I'm so sorry. I could not do anything. The demons were telling each other that you were very green and inexperienced and that they would be successful if they just persisted. My body felt like it was torn. But I am free now!"

The lady began screaming again—this time with joy. She had also been healed of her paralysis. This miracle led her husband to commit his life to Jesus.[1]

C. OCCULT-LEVEL SPIRITUAL WARFARE

This level deals in intercessory confrontations with demonic forces that operate through Satanism, witchcraft, New Age, shamanism, esoteric philosophies (such as secret societies or Tibetan Buddhism), humanism, rock music, occult movies and blood sacrifices.

This level of warfare tends to be much tougher, because although some victims have been trapped by subtle demonic deception, others have openly solicited the power of Satan. In Acts 16:16-23, we read how Paul dealt with a young woman who had a spirit of witchcraft.

> *Once when we were going to the place of prayer, we were met by a slave girl who had a spirit by which she predicted the future. She earned a great deal of money for her owners by fortune-telling. This girl followed Paul and the rest of us, shouting, "These men are servants of the Most High God, who are telling you the way to be saved." She kept this up for many days. Finally Paul became so troubled that he turned around and said to the spirit, "In the name of Jesus Christ I command you to come out of her!" At that moment the spirit left her.*

When the owners of the slave girl realized that their hope of making money was gone, they seized Paul and Silas and dragged them into the marketplace to face the authorities. They brought them before the magistrates and said, "These men are Jews, and are throwing our city into an uproar by advocating customs unlawful for us Romans to accept or practice."

The crowd joined in the attack against Paul and Silas, and the magistrates ordered them to be stripped and beaten. After they had been severely flogged, they were thrown into prison, and the jailer was commanded to guard them carefully.

Observations:

- Paul and Silas were going to the place of prayer when the girl met them and began shouting her message. The Bible says she kept this up for many days.
- Paul knew that this slave girl had an evil spirit of fortune-telling. When she spoke about Paul and Silas, she was telling the truth. But we must see beyond the obvious to understand that the purpose of Satan working in her was to discredit the message of the apostles. Satan was trying to make people think that the prophecies of Paul and Silas came from the same source as the girl's prophecies. This would discredit the Gospel and the apostles.
- Although Paul knew the girl was demonized, he did not do anything to stop her until God gave him both the compassion and His direction to exercise spiritual authority in the matter. Just because we have a revelation about a matter, or even the spiritual authority or power over it, does not mean we have permission to act. Diagnosis is not assignment.[2] (See Luke 10:19)

In a small conservative city of Canada, there are many evangelical churches but also a Church of Satan. One year at the provincial conference of the Satanists, the Church of Satan from this city was honored for its distinguished achievements. They claimed that during the past year they had prayed to Satan for the elimination of a select list of evangelical leaders in the city through immorality or marriage and family breakdowns. In one year they had *succeeded* in seeing five of the finest Christian leaders in the city resign from their positions. The Lord obviously moved some of the pastors to new and even larger assignments but the Satanists claimed this as *their* doing. For a parallel principle see 2 Samuel 24:1: *"The LORD...incited David...saying, 'Go and take a census of Israel'."* Compare this to 1 Chronicles 21:1: *"Satan...incited David to take a census of Israel."* Both passages confirm God's sovereign control over man's—and Satan's—evil acts.

The enemy loves to distract us from prayer.

Asian missionaries working in a rural and remote village of Indonesia came up against occult powers after they prayed for a sick lady in the name of Jesus and she was miraculously healed. The local occult leader was threatened by this turn of events. When the missionaries came to that village on their next visit, he challenged them to a power demonstration like the prophet Elijah on Mount Carmel.

He took off his ring, which in his mind and experience was a spiritual power source, and set it down on top of the old wood table. He then challenged, "Let's pray to our god. Whichever god can make the ring on the table turn in circles is the most powerful, and the followers of the other god must then leave and never return to this village. I will go first."

With a sardonic smile, the occult leader pointed at the ring from the distance where he sat. The ring immediately began to spin around in a circle much to the horror of the onlooking Christian missionaries.

It was now their turn. As the small group softly sang, "He is Lord," the leader prayed in a loud voice asking God to show Himself strong and prove His power beyond a shadow of a doubt.

To everyone's amazement both the ring and the occult leader began to revolve in circles faster and faster until the occult leader screamed in agony for the power to stop.

The occult leader left that village forever and many of the villagers came to Christ that night as a result of this spiritual warfare encounter.[3]

D. STRATEGIC OR CITY-LEVEL WARFARE

There is considerable interest and teaching in the Christian community about "territorial spirits," that is, spiritual warfare waged against high-ranking principalities and powers assigned to a locale—evil spirits we should know and engage by name.

From Daniel 10:12-14, it appears that a particular evil spirit was assigned to his own human government or territory. The Bible never gives an example of anyone engaging spirits directly by name. Neither does it command us to address them by name. Daniel, for example, did not pray against the spiritual powers over the nations. He prayed to God who sovereignly directs angels to war against the territorial rulers.

Bible scholar Clinton Arnold notes that the Apostle Paul "himself never connected the powers of darkness with any specific country or territory. For instance, he never entreated God to thwart the angelic prince over Rome or to bind the demonic ruler over Corinth.... What Paul stressed is the recognition that there are powerful demonic emissaries who attack the church and hinder its mission and that they can be overcome only through reliance on the power of God."[4]

The city of Luxor in Upper Egypt, known as Thebes in Bible times, is located on the Nile River about 800 kilometers south of Cairo. It is the site of the Valley of the Kings where the tombs of King Tut and other leaders of the ancient Egyptians are. In Jeremiah 46:25, Amon, the ruling god of Thebes, is described in terms that clearly equate to a regional principality. In the more than 4,500 years of history of the city, there is nothing to indicate that any body of praying, fasting, and praising believers ever challenged the rule of the powers of darkness.

In late 2000, about seventy Egyptian intercessors gathered from across the southern areas, where there is little church activity, to fast and pray for Egypt. They also prayed for God to prevail against the power of Amon. Several prayer walks were made with intercession in the "holy place" of the local temple.

Evening meetings were also held in a local church. On the second night, the Holy Spirit moved in power and dozens of believers came forward to repent of involvement in witchcraft and magic, which is common in that region. The service lasted until 1:30 a.m. with intercessors at the front of the church praying with people about repentance, release from bondage and anointing for ministry. The intercessors believe the power of the territorial spirit, Amon, was broken.

E. HOW TO WAGE SPIRITUAL WARFARE

The temptation in studying this subject is to over-emphasize the significance of demonic levels and categories of warfare. We realize that this can be a controversial teaching. At the same time we must not sell short human sinfulness by treating people as hapless victims of invisible forces rather than as moral agents responsible before God.

We must be completely aware of the nuances of the battle we are in as well as learn the skills of warfare prayer and deliverance. In the following chapters, we look more closely at the powerful spiritual weapons at our disposal and how we can effectively use them.

The secret of victory is to use spiritual weapons effectively and produce the fruit of the Spirit in your life.
Galatians 5:22

Warfare prayer for our neighborhoods and cities is also vital when we ask God that the ruling powers of darkness will be exposed and defeated. Also that "Gospel blindness" veiling the minds of unbelieving men, women and children will fall. All this so we can faithfully preach the Gospel to our generation.

The current prevailing thought about warfare prayer is that spiritual warfare consists only of direct, frontal assaults against the devil and his demons. In truth, spiritual warfare is far more than that. It encompasses any attitude or action that lines up with the plans and purposes of God's kingdom. Some of the effective weapons we use against Satan are:

• Watch and warn	Isaiah 62:6-7
• Praise and worship	2 Chronicles 20:21-22 Psalm 68:1-35
• Loving God more than life	Revelation 12:11
• Fasting	Isaiah 58:6
• Intimacy with God	Psalm 84:1-4
• Resisting the devil	James 4:7
• Personal power evangelism	Acts 16:16-40

Since the battle is a spiritual battle, the weapons we use to wage this warfare are also spiritual weapons. These spiritual weapons will be our focus in the following section.

STUDY GUIDE/DISCUSSION QUESTIONS

PASTOR FOCUS

1. If Satan is an already defeated foe, why do we keep struggling with him and his demonic forces?

2. What can you and your fellowship do to heighten your awareness of spiritual warfare even more?

WOMEN'S FOCUS

Explain how you do (or could) use the following Scriptures against Satan in your life:

- Intercession: Isaiah 62:6-7
- Praise: 2 Chronicles 20:21-22; Psalm 68:1-35
- Love God more than life: Revelation 12:11
- Fasting: Isaiah 58:6
- Intimacy with God: Psalm 84:1-4
- Resisting the devil: James 4:7

- Evangelism: Acts 16:16-40

YOUTH FOCUS

1. "As Christians, engaged in a real battle, it is crucial that we focus not on the demonic but that we focus on the living God." Why is this so important today? Is there any reason for the Christian to be afraid of Satan's powers?

2. "Spiritual warfare more closely resembles guerrilla warfare than conventional fighting." Give examples to show this is true. (Ephesians 2:6; 2 Corinthians 4:18)

3. You are praying in your fellowship and suddenly a demon reveals itself in a member of the group. What will **you** do? How long will you persist in your activity plan? Who would you call for help if you cannot seem to deal with the problem? Is it worth persisting for full liberation for the victim?

MEN'S FOCUS

1. If Satan's primary strategy is to "divide and conquer" how does he do this?

2. How does a person relate to demons today?

   - Galatians 6:7-8

   - Acts 19:18-19

   - Mark 9:17-27

   - Numbers 14:18

3. What does Acts 16:16-23 tell us about our role in spiritual warfare?

4. Read Matthew 12:29. What does Jesus mean when He says that it is useless to try and deliver a person unless you first bind the strongman?

SECTION TWO

Provisions for Victory

The Bible, Prayer and the Holy Spirit

5

GOD'S PROVISION: FULL ARMOR

Put on the full armor of God so that you can take your stand against the devil's schemes.

EPHESIANS 6:11

In the valley stood a ten-foot-tall giant, bellowing out threats against God's people and mocking their God. "Send one man out to fight me," he roared. "If I win, you will serve us. If he wins, we will be your slaves."

If the physical presence of Goliath wasn't daunting enough, the stakes for Israel were. It would be an all-or-nothing fight for the future of the people. On top of that, he mocked God. The fight would be a showdown between the giant's pagan gods and the God of Israel.

Courageous David decided to face the monster. King Saul, looking at David's physical disadvantage, insisted the young man take his armor. But David knew the spiritual battle was more crucial than the physical battle. Faith in God, not superior weaponry, would be his salvation. David stepped out in the name of God, and the giant fell.

Most of us are so focused on our physical circumstances that we fail to see the basic spiritual challenges before us. We spend our energies trying to make ends meet. We exhaust ourselves by constant activity. We are so distracted and frightened by what we see that we miss our chance to slay the giant. Instead, we find *his* foot on *our* neck.

Christian attempts to live victoriously in Christ when in a hostile environment could become frightening if we did not believe that God provides for us in every trial. The sovereign God of eternity knew every kind of attack the enemy would use before time began. And He has provided His spiritual armor—His Word, prayer and the Holy Spirit—so that we might be victorious when these attacks come to us.

Therefore put on the full armor of God, so that when the day of evil comes, you may be able to stand your ground, and after you have done everything, to stand.
Ephesians 6:13

God has equipped you as a servant-soldier of Jesus Christ with these spiritual weapons, the resources you need to defeat the enemy and gain great victories for His kingdom.

Paul instructed Christian converts to put on the impenetrable armor of God—coverings God provides—so that we can stand *victorious* in every situation we face as we move forward confidently in the work God has called us to do. He also understood it to be a protective covering for the mind and spirit, ensuring that injuries to the body will not embitter or destroy the soul.

In Ephesians 6:10-18, we have the classic teaching of the Apostle Paul about the resources we have for spiritual battle. In verse 14, he begins to deal with specific pieces of spiritual armor based on the imagery of a Roman soldier.

> *Stand firm then, with the belt of truth buckled around your waist, with the breastplate of righteousness in place, and with your feet fitted with the readiness that comes from the gospel of peace. In addition to all this, take up the shield of faith, with which you can*

extinguish all the flaming arrows of the evil one. Take the helmet of salvation and the sword of the Spirit, which is the word of God. And pray in the Spirit on all occasions with all kinds of prayers and requests. With this in mind, be alert and always keep on praying for all the saints. (Ephesians 6:14-18)

A. DEFENSIVE SPIRITUAL ARMOR

From this passage we learn that defensive or protective pieces form your spiritual armor, although some of the protective pieces, such as the sandals and the sword, also enable us to be effective on the offense. Later we will look at the offensive aspects of the armor.

1. Belt of Truth

The soldier's wide leather belt held the various garments and pieces of armor securely in place. Loose armor was not only uncomfortable, but also unsafe. The belt also held the scabbards for swords and daggers. It was foundational to keeping everything balanced and in place.

Truth secures everything in our spiritual life. We can't know what is right or wrong apart from truth.

In this spiritual warfare we wage, we first *put on* Christ, who Himself is the *truth* (John 14:6). Putting on Christ is our positional application of the belt. Putting on Christ enables us to talk, walk and fight the spiritual war proclaiming Christ, the truth.

On another application level, buckling the belt of truth around the waist is more than just seeking truth to find out facts. The servant-soldier of Christ who puts on the armor of God must be willing to overcome his own prejudices to find out the truth. He must struggle against pride, which clings to his preconceived ideas and makes him unwilling to re-examine those ideas and change his opinions.

Second, to wear the belt of truth means to bind one's whole

Figure 7: The Whole Armor of God

Ephesians 6:11

THE ARMOR OF GOD	KNOW THE TRUTH ABOUT...	AFFIRM KEY SCRIPTURES
Belt of TRUTH	God (Jesus)—His sovereignty, love, wisdom, and holiness	Deuteronomy 4:39; Psalm 23:1; Psalm 18:1-3
Breastplate of RIGHTEOUSNESS	Your personal righteousness is Jesus Christ and His blood	Psalm 100:3; Romans 3:23-24; 6:23; Galatians 2:20-21; Philippians 3:8-10.
Sandals of PEACE	Inner peace and readiness... through our relationship with Jesus Christ	Romans 5:1; Ephesians 2:14; John 14:27; 16:33; 20:21.
Shield of FAITH	Living by faith...with continual trust in God and His Word	Romans 4:18-21; Hebrews 11:1; 1 Peter 1:6-7
Helmet of SALVATION	God's promises of daily and eternal salvation in Jesus Christ	**Daily:** Psalm 16; Psalm 23; Hebrews 1:1-6 **Eternal:** 2 Corinthians 4:16-18; 1 Thessalonians 4:17; 1 John 3:1-3
Sword of the SPIRIT	The power of God's Word to counter spiritual deception and accusations	Hebrews 4:12; Matthew 4:1-11; 1 Peter 3:15; Psalm 119:110-112 See Endnote[1]

nature together with integrity, that is, honesty. Wearing the belt of truth causes us to know that we are inherently wicked, weak and born with a predisposition to sin (Matthew 15:19; 7:4). King David said, *"Surely you desire truth in the inner parts; you teach me wisdom in the inmost place."* (Psalm 51:6)

Therefore, a servant-soldier must maintain a humble spirit and a longing for God. He must continually seek to be meek and to hunger for righteousness.

Truth directly opposes Satan, the father of lies. His first challenge to Eve was to question God's truthfulness. When we know and walk in God's truth, it sets us free (John 8:32). This is why Jesus concluded His great sermon in Matthew chapters five, six and seven with the admonition to not just hear His words but to act upon them. By living the truth when we hear it, we put a solid-rock foundation under our faith.

Jesus is the Truth. Truth is on your side. Truth will win over the enemy's lies. Fill your heart with Truth and stand by it.

2. Breastplate of Righteousness

The soldier's breastplate of the Roman times protected his vital organs. It was usually made of hardened slabs of leather or pounded bronze or a combination of both. The soldier's rank and his country's seal were attached to it. The breastplate was designed to cover the soldier's chest and abdomen, not his back. This meant the soldier must face his enemy, not run from him. To run away would have left him with no covering.

> *When God sees you, He sees Jesus. Stand tall before the enemy.*

Because we are waging a war against an invisible enemy, we must always be armed. Our real "breastplate"—righteousness—is not made of heavy metal. Rather, it is molded by the Spirit of the living God to fit our inner being. It is the righteousness of Jesus Christ, given to us by Him so that He might be seen in us in our day-to-day relationships and circumstances.

Our enemy will point out your failures and shortcomings. He will try to convince you that you are unworthy to be a child of God. He is right. But your relationship with God is based on Jesus' uprightness before God, not yours. Your sins have been wiped out.

3. Sandals of Peace

The cry for peace is as old as the dawn of history and as fresh as the morning newspaper. Several centuries before Christ, the prophet Isaiah said, *"How beautiful on the mountains are the feet of those who bring good news, who proclaim peace…."* (Isaiah 52:7)

When the Hebrew prophets foretold the coming of a divine deliverer, they said one of his names would be *"Prince of Peace."* When the Savior was born, the note struck by the angelic chorus in the nativity story of the shepherds was *"…and on earth peace to men on whom his favor rests."* (Luke 2:14)

Therefore, it is not surprising that when describing the armor of God, Paul included the element of peace. As God's peacemakers, our sandals enable us to march into circumstances to bring peace, not destruction. Christ calls people who have made their peace with God to fight *for* fellowship, not against it (Hebrews 12:2-3). So we must be ready to go where God sends us with the message of peace, forgiveness and hope. We may be called to march right to the gates of hell—which He promised would not hold us back (Matthew 16:18 KJV). It is in this sense that we can be considered "waging" peace.

Your life thus centers on the good news of the kingdom. Everything else comes second. Know how to share the good news. Understand what it has done in your life. See how it can help others. Ask God to give you opportunities to share with others. Be alert for the opportunities. Be prepared to take advantage of them.

4. Shield of Faith

The Roman shield was the defensive piece of armor that was almost always used together with the sword. It was used to ward off a blow from the opponent while making your own sword-thrust. Likened to a shield, our faith in God is that piece of spiritual armor that enables us to withstand attacks by the enemy that are too much for the mind and body. The shield of faith has a three-fold duty.

- It is a saving faith that is the inward confidence in God.
- It is a serving faith that inspires our servanthood.
- It is a sanctifying faith that lays hold of the power of God for our daily lives.

When you come under enemy fire, take shelter behind your faith in God. Do not be deceived by circumstances and events. Walk by faith, not by sight. Be confident that God has secured victory. Stake your life on His faithfulness. Trust Him to deliver you.

5. Helmet of Salvation

In describing the Christian's helmet, Paul wrote in 1 Thessalonians 5:8, "*…and the hope of salvation as a helmet.*" The best armor you can give a soldier is the kind that cannot be destroyed by the enemy. Paul, knowing the eternal nature of God's salvation, exhorts the servant-soldier to put on—that is, believe in—the hope of life beyond this world. Soldiers without fear of death? What a mighty force!

God also provides the helmet to protect our minds. When the enemy tries to infiltrate our thinking with doubts about our salvation, the helmet becomes our protection.

You are God's own child. He Himself redeemed you from slavery. He does not want the enemy to overcome you. You are secure in your relationship with God. The power within you is greater than the power in your enemy. Give no place to doubt. Take your stand for God in confidence.

B. OFFENSIVE SPIRITUAL ARMOR

Two items from the text and context of armor pieces in Ephesians chapter six are very important offensive resources. We will look at these two items in detail in subsequent chapters.

1. Sword of the Spirit (both offensive and defensive)

Scripture is God's word to us. Get to know it. It is the source of truth, assurance and comfort. Learn its lessons. Let God use it to speak to your heart. Look to it to cut through the enemy's lies and spiritual deception, and to reveal the truth. Use it to persuade others about God's love and forgiveness.

Spiritual victory requires hiding God's Word, that is, knowing it, even memorizing it, in your heart and obeying it–whatever the cost. Psalm 119:105; Mark 8:34-35

When God's Spirit impresses us with a verse or a passage of Scripture to use in our battle against the enemy in a particular conflict, the Bible calls this taking the *sword of the Spirit.*

Jesus defeated Satan the three times he was tempted in the wilderness by using the sword of the Spirit. (see Matthew 4)

2. Prayer

Prayer is mentioned in the context of the wardrobe of the Christian warrior but not as a specific weapon of war or a piece of armor. That's because prayer is the key to consistent victory in our warfare. Therefore, prayer is one of the most important things we can do when fighting the enemy.

David's battle with Goliath was not won when the stone flew from the sling. It was won in David's close relationship with the Living God. Our battles are won or lost in the way we walk with God. Prayer is talking with God and letting Him talk with you. Prayer is taking a stand against the spiritual forces of darkness that influence events and circumstances in the world. Prayer is asserting God's victory before we walk into battle.

Prayer is living every moment in the presence of God.

But prayer is more than kneeling before God. Prayer is as much an attitude as it is an act. Prayer is keeping your heart open to His leadership. Prayer is the constant communion with God needed to face the challenge of completing Jesus' mission.

C. THE FULL ARMOR OF GOD

The Bible clearly says to use the *full* armor. We usually feel we are doing okay if we have *most* of the pieces of armor in place. Yet, if even one piece is missing, we have a weak spot where Satan can injure us, causing us to lose ground rather than standing firm. (1 Peter 5:8-9)

The New Living Translation in Ephesians 6:11 puts it this way: *"Put on all of God's armor so that you will be able to stand firm against all strategies and tricks of the Devil."* It further says in verse 13, *"Use every piece of God's armor to resist the enemy in the time of evil, so that after the battle you will still be standing firm."*

Again, from *The New Living Translation, "Stand your ground, putting on the sturdy belt of truth and the body armor of God's righteousness. For shoes, put on the peace that comes from the Good News, so that you will be fully prepared. In every battle you will need faith as your shield to stop the fiery arrows aimed at you by Satan. Put on salvation as your helmet, and take the sword of the Spirit, which is the word of God. Pray at all times and on every occasion in the power of the Holy Spirit. Stay alert and be persistent in your prayers for all Christians everywhere."* (Ephesians 6:14-18)

We need to think about these things. Do we always live in the truth, both in thought and in word, or do we allow ourselves to be deceived or do we deceive others? Do we cover ourselves in God's righteousness, or do we live our lives according to our own rules? Do we live in the peace and confidence of salvation? Are we prepared to be active peacemakers? Do we work in faith, or in fear?

Do we speak the words of God, or our own words? Do we pray in the power of the Holy Spirit, or are our prayers shallow, selfish and meaningless? Are we alert to what is happening in the battlefield around us, or are we distracted by other things? And, are we persistent in praying for our brothers and sisters in Christ? Do we pray that they will receive strength and power from the Holy Spirit so they can join us in the spiritual battle?

If any one of these areas is weak, we must fortify it. We must work to strengthen that area so that we can consistently obey God's commands and be victorious over sin and against the Evil One.

STUDY GUIDE/DISCUSSION QUESTIONS

PASTOR FOCUS

Discuss together the practical application in your lives of using each piece of the armor of God.

WOMEN'S FOCUS

How can we be assured practically that we are operating in the *full* armor of God?

YOUTH FOCUS

What imagery in your culture today could you use as a counterpart to the Roman soldier's armor to explain protection as well as the position and practice of strength in spiritual warfare?

MEN'S FOCUS

Read 1 Samuel 17 and list the principles of spiritual warfare found in this chapter. Discuss in what ways David uses each element of the whole armor of God as outlined in Ephesians 6.

"The Warrior's Prayer"
(If in a group, read aloud together)

Heavenly Father,
Your warrior prepares for battle.
Today I claim victory over Satan by putting on
the whole armor of God!

I put on the Belt of Truth.
May I stand firm in the truth of your Word
so I will not be a victim of Satan's lies.

I put on the Breastplate of Righteousness.
May it guard my heart from evil
so I will remain pure and holy,
protected under the blood of Jesus Christ.

I put on the Sandals of Peace.
May I go out and proclaim the good news of the Gospel
so your peace will shine through me
and be a light to all I encounter.

I take the Shield of Faith.
May I be ready to deflect Satan's fiery darts of
doubt, denial and deceit
so I will not be vulnerable to spiritual defeat.

I put on the Helmet of Salvation.
May I keep my mind focused on you
so Satan will not have a stronghold on my thoughts.

I take the Sword of the Spirit.
May the two-edged sword of your Word
be ready in my hands
so I can use it to take authority over the Enemy.

By faith, your warrior has put on
the whole armor of God.
"Let not him who puts his armor on
boast like him who takes it off."[2]
Amen.

6

GOD'S PROVISION: THE BIBLE

Above all, you must understand that no prophecy of Scripture came about by the prophet's own interpretation. For prophecy never had its origin in the will of man, but men spoke from God as they were carried along by the Holy Spirit.

2 Peter 1:20-21

Daniel, a Chinese living in Singapore, sat in the chair still shaking his head in unbelief. He had just returned from his first extensive visit to the People's Republic of China. Now in the freedom of his home city, he was trying to assimilate and communicate all the impressions and messages he had received.

"How would you summarize what you learned on your visit, Daniel?" he was asked. He continued to shake his head and smile. Finally he began to speak.

"Probably by my visit to one particular house church," he slowly replied. "It numbers several hundred believers who have had a lot of persecution over the past years. I asked them how they had been victorious and even grown in numbers during such terrible experiences. They quickly replied, telling me three things," he continued. "First, obedience to the Word of God; second, communication with

God, that is, prayer. And third, love for the brothers and sisters."

This group memorized one chapter of the Bible every week. They began doing this because of a lack of Bibles, but continued doing so after they realized the blessing it brought to their lives.

A. PRIMARY SOURCE

The Bible is God's written revelation of Himself and His desire for a relationship with people. It is more than just a revelation of God's character. It is also a revelation of His intricate plan for the world. We could never have understood our great God if He had not chosen to reveal Himself.

His greatest revelation of Himself was when He came to live among us in a human body and was known as Jesus Christ. But even our knowledge of that revelation depends upon His written Word, the Bible.

Satan has conducted a massive propaganda campaign in the last century in an attempt to discredit the Bible. He would love to see Christians lose faith in the Word of God. In spite of his efforts, however, no one has ever been able to disprove its reliability. It remains the only absolute truth known to humankind.

The Bible is our God-given basis for faith, doctrine and practice. Many times Christians have knowingly departed from its teachings and suffered because of doing so. Many times when Christians depart from the Word, it is because they do not know or understand it.

The church can only be true to the revealed Word of God when its people know what it teaches. Study of God's Word is an essential part of the Christian life. When Christians doubt, ignore or fail to understand the teachings of Scripture and depart from its principles, they lose their spiritual power.

Many human organizations originally built on scriptural principles have lost their spiritual impact for this reason. Only a return to the authority of the Word of God and a faithful teaching of its principles can restore the spiritual life that should be present in a true member of the Body of Christ. The Bible makes a very clear claim that it is the revealed Word of God. *"All Scripture is God-breathed and is useful for teaching, rebuking, correcting and training in righteousness, so that the man of God may be thoroughly equipped for every good work."* (2 Timothy 3:16-17) (see also 2 Peter 1:21; John 6:63)

All that we teach in the church must be based on the Bible. You have probably noticed that in this text, every principle is supported by a reference to the Bible. Look up these passages and be sure that these lessons tell you only what the Bible teaches. Unless the church has a clear understanding of the teaching of Scripture, it cannot be a victorious church. (see Matthew 5:18)

B. AUTHORITY OF SCRIPTURE

Sometimes Christians in free societies acknowledge the importance of the Bible, but because they have such easy access to it, they may take it for granted. What if it was not available to you? Do you have it *"hidden in your heart"* (see Psalm 119:11)? Do you have such a clear understanding of the basic teachings of Scripture that you could stay true to the Lord if you did not have continued access to a Bible?

Jesus is our best example of dependence on the written Word of God. He quoted Scripture repeatedly. When Satan tempted Him in the wilderness, for example, He quoted Scripture in answer to each of Satan's temptations (Matthew 4:1-11). Jesus based His teaching on the Old Testament Scriptures and referred to them frequently for historical examples. Jesus validated almost every book in the Old Testament by quoting from them at least once as divine authority.

Note how Jesus used the Scriptures after His death and resurrection. While walking with some of His followers on the road to Emmaus, He began *"with Moses and all the Prophets"* explaining *"to them what was said in all the Scriptures concerning himself."* (Luke 24:27)

The central place Scripture held for the early church is evident throughout the book of Acts. Scripture was used to explain the events of Pentecost (Acts 2:16-21), to identify Jesus as the Messiah (2:25-28), to determine their response to persecution (4:23-26), to state the church's position in the face of persecution (7:1-53), to preach Christ (8:29-35), and to determine how to accept Gentile believers. (15:13-21)

The New Testament Christians and the writers of the Epistles quote the Old Testament Scriptures hundreds of times to prove their positions.

This practice is so basic to sound biblical teaching that it is still common in evangelical circles today. The Bible is our source.

The books of the Old Testament were compiled over a period of more than 1,000 years and Christ accepted their authority. The early church gradually assembled the books of the New Testament and the Holy Spirit affirmed their authority.

In the first and second centuries, to prove their teachings, early church leaders began to quote from the writings of various New Testament apostles and the Gospel accounts, just as Jesus had referred to the Old Testament Scriptures. Every book in our New Testament gradually gained this kind of authority, while hundreds of other books of the era were set aside.

By the third century, there was widespread acceptance by the spiritual leaders of the church of the books now called the New Testament. An international church council also confirmed that these particular books were to be the "canon," or official contents of the New Testament, but the church acknowledges that the selection was made by the Holy Spirit and merely confirmed by humans.

Satan does not question the importance of the Bible. He has attempted to destroy it throughout history. Whether Romans in New Testament times, barbarians in the Dark Ages, Spanish Inquisitors in the Middle Ages, French radicals in the eighteenth century, Nazis in World War II, Soviet Communists or Chinese revolutionaries, each group has tried to destroy the Bible. It is not unusual throughout history to read about Bibles burned in bonfires.

Yet the Bible remains the most widely published and read book of all time. Satan has not only attempted to physically destroy the Bible, he has also tried to destroy people's faith in the Bible. One generation after another has produced pseudo-intellectual attacks on the Bible.

The greatest waste of paper is an unread Bible.

But Satan's most effective attack has been indifference. He is as pleased to see the Bible remain unused on a Christian's bookshelf as he is to see it burned by extremists.

Even if the Bible is considered a good book or fine literature, Satan is pleased. His fear is that it will be recognized for what it truly is—God's Word to lost men and women and to maturing Christians.

C. THE POWER OF SCRIPTURE

One of the strongest arguments in support of the Bible is the intense hatred for it displayed by such diverse groups as barbarians, liberal intellectuals, fascists and communists. Why are all these groups so afraid of the Bible? Why have so many repressive societies attempted to stop its importation and distribution?

Some time ago, two young ladies from Scandinavia were caught trying to give Bibles away in the Soviet Union. They were roughly treated by the police, all their possessions, including their automobile, were confiscated, and they were expelled from the country. In another case a few years ago, an Englishman was sent to prison for the same "*crime.*" Why? Oppressive authorities are afraid of the power of the Bible, a power not seen in holy writings of other faiths.

We discussed earlier the attempts by oppressive regimes to destroy Christianity. First, leaders in such regimes usually claim that the teachings of Jesus are compatible with their doctrines. Next, they try to make young Christians believe that they can be Christians and followers of the ideology of the regime at the same time. They also repeatedly claim that the Bible is full of contradictions and no longer valid.

They frequently mock the stories found in Scripture calling them "fairy tales" and demand rational explanations for teachings that are based on faith. Very few Christians are prepared for this kind of two-pronged attack.

Some Christian students at a major university in China did a wonderful job of confounding such attacks, but later the government abandoned "persuasion" and simply forced submission. When Christians find themselves in this kind of situation, they must turn to serious Bible study, knowing that the time they have to openly study Scripture will be brief. Soon Bibles will disappear from the bookstores and shops. One favorite trick used by the authorities in a number of repressive societies has been to allow Bibles to be displayed for sale, but no one can buy one until they have "permission." This means that if anyone should be so bold as to try to get "permission," the police have a record of which Christians want them. This ruse has great propaganda value.

Of course, the government-controlled printing presses will not normally produce Bibles. One major exception is China's permission for the Amity Bible Press to print Bibles. This press claims to have now printed more than thirty million copies (end of 2002). Most of these are for sale only in registered churches. The house church need for Bibles in China is still well over forty million copies.

In restricted countries where Bibles are in short supply, pastors are often in a quandary as to which of the many spiritually needy he should share these precious books with. Progress in Bible memorization is one method they can use for determining who will receive the available Bibles.

One house church group in Vietnam decided to give them to the believers who were most determined to use them. The criterion used was memory work. So Bibles were shared only with those who recited flawlessly Psalm 119—all 176 verses!

Open Doors is committed to provide God's Word to those for whom it is not available. *"It is the power of God for the salvation of everyone who believes...."* (Romans 1:16)

D. INTERNALIZING THE BIBLE

When China's best-known pastor, Wang Ming-dao, was finally released from prison, he stated, "In these past 20 years, I have not had a copy of the Bible. Happily between the ages of 21 to 24, I spent my time at home doing the housework and studying the Scriptures. I memorized many passages. These passages in my heart came out one by one and strengthened me. Had it not been for those words of God, then not only I, but many others, would also have been defeated."

Pastor Lamb in southern China was in prison for many years at that same time. "I understood then why I had memorized so much of God's Word while in Bible school," he says. "I kept my sanity only by repeating Bible verses over and over."

1. Bible reading, studying and meditating

The best way the church can prepare for trials and persecution is by seriously studying and learning the Word of God. Christians need an overview of the whole Bible. Understanding God's outline for mankind in the Bible aids in memorization as well.

What is the right attitude to bring to Bible study? Some read and study the Bible with the intent to get something from it to teach to others. But first, we should approach the Bible with the desire to see the goodness and loving-kindness of God and understand how *"wide and long and high and deep"* is His love for us (Ephesians 3:17-19). Let His love show you His supply for your own need and then you are better able to meet the needs of others.

Don't try to make the Bible say what you would like it to say.

Second, approach the Bible with humility. Study the Bible to discover what God has said. Bible study is meant not merely to inform but to transform.

Over and over the Scriptures direct us to *meditate* on God's Word. This activity takes time and discipline but brings much spiritual benefit and reward. Meditation is focused thinking about a Bible verse or passage in order to discover how we can apply its truth to our own lives. In applying Scripture, we need to ask three primary questions.

- What did it mean to the original hearers?
- What is the underlying timeless principle?
- Where or how should I practice that principle?

Here are six specific ways to *meditate* on a verse or passage:

- **Picture it.** Visualize the scene in your mind.
- **Pronounce it.** Say it aloud each time, emphasizing a different word.
- **Paraphrase it.** Rewrite the verse in your own words.
- **Personalize it.** Replace the pronouns or people with your own name.
- **Pray it.** Turn the verse into a prayer and say it back to God.
- **Probe it.** Ask the following questions:
    - Is there any sin to confess?
    - Is there any promise to claim?
    - Is there any attitude to change?
    - Is there any command to keep?

- Is there any example to follow?
- Is there any prayer to pray?
- Is there any error to avoid?
- Is there any truth to believe?
- Is there something for which to thank God?

2. Bible Memorization

Scripture memorization is also very important. Every Christian should know key verses by heart such as: John 3:16, John 5:24 and Ephesians 2:8-9.

A good approach is to memorize at least one key verse each week. One per day is even better. Your fellowship, for example, could begin a plan of memorizing whole chapters. The same chapter is assigned to two or three people. Then at a later date, they can get together and write it out. With a little practice and constant review, even a small fellowship can memorize whole books like 1 John or Philippians. It is important to begin this kind of activity right away. Memorization of Scripture is well worth the effort, even if you are never denied the use of a Bible. Start now!

A young Christian lived in the northern part of Vietnam that fell to communist control. He vowed that if he ever again had the opportunity to live in a free area, he would learn Bible teachings thoroughly. Later, the South Vietnamese forces took his area and he set out to keep his vow. He memorized Scripture earnestly and also studied basic Bible theology. A few years later, his area again came under communist control. This time he was prepared.

Following his escape to the West, his testimony was that the Scripture was his comfort and strength. He and a few fellow believers were able to worship together and strengthen each other through the use of memorized Scripture.

One of the more effective ways to memorize Scripture is through music. We tend to learn Scripture easier and remember it longer when we learn it in song. The Holy Spirit also uses Scripture set to song to encourage us in our spirits and to enable us to recall it when we face a situation in our everyday lives to which it applies.

But, just memorizing some verses is only the beginning. Believers have found that the effort involved in memorizing passages and later writing them out is a great aid in understanding their meaning. If you think hard about each word as you are memorizing, the related meanings of the words will become clearer.

Children should be made an important part of any group's memorization plan. They are frequently able to memorize better than adults and the Scripture they learn can be passed on to the next generation.

Passages that have been memorized should be reviewed at least once a month. When all in the church have memorized different parts of a lengthy passage of Scripture, each person should write out the portion he has memorized. All these pieces of paper should then be put together. Doing this will show the group how to produce a passage of Scripture from memory if the need ever arises.

The varieties of handwriting and the different kinds of paper used would help conceal the importance of the copy. A disadvantage of typed or computer-printed copies of Scripture is that they look too "important" to a searching official who would confiscate them.

The church must recognize the true value of Scripture if it is going to be victorious. A story about an elderly lady from Hong Kong and a church in China shows how they valued Scripture. The elderly lady made frequent visits to China and spent all her spare time there writing out Scripture she had memorized. Her friends in China eagerly collected the passages and guarded them like treasure.

In some countries, many Christians cannot read and write. But these nonliterate people can still play an important part in the Scripture memory program. They are able to memorize Scripture if they hear the passage on audio tape or others read it to them over and over again. Then they can pass it on to others in the same way that oral traditions and customs have been passed on for thousands of years. We can thank God that in many oral societies, audio cassettes are becoming an increasingly useful form of Scriptures.

Following the psalmist's advice—hiding God's Word in our heart—is one of the main resources we have in the spiritual battle. Christians in restricted situations seem to be more aware of this principle than Christians in so-called free countries. Christians who spend many years in prison without a copy of the Bible leave a lasting impression of the importance of memorizing God's Word.

In the former Soviet Union, Pastor Ivan Antonov spent a total of twenty-four years in a prison camp for preaching the Gospel. He was released from Siberian exile in November 1988. In looking back he says:

> *Most important of all, you should study and memorize the Word of God. When I was in prison and camp, I had no Bible, but I was able to review what I had stored in my heart. I went over two chapters from the Old Testament and two chapters from the New Testament every day.*
>
> *This experience reminded me of Joseph in Egypt. During the time of abundance, he was laying aside stores of grain. When the famine came, he distributed grain from these stores, and the people were saved from starvation.*
>
> *The Scriptures I had memorized were food for my soul.... God always woke me up early in the morning.... This gave me time to pray and to meditate in peace.*[1]

Another Russian brother, Veniamin Markevich, reported after his release from prison camp, "[My]...main comfort and encouragement [while in prison] came from Bible chapters I had memorized. These verses gave food to my soul and helped in the struggle against demonic powers.... Those were just such evil days when special strength was needed in order to, *having done all,* stand."[2]

E. PRESERVING THE BIBLE

In addition to a memorization program, your fellowship can start now to protect and preserve printed copies of Scripture. Do not assume that copies will always be readily available. Each believer should have at least one copy and determine to read in it daily.

While living in a free society, you can openly carry a Bible as a witness of your faith in Christ. If the time comes when you are forced to live in a hostile environment, your Bible may be confiscated if it is seen and recognized. Would you know how to keep it from falling into the hands of the authorities? Some believers have found that simply covering it with brown paper is sufficient. Others have cut the binding and divided it into several small books. Very few non-Christians will recognize such isolate portions as part of a Bible.

Each Christian family should commit itself to carefully preserving a copy of the Bible. Although many Bibles may be discovered and lost, if only one copy remains available to each fellowship the purity of teaching can be maintained.

Remember, both memorization and attempts to preserve printed copies of the Bible are important to Christians in a hostile environment. If you and your fellowship will begin now to work on both

Tips on distribution of Bibles

(learned by many Christians the hard way)

- Portions are easier to distribute than the whole Bible.
- Pass on a copy with the understanding that the person receiving it will copy the portion and then pass it on to someone else.
- Few restrictive societies can monitor all internal mail. Small portions can be sent from one place to another by mail. Copies that are mailed should be handwritten on common-sized, locally available paper.
- Use of audio versions may be less suspicious, especially if set to music.
- With the growing proliferation of computers, Scriptures on disk are a valuable tool for those who have computers.

programs, you will find that it will strengthen the spiritual bonds of your group, it will sharpen your sense of urgency, and it will give you all a deeper sense of commitment to the Word of God.

When and if the Bible becomes a restricted item, you must face the responsibility of distributing the knowledge of God's Word you have preserved. When you learn of other Christians who have no access to a Bible, you will want to help meet that need.

People who reproduce and distribute Scripture in a restricted society take great risks. But, as in the case of memorization, the reproduction and distribution of Scripture also brings spiritual rewards. The Lord will bless your commitment to spread His Word.

Even today, as you live in a free society, you can be involved in getting the Scriptures to Christians inside restrictive societies. You will realize that a high regard for the teaching and spreading of the Word of God can be a key to victory!

In 1980, Chinese Christians in southern China requested one million Bibles from Open Doors. The project to fulfill that request was called "Project Pearl" by Open Doors. Those Chinese Christians were so desirous of God's Word that they created a prayer song asking God to send those Bibles. It is reported that they sang the song every day.

Lord, send a Bible for that's your gracious light,
True love and teaching and the bread of life.
I know for sure that your Word will lead me on,
Brighten the way all through my journey home.

STUDY GUIDE/DISCUSSION QUESTIONS

PASTOR FOCUS

1. One house church group in Vietnam decided to give Bibles to the believers who were most determined to use them. The

criterion used was memory work. So Bibles were shared only with those who recited flawlessly Psalm 119—all 176 verses! Try writing as much of Psalm 119 as you can from memory.

2. How do we know Jesus Christ considered the Old Testament Scriptures important? Consider His teachings on the following:

   Marriage (Matthew 5:31 and Matthew 19:4-9)

   Temptation (Matthew 4)

   Flood (Matthew 24:36-44)

WOMEN'S FOCUS

1. In applying Scripture, we need to ask three primary questions: What did it mean to the original hearers?

What is the underlying timeless principle?

Where or how should I practice that principle?

Use these three questions (above) to study Romans 8.

2. Most Scripture memory plans suggest key verses to memorize. Why is it important to learn whole chapters as well? Identify chapters **you** have committed to memory.

YOUTH FOCUS

1. In applying Scripture, we need to ask three primary questions: What did it mean to the original hearers?

What is the underlying timeless principle?

Where or how should I practice that principle?

Use these three questions to study 2 Timothy 2.

2. What are reasons for memorizing Scripture?

MEN'S FOCUS

1. Why do Christians need a Bible as part of their spiritual *armor*?

2. Why does Satan hate the Bible so much?

3. Why do government authorities and intellectuals hate the Bible?

4. Have you heard the Bible criticized? How should a Christian respond to such an attack?

7

GOD'S PROVISION: PRAYER

Devote yourselves to prayer, being watchful and thankful.

COLOSSIANS 4:2

Pastor Ha's church in Vietnam grew from twenty-nine to more than 5,000 in the first few years of the communist regime. When asked the secret of this extraordinary church growth, Pastor Ha replied, "I have a very simple theology: When you have problems, pray! When you have more problems, pray more!" Every morning at 6 a.m., this church held a prayer meeting and many people came to it. And the church grew and grew. Despite living under constant pressure, the church people chose one Scripture text to put on the wall of their sanctuary: *"In everything give thanks."*

After years of imprisonment, Pastor Ha said, "When I had my freedom, I worked with prayer sometimes in the background. In prison, I discovered how important prayer is. It's like a pilot using a checklist before he takes off. If he skips the first item, many lives might be in danger. **The first item on our checklist should always be prayer. If we skip it, the whole mission is in jeopardy."** (emphasis added)

Vietnamese pastor Cuong also spent more than six years in prison. He says this about prayer:

"In my work I was so busy I had no time to pray. But in prison, I was thankful to God that He gave me time for prayer. I had about six hours of prayer every day. I had time to recall every member of my congregation and to pray for them. Before that, although I served the church, I didn't have enough time to pray for them. **I learned about the real presence of God in prayer there. When you kneel down and pray wholeheartedly with the Lord, you feel His answer right there."** (emphasis added)

A. EMPOWERING THROUGH PRAYER

Although they do not believe anyone is listening, the Buddhists repeat their prayers fervently. The Hindus pray regularly, believing one of their many Hindu gods may be listening, but they do not really expect any response to their prayers. The Muslims pray five times a day. They believe that Allah is listening, but he will not alter his plans to meet their needs.

Devout Buddhists, Hindus and Muslims consider Christianity a *prayerless* faith, because they rarely see Christians praying. Some Christians have been observed "rubbing their foreheads in public" while whispering a prayer before they eat a meal. Yet Christians believe they have a God who not only hears their prayers offered from the heart in secret in their "quiet place" (see Matthew 6:5-15), but also will answer these prayers in public, in mighty power!

The Christian concept of prayer is deeply rooted in the Old Testament. David gave the church a rich heritage of prayer in the Psalms, and many modern Christians have added new meaning to their prayer lives by studying them. But the Christian learns his greatest lessons about prayer from Jesus Christ. Generations of Christians have come to Christ, as His disciples did, and said, *"Lord, teach us to pray."* (Luke 11:1)

Jesus taught by both word and example. His life was full of prayer. The Bible records that He rose very early in the morning to pray (Mark 1:35). He is seen spending time in prayer either before or after every important event of His life (Luke 6:6-13; Luke 9:28-29; Matthew 14:19 and 15:36; John 17). Prayer was certainly a regular part of His life, and a very prominent feature of His death. From His prayer in the Garden of Gethsemane (Mark 14:32-41) to His final words of prayer on the cross, Jesus moved in an atmosphere of prayer.

In addition to the deep impact that His prayerful life had on His disciples, Jesus commanded them to pray (John 16:24) and taught them many things about prayer (Matthew 6 and 7). Jesus even gave His followers a model prayer (Matthew 6:9-13). In this prayer, we are taught to glorify God, seek His perfect will, look to Him for our daily needs, seek His forgiveness as we give our forgiveness to others, rely on Him in temptation and praise Him.

Jesus taught that our motive in prayer is more important than the form of our prayer. James 4:3 also says that we don't receive when we ask with wrong motives.

Then, in Matthew's Gospel, Jesus says, *"And when you pray, do not be like the hypocrites, for they love to pray standing in the synagogues and on the street corners to be seen by men..."* (Matthew 6:5). Rather, we are to go to a private place and pray. God, who hears everything done in secret, will hear our prayers and reward us.

Jesus Christ also gave us the thrilling privilege of praying in His name. This is not a "magic formula" that guarantees results if tacked onto the end of a list of demands. It is the privilege of going into the very presence of God and being received as Jesus is received.

Praying in Jesus' name implies that our will and purposes are one with His. It is in this sense that Jesus was able to say, *"You may ask me for anything in my name, and I will do it"* (John 14:14). Jesus chose to use one of His greatest miracles, the raising of Lazarus from the dead, to teach an important point. John tells us that Jesus looked up and said, *"Father, I thank you that you have heard me. I knew that you always hear me, but I said this for the benefit of the people standing here...*" (John 11:41b-42). Note that God always hears Jesus' prayer. He also hears every prayer prayed in Jesus' name.

The Muslim idea that Allah is so great that he has everything under his control, and therefore won't change anything in answer to prayer, seems impressive at first. But this teaching of Jesus is even greater. Our God has chosen to use prayer as a means of displaying His power from a desire to be in relationship with us. As His children call upon Him, He will change circumstances and events that are adversely affecting His work. He has eternally planned to do this.

"Much prayer, much power; little prayer, little power." Chinese Christian maxim

B. WHEN TO PRAY

The simple faith of those in the New Testament church is most dramatically evident in their attitude toward prayer. While awaiting the promised Holy Spirit, they prayed (Acts 1:14). When seeking a replacement for Judas, 120 of the believers gathered to pray, and they were in prayer again when the Holy Spirit was poured out upon them (Acts 2). Following this great event, they returned to prayer (Acts 2:42). When the authorities threatened them, they prayed. (Acts 4:23-31)

This prayer in Acts 4 is a model prayer for Christians facing persecution. Here, the church recognized the sovereign power of God, and they recalled the Scriptural prophesies that persecution would come and accepted this fact. They did not pray for deliverance from persecution, but asked for boldness and power. Note that God was pleased with their prayer and dramatically answered. (Acts 4:31)

The early church's dependence on prayer is evident throughout the book of Acts. Whether faced with persecution from without (Acts 7:59-60), strife within the fellowship (Acts 6:1-4), or the need to empower new believers (Acts 8:14-17), they turned to prayer.

When the Lord desired to make changes in the course of the church, He did it through their prayers. He sent Peter to the first Gentile believers as Peter prayed (Acts 10:9), and set apart Paul and Barnabas as the first missionaries as the church in Antioch prayed. (Acts 13:2-3)

The Apostle Paul set a consistent example in prayer from the beginning to the end of his ministry. He considered prayer so important that he made some reference to it in every one of his letters. His teaching enlarges upon the brief teachings of Christ. Especially important are the following verses.

- *Devote yourselves to prayer, being watchful and thankful.* (Colossians 4:2)
- *Pray continually.* (1 Thessalonians 5:17)
- *I urge, then, first of all, that requests, prayers, intercession and thanksgiving be made for everyone—for kings and all those in authority, that we may live peaceful and quiet lives in all godliness and holiness.* (1 Timothy 2:1-2)

Paul had a great deal of personal experience with persecution and his response was to pray (Acts 16:25). God miraculously delivered him, and he believed that the deliverance was in answer to prayer. (2 Corinthians 1:9-11)

James also emphasizes the practical importance of prayer. He teaches that we can expect to receive needed wisdom in answer to prayer (James 1:5). He also gives clear teaching on praying for healing. (5:13-16)

C. HOW AND WHAT TO PRAY

As we study the things that the Bible teaches about prayer, we see that prayer is basically talking with God. Based on the prayer model that Jesus taught His disciples in Matthew 6:9-13, there are six parts to His prayer.

1. Praise

"Our Father in heaven, may your name be honored." (NLT)

When praying, we should honor God by thanking and praising Him for His grace, mercy and blessings. Praise and thanksgiving are important aspects of prayer. God deserves our praise, and the Scriptures repeatedly encourage us to praise Him (Psalm 34:1-3; Psalm 105:1-2; and Exodus 15:11). God does not need our praise, but we need to praise Him. Our praise is a testimony of our faith in His sovereign power, even when our circumstances are very difficult.

Mature Christians living under persecution have frequently urged us to turn our hearts to praise, because in this way we are acknowledging the sovereignty of God, bringing glory to His name and strengthening ourselves. They assure us that God honors our faith when we praise Him in spite of difficult circumstances.

There are many specific cases where God has responded to the prayer of praise by divine intervention. And remember, whether God changes the circumstances or not, He is God and He deserves our praise.

2. Purpose

"...your kingdom come, your will be done on earth as it is in heaven."

In prayer you commit yourself to do God's will—in your personal life, your family, your church, your ministry, your employment, your future, your city, your nation, and the world.

3. Provision

"Give us today our daily bread."

In prayer you ask God to provide for your daily needs. There are numerous Scriptures that indicate we should take *all* our needs first to the Lord.

4. Pardon

"Forgive us our debts..." (NLT: ***"...and forgive us our sins..."***)

Another important aspect of prayer is confession of sin. Since all of us fail the Lord by sinning, we rejoice in His promise to cleanse us when we confess to Him (1 John 1:9). When we enter the holy presence of God through prayer, we should allow the Holy Spirit to convict us of those things that are displeasing to God and immediately confess them, confident that He will forgive. Our confession should be specific and include a willingness to make amends the Lord may lead us to make. A scriptural illustration of this is found in the story about Zacchaeus. (see Luke 19:8)

5. People

"...as we also have forgiven our debtors." (*"debtors"* in the Living Bible: ***"those who have wronged us"***)

Praying for other people is an important part of prayer as is the positive act of forgiveness to those who have wronged us. (see Matthew 5:44)

6. Protection

"And lead us not into temptation, but deliver us from the evil one."

We face a spiritual battle every day. Satan wants to defeat you through temptation and fear. By praying for protection from the evil one's attacks, you will have the confidence to face every situation during the day. (1 John 4:4)

D. OTHER DYNAMICS OF PRAYER

1. Promises

One of the amazing things about the Bible is the number of great promises it makes concerning prayer. If it only promised occasional answers, we would pray much as a person gambles, hoping to be one of the fortunate ones. But the Bible makes such broad promises as:

- *And I will do whatever you ask in my name, so that the Son may bring glory to the Father.* (John 14:13)
- *Ask and it will be given to you; seek and you will find; knock and the door will be opened to you.* (Matthew 7:7)
- *Call to me and I will answer you and tell you great and unsearchable things you do not know.* (Jeremiah 33:3)

These promises should encourage us to bring every need to the Lord, as long as our motives are correct. (see James 4:3)

2. Listening

Throughout our prayer time, it is important to be open to the Spirit's guidance. The Holy Spirit will help us to praise God. He will remind us of needs for which we should be praying. Sometimes He will clearly show us specifically what we should do in connection with matters we are considering in prayer (John 16:13-14). Often He will guide us to a passage of Scripture that will show us what we should do. The Living Bible translation of James 1:5 is very clear on this point. *"If you want to know what God wants you to do, ask Him, and He will gladly tell you, for He is ready to give a bountiful supply of wisdom to all who ask Him; and He will not resent it."*

3. Specific and Expectant

When we pray, we should be specific and expect answers. Only through praying specifically can we experience the faith-building thrill of seeing needs met in our lives, in the lives of our church family, and in the lives of our friends and loved ones. It is helpful to keep a record of these requests so that we can later record the Lord's answers to our prayers. This, of course, implies we will be praying expectantly.

Some Christians are afraid to ask God to meet specific needs, because they don't expect Him to answer. Their faith is weak, and they do not want to face the possibility that their prayers may not be effective. When we study the Scriptures, we find that God wants us to pray with expectancy. *"Therefore I tell you, whatever you ask for in prayer, believe that you have received it, and it will be yours"* (Mark 11:24). The same would apply to the victory of any group of believers in hostile circumstances.

How can a group of Christians develop this kind of effective prayer communication with God? First, they must study what the Bible teaches about prayer. Review the examples given in the Scriptures of those who exercised power with God through prayer. You must know the teachings of Scripture before they can affect your life. Sound biblical teaching about prayer should be continuously presented and practiced in your fellowship group. There are valuable passages in both the Old and New Testaments that show the practical application of prayer.

Whether or not Christians have learned to have real communication with God in prayer may be the single most important factor in determining if they will be victorious Christians.

If at all possible, it is a good policy for each new believer to be assigned a mature Christian as a prayer partner. The new believer and his prayer partner should meet regularly to pray together and to learn the various types of prayer by study and practice. When young believers have become seasoned prayer intercessors, they should become prayer partners of other new believers.

E. THE SPECIFIC NATURE OF PRAYER

To become strong in prayer, the church must learn to recognize needs that should be prayed for. Crisis prayer is found in the Bible, and such prayer is encouraged. But frequently, our crises are the result of our lack of prayer earlier. If we bring our needs to the Lord when they are still small, fewer crises may develop. Our God is not too busy to be interested in our small problems. The Scripture specifically tells us that our God is interested in such little things as one sparrow and the number of hairs on our heads.

Sometimes young believers get the idea that they can only pray about *important* things. We need to show them that our God is interested in every detail of our lives. Repeated teaching of the promises of God is important. We expect God to answer our prayer because He promised to do so. The sense of expectancy can become exciting.

1. Specific Needs

It is important to understand the difference between needs and wants. Many weak Christians fail on this point. They demand that God give them their wants, but God knows when something is not the best for them and He denies it. So they become discouraged, and therefore are easy prey for the enemy.

When we pray for specific needs in our lives and base our prayer on a specific promise of Scripture, we will see the answer and our faith will be strengthened. This is one reason why it is important to make specific requests and keep track of them. New believers are always encouraged when God answers their specific prayers. Seeing God answer prayer encourages them to continue praying and to expect God to keep answering their prayers.

2. Forms

What about the position of prayer? The Bible records examples of people praying while bowing (Genesis 24:26), kneeling (1 Kings 8:54), on their faces before the Lord (Matthew 26:39), and standing (2 Chronicles 6:12). Apparently, the physical position is not too important. In fact, in Nehemiah 2:4-5, a man questioned by the king quickly prays before he responds. He did not assume a prayer position as he made this brief prayer, yet the Lord certainly heard and answered him.

Many Christians under pressure or persecution have found this type of prayer very effective. When we are faced with difficult situations, we can call upon the Lord in our hearts and know He hears. While it is often useful to pray out loud with others so they can pray with us, it is also important that we learn to pray silently.

Nehemiah's short prayer before he answered the king was certainly a silent prayer. The church needs to learn that sometimes it is best to pray fervently, yet silently. When Christians pray out loud, they might be heard by the authorities and stopped. Silent prayer that expresses the deep desire of the heart can be presented to the Lord completely undetected. We can pray silently while working in the fields, standing at a machine, or even while attending a propaganda meeting.

3. Patience and Perseverance

Another lesson the church needs to learn about prayer is to pray patiently. God meets our needs *"at the proper time"* (Galatians 6:9). Too often Christians grow tired of praying and give up. They often justify this on the basis that God's failure to answer means the request is not according to His will. Remember, God can:

Deliver—whatever we ask in His name;

Delay—to fit His perfect timing (only He sees the end from the beginning);

Deny—and say "No" because we ask amiss or

Defer—to a better answer.

Jesus urges us to be persistent in prayer (Luke 11:5-8). This does not mean that God does not want to meet our needs and that we need to try to persuade Him. It simply means that only God, who completely understands the whole situation, can know when and how to answer. Only when we have assurance in our hearts from the Lord should we remove a matter from our prayer list. Let's say with Samuel, *"As for me, far be it from me that I should sin against the LORD by failing to pray...."* (1 Samuel 12:23)

Many times Christians lose heart in prayer because they do not recognize it when the Lord does answer their prayers. Sometimes this is due to the fact that they did not pray specifically enough. Other times it may be because they have decided in advance how God must answer. Or maybe they think that only a great miracle can meet their need.

But the Lord may change the circumstances so that the need seems to be answered naturally. Mature believers should recognize that the events of everyday life also come from the Lord. Our daily bread and safety are miracles of God in this troubled world. Let us not presume to tell God how to answer, and let us praise Him for His daily care. The old saying is certainly true, "God gives His best to those who leave the choices to Him."

4. In hostile situations

The church that is threatened by bitter opposition must allocate extended time for prayer. It is a great mistake for a body of believers to set aside only a brief portion of one weekly meeting to share prayer requests, rejoice in answers to prayer, and join together in prayer. It would be much better if time were provided in every gathering of believers for this critically important activity. Even informal meetings of Christians should be seen as an opportunity to pray together.

The church is wise to schedule small group prayer meetings and a meeting for prayer partners every week, as well as strongly encouraging daily personal prayer by every member. Some churches in the free world have begun to decentralize their mid-week prayer meeting. Instead of one meeting at the church, the prayer sessions are held in homes scattered throughout the community. This encourages lay leadership, stimulates personal involvement, and makes young Christians realize that the Lord can be present in meetings outside of the formal sanctuary.

In addition to home prayer meetings based on geographical

areas, the church can encourage various groups within the fellowship to gather for prayer together: housewives, farmers, students, factory workers....

If open persecution comes to a local assembly that has learned to pray in these various ways, the prayer life of the church will continue. Even if Christians are scattered, they can continue to share prayer requests and answers to prayer with one another by mail. It is easy to write about such things in a way that will not draw the attention of the authorities.

The prayer and devotional life of the Christian family, however, remains the basic unit of spiritual power. If Satan wins a temporary victory of completely scattering a local body of believers, the prayer fellowship of the family remains.

Individual Christians have found prayer their main source of strength when they have been unjustly imprisoned or exiled. Prayer is the Christian's first, highest and perhaps most powerful spiritual experience. Learning to pray effectively is certainly one of the greatest lessons a Christian can learn.

5. For your persecutors

One of the great lessons from the Persecuted Church is praying for those who persecute you. This is a parallel principle with loving your enemies. Multiple examples can be shared how God has honored this principle of prayer.

Noskie, a Muslim imam in the southern part of the Philippines, was greatly respected in his small community. Coming home from a fishing expedition one day, he was shocked to discover that his two daughters had converted to Christianity. He knew that this would bring shame to the whole community. In his anger, he mercilessly beat his daughters hoping they would renounce their new faith. But the daughters remained faithful. They loved their father and knew that nothing was impossible with God so they started praying for their father's conversion.

Sometime later, while fishing, Noskie felt a sudden piercing pain in his stomach. As the pain intensified, his belly began to swell up like a balloon. He writhed in unbearable pain. He prayed to Allah but nothing happened. In desperation he cried out to the God of his daughters, Jesus Christ, and was instantly healed.

Noskie emerged from the experience a new person. He surrendered his life to the lordship of Jesus Christ. Today he faithfully serves the Lord as a lay pastor and his daughters help in the ministry.

F. FASTING AND PRAYING

Fasting is a significant spiritual activity that goes along with intensive prayer times. Let's examine this topic by answering some common questions.

1. What does it mean to fast and pray?

To fast means to put God first. Fasting is an attitude of the heart in which we interrupt our normal life to pray for a specific matter or cause. It means to abstain from food—and for some, even drink—so that we can focus on God and be more sensitive to spiritual matters. Fasting is also perseverance in prayer until you have received an answer—be it yes, no, wait or something different.

2. Is fasting biblical?

Consider the following:

- Moses fasted twice for forty days. (Exodus 34:28)
- Daniel fasted (partially) for twenty-one days. (Daniel 10:3)
- Joel called for a day of fasting. (Joel 1:14; 2:12)
- Ezra withdrew for a period of fasting and mourning. (Ezra 10:6)
- Elijah fasted for forty days. (1 Kings 19:8)
- Leaders of the church in Antioch fasted. (Acts 13:2-3)
- Jesus fasted for forty days. (Luke 4:2)
- Paul and Barnabas fasted. (Acts 14:23; 27:33)

In essence, fasting means that we rend our hearts before God, confess our sins and turn to the Lord anew (Joel 2:12-13). In Matthew 6:16-18, Jesus teaches His disciples about what to do when fasting. It is interesting that He assumes they *will* fast and gives instructions for *when* they fast.

3. Are there different types of fasting?

First, there is an *ordinary fast* when you take no solids for a certain period of time and drink only water (up to forty days maximum).

Second, there is a *complete fast* when you take no water or any other form of food for a certain period (normally not more than three days).

The third type is a *partial fast,* where you omit certain foods for a certain period of time, for example, sweets or eating and drinking less. During a partial fast someone might decide, for instance, to only eat bread and drink water for a certain period of time.

4. Guidelines for fasting

Check with your doctor before you start a fast. People with heart problems or diabetes are recommended not to fast.

Be aware that your body will excrete excessive amounts of toxic waste.

People on an ordinary fast normally drink different kinds of fluids. Do as your conscience permits you. But do not fast for more than three days without fluids. Avoid water with chemical additives like chlorine and fluorides.

Most people find that the first three days of any fast are normally the most difficult. It is an enormous encouragement to have other believers fasting and praying with you, especially for longer fasts.

If you are fasting while maintaining your normal work schedule, use the times you usually spend eating for prayer. Find as much time for prayer as possible.

G. A DAY FOR PRAYER AND FASTING

Here are a few ideas on how to schedule a day of prayer and fasting. These are only ideas to stimulate you and your fellowship group.

- You may want to start by setting aside a morning, or an afternoon, or an evening. If you can fill half a day, you may want to extend the period.
- Get a Bible, a notebook and a pen and, if you want to, a good spiritual book. Pick a quiet place with no telephones where you cannot be disturbed. Decide beforehand how long you want this time to be and stick to it.
- Start your time with the Lord with exaltation and worship, and then sit quietly in His presence.
- If your mind wanders and you think of everything you have to do, write it down on a sheet of paper. This will let you concentrate on those things later.
- Select a book of the Bible and start reading it from the beginning. Don't be in a hurry. Read it verse by verse. Seek to see Jesus in whatever passage you are reading. Ask the Lord what He wants to teach you from each verse. Pray about it. Go on to the next verse. In your notebook, write down the things the Lord speaks to you about.
- After an hour of Bible study enter into direct prayer. Take time for confession. Be specific about your personal and family or ministry needs. Then enter into intercession for others. It is important not to hurry. The emphasis is on being with and talking with the Lord Jesus.
- Set aside time to specifically pray for urgent matters and seek the Lord's guidance.
- Vary your time with Bible study and prayer. Also you might take time to read a few chapters from a spiritual book.

- If possible, listen to some good, uplifting Christian music from time to time during the day.
- You might even sleep a while if you feel drowsy. At the end of the day, you will be revived and refreshed and ready to go to work again.

Besides one-day fasts as described above, many Christians practice three-day, seven-day and forty-day fasts.

I asked for strength that I might achieve, I was made weak that I might endure;
I asked for health to do larger things, I was given infirmity that I might do better things;
I asked for power that I might impress men, I was given weakness that I might seek God;
I asked for wealth that I might be free from care, I was given poverty that I might be wiser than carefree;
I asked for all things that I might enjoy life, I was given life that I might enjoy all things;
I received nothing I asked for. I received more than I ever hoped for.
My prayer was answered! I am blessed!

—*Author Unknown*

STUDY GUIDE/DISCUSSION QUESTIONS

PASTOR FOCUS

1. One pastor at an SSTS seminar commented, "I have been a pastor for over thirty years and I have never fasted." In Matthew 6 our Lord teaches:
   6:2—*"So **when** you give...."*
   6:5—*"And **when** you pray...."*

6:16—"***When*** *you fast....* "
From your perspective as a pastor, why are *giving, praying* and *fasting*—each of which is to be done *"in secret"*—such a challenge for Christians in free societies?

2. As the leader of your fellowship you are planning a day of prayer and fasting. Discuss and plan variations that would suit you or your group best. Plan your group prayer session together where all of the above teaching recommendations are implemented. Let the gifts of the Holy Spirit be exercised around your specific prayer requests.

3. Explain the following promises as they relate to prayer:
   - *"I will do whatever you ask in my name, so that the Son may bring glory to the Father."* (John 14:13)

   - *"Ask and it will be given to you; seek and you will find; knock and the door will be opened to you."* (Matthew 7:7)

   - *"Call to me and I will answer you and tell you great and unsearchable things you do not know."* (Jeremiah 33:3)

WOMEN'S FOCUS

1. Write a definition of "prayer" that you could share with a new believer. "Prayer is…

2. Why is "listening to God" such an important part of prayer?

3. Explain the six parts of the "model" prayer Jesus taught His disciples in Matthew 6:9-13, as you would for a new convert.

   PRAISE
   "Our Father in heaven, hallowed be your name…."

   PURPOSE
   "your kingdom come, your will be done on earth as it is in heaven."

   PROVISION
   "Give us today our daily bread."

PARDON

"Forgive us our debts..."

PEOPLE

"...as we also have forgiven our debtors."

PROTECTION

"And lead us not into temptation, but deliver us from the evil one."

YOUTH FOCUS

1. What do the following Scriptures tell us about "when" and "how" to pray?
   - Pray with ____________, exaltation, thanks and ____________ to God. (1 Chronicles 29:10-13)
   - Pray with ____________ confession/repentance. (2 Chronicles 7:14)
   - Pray with a pure, clean ____________ and motive. (Psalm 66:18-20)
   - Pray in ____________. (Matthew 6:6)
   - Pray as ____________ taught us to pray. (Matthew 6:9)
   - Pray according to God's ____________. (John 15:7)
   - Pray with ____________. (Romans 12:12)

- Pray with ____________. (Philippians 4:6)
- Pray with care and ____________. (Colossians 4:2)
- Pray continually with ____________. (1 Thessalonians 5:17)
- Pray in peace lifting up holy ____________. (1 Timothy 2:8)
- Pray when in trouble, or ____________. (James 5:13-16)
- Pray from a right relationship with your ____________. (1 Peter 3:7)
- Pray with ____________. (1 Peter 4:7)
- Pray according to God's ____________. (1 John 5:14-15)
- Pray in the ____________. (Jude 1:20)

2. What are the hindrances to prayer based on the following Scriptures?
   - Praying with selfish ____________. (James 4:3)
   - Praying without first confessing known ____________. (John 9:31)
   - Praying while ____________ God's Word. (Jeremiah 14:10-13)
   - Praying without responding to God's ____________. (Proverbs 1:24-33)
   - Praying without practical responses to the ____________. (Proverbs 21:13)
   - Praying while full of ____________ (equals being a murderer). (Isaiah 1:15)
   - Praying while serving any ____________. (Jeremiah 11:11-14)
   - Praying with ____________. (James 1:6-7)
   - Praying with godlessness or ____________. (Job 27:8)
   - Praying while full of ____________. (Job 35:12)
   - Praying while being ____________. (Luke 18:9-14)
   - Praying while being an enemy of the ____________. (Psalm 18:40-41)

MEN'S FOCUS

1. Why is it important to be specific in our prayers?

   Note the following specific prayer commands:
   - Psalm 122:6—Pray for the peace of ________________.
   - Matthew 5:44—Pray for those who ________________ you.
   - Matthew 6:13—Pray for deliverance from the evil ____________.
   - Matthew 9:37-38—Pray for Christian ________________ worldwide.
   - Matthew 26:41—Pray for victory over ________________.
   - John 17—Pray for the protection, sanctification and unity of ____________.
   - Ephesians 6:18—Pray for all the ________________.
   - 2 Thessalonians 3:1—Pray for world ________________.
   - 2 Thessalonians 3:2—Pray for the ________________ of Christian leaders.
   - 1 Timothy 2:1-7—Pray for all those in ________________.
   - James 1:5—Pray for spiritual ______________.
   - 1 John 5:16—Pray for a brother who errs in his ______________.

2. How should you respond to apparently "unanswered" prayer or answers that are not what you desire?

3. One of the great lessons from the Suffering Church is praying for those who persecute you. Identify your greatest human "persecutor." Write out **your** prayer for this person.

4. What is the difference between:
   - A partial fast and an ordinary fast?

   - An ordinary fast and a complete fast?

5. America is considered by many in other countries to be a "Christian" nation: In Bill Bright's book *The Coming Revival: America's Call to Fast, Pray, and "Seek God's Face,"* he says: "50% of the 100 million Americans who attend church each Sunday have no assurance of their salvation.... And 95% are not familiar with the person and ministry of the Holy Spirit.... Only 2% of believers in America regularly share their faith in Christ with others."[1] Are we pretending to be Christians yet living all week in our natural environment with morals, principles and a lifestyle that is a twisted three-cord strand of duplicity, hypocrisy and apostasy? How should we then live?

6. The church in China is growing with committed believers, willing to risk all, including career, economic advantage, prison terms, health and family—in essence everything we cherish in the Western world—for the basics of prayer, the Word, witnessing and being filled with the Spirit. Billy Graham has said that, according to his research, "at least 90 percent of all Christians in America are living defeated lives...." [2] Why?

7. Consider the following physical and spiritual benefits of fasting by choosing the best word for each blank space:

Physical Benefits of Fasting—choose from:
rest, eating, waste, toxins, revitalization

- Provides physiological ________________ (digestive, glandular, circulatory, respiratory systems).
- Allows elimination of ___________/____________ and purification of blood and lymph systems.
- Promotes discipline in __________________.

Overall ____________________.

Spiritual Benefits of Fasting—choose from:
humbling, discernment, alone, values

- Time to be _____________ with the Lord in His presence.
- A ________________ of oneself before the Lord in prayer.
- A heightened level of spiritual sensitivity, alertness and __________________.
- A time of personal re-examination of one's motives, goals and _____________.

8. What did Paul mean when he said, *"Pray continually"* (1 Thessalonians 5:17)? Is this possible?

9. How does keeping a journal of prayer requests challenge our faith? Are you willing to accept the challenge?

8

GOD'S PROVISION: THE HOLY SPIRIT

If you then, though you are evil, know how to give good gifts to your children, how much more will your Father in heaven give the Holy Spirit to those who ask him.

LUKE 11:13

In China, a Christian woman was in charge of security at a coal mine. The woman suddenly felt the Holy Spirit urging her to pull the alarm lever, even though there was no apparent reason to do so. Although everything seemed quiet and normal, she obeyed the prompting within her. The whole mine was evacuated as a result of the alarm sounding. But when all the men had assembled on the surface, it seemed as if a huge mistake had been made. Just moments later, the ground beneath their feet shook and a large section of the mine collapsed from an earthquake.

Because of this sister's sensitivity and willingness to obey God's Holy Spirit, everyone's lives had been saved. After recognising that God had miraculously saved them from death, four hundred of the miners surrendered their lives to Christ.[1]

A. THE WORK OF THE HOLY SPIRIT

Throughout the history of the church, one of the most important doctrines has been the concept of the Trinity. The living God of the Bible is one God, yet He has revealed Himself to us as three distinct persons: God the Father; God the Son, whom we call Jesus Christ; and God the Holy Spirit. This crucial doctrine is a spiritual mystery that can only be understood by faith, not by human reason.

The thrilling fact is that many believers around the world who have never understood this doctrine, and some that have never even heard of it, have nonetheless experienced and known the triune God.

Most believers recognize God the Father as the ruler of the universe, the eternal divine power on high. It is also generally understood among Christian believers that the God of the universe chose to reveal Himself, first through the written Word, the Bible, and then more dramatically by entering the world in physical form as our Savior, Jesus Christ, and on a personal level, as the Holy Spirit.

There seems to be much less understanding by believers of the third person of the Trinity. Yet, according to the Bible, it is the Holy Spirit who is so vitally involved in our efforts to live victoriously. Upon our invitation of Jesus as Lord of our lives, the Holy Spirit came to reside within us to enable the living-out of that commitment.

This lack of teaching and understanding about the person and work of the Holy Spirit can probably be traced to two primary misunderstandings. First, there are those who think that when Jesus said of the Holy Spirit, *"He will bring glory to me"* (John 16:14), He meant that all Spirit-guided teaching will be about Christ. Therefore these people do not teach about the Holy Spirit. This is a sincere desire to follow the Scriptures, but it fails to notice that there are many references to the person and the work of the Holy Spirit in the New Testament. Were these New Testament writers led of the Holy Spirit when they wrote these passages? Of course they were. So it seems that the Holy Spirit wants us to know and understand His ministry to the church, which will bring glory to Christ. In fact, when Christians realize what the Holy Spirit can do for them, their lives are much more likely to glorify Christ.

The second reason that the person and work of the Holy Spirit are often disregarded in Christian teaching is because the ministry of the Holy Spirit may seem too dynamic and unpredictable. The book of Acts reveals that the Holy Spirit's work does not follow a consistent pattern. He responds to apparently similar situations in a variety of amazing ways. This dynamic inconsistency cannot be programmed or controlled and is often unwelcome in institutional churches.

Jesus said He would not leave us alone but would give us a Helper to be with us forever (John 14:16-18). He taught us that the Holy Spirit would be our Counselor (John 14:26). Jesus also called Him the Spirit of Truth (John 14:17). The work of the Holy Spirit is so practical to us that it will be useful to begin by listing His functions.

• Assuring us	Ephesians 1:14
• Comforting	John 14:16
• Convicting	John 16:8
• Teaching	John 14:26
• Reminding	John 14:26
• Testifying of Christ	John 15:26
• Guiding	John 16:13; Romans 8:14
• Revealing	John 16:14; Luke 2:26
• Glorifying Christ	John 16:14
• Supplying power	Acts 1:8
• Speaking through us	Acts 4:31
• Speaking to us	John 16:13
• Bearing witness in us	Romans 8:16
• Helping	Romans 8:26
• Interceding	Romans 8:26

• Giving spiritual gifts	1 Corinthians 12:4-11
• Renewal	Titus 3:5
• Confirming our salvation	Ephesians 1:13
• Producing His fruit in us	Galatians 5:22

It is evident from this list that both common errors of ignoring the Holy Spirit and looking to Him only for the sensational must be avoided. The functions of the Holy Spirit are essential to Christians whether or not they are in a hostile environment.

If the Holy Spirit did not work in our lives in the ways listed above, we would have no power to offer anything to a lost world. The goal of all Christians should be to live so completely under the control of the Holy Spirit that it can be said we are walking in the Spirit (Galatians 5:25). As Paul reminded the Galatian Christians, they began their Christian lives by a miracle work of God—new birth in Jesus—and they could only expect to continue to grow in Christ by God's power. This fact is even more evident in a hostile environment.

It would help you to memorize this list of the functions of the Holy Spirit, so you know what you can expect God to do for you when you are under pressure.

A courier to China was once put in a difficult position by the probing questions of a border guard. He didn't know what to say. He recalled the scriptural promise that the Holy Spirit would tell him what to say, and with only a second's hesitation, he mentioned a fact of Chinese history to the guard that changed the whole direction of the conversation. He later commented that he didn't remember ever having heard that detail of history before. The Holy Spirit had put it into his mouth.

Remember that the Bible teaches, *"...he who began a good work in you will carry it on to completion until the day of Christ Jesus"* (Philippians 1:6). This means that the Holy Spirit is actively functioning in you if you are a believer. Are you aware of what He has been doing?

B. THE EMPOWERMENT OF THE HOLY SPIRIT

Notice how many of the functions of the Holy Spirit are vital for leadership in the church. Spirit-led leadership is most important when the church is facing a hostile situation. The type of church leadership that is widely accepted in the institutional churches in free societies today, with one person as the center of all activity, cannot continue in a repressive society. Apart from the fact that this type of leadership is probably not biblical, it is easy for the authorities to remove the key person and stop that church's impact.

Whether a local church group chooses to co-exist, protest, or go underground in the face of repression, the pastor-teacher style of church leadership must change. While co-existing churches or even protest churches may have pastors, their activities will be closely monitored.

While pastors are the center of attention of the authorities, it is hoped that other believers will assume such key roles as visiting the sick and teaching the young. Without the pastor being able to move freely among the members to encourage, comfort, and exhort, will other members meet these needs? The Holy Spirit, if He can find willing vessels, can fill and use members who have never before attempted such leadership responsibilities.

When one oppressive regime took over a country, government officials had already identified the key Christian leaders on the local as well as the national levels. Anyone who was a "full-time" Christian worker before the takeover was a "marked" person.

In Vietnam, even Christian businessmen who were not "full-time" Christian workers, but who had exercised lay leadership, were "marked." These people did not have the option of going underground. They had to stand for the Lord openly and face the consequences or suffer spiritual defeat.

People in such positions deserve the prayerful support of Christians everywhere. Imagine the Christian movement in your country suddenly cut off from all those who are now its leaders. In the period of confusion that immediately follows a takeover by a hostile regime, some small groups of Christians may be able to move to a different locality and become underground churches, but they must leave their "institutional forms" behind.

But who would lead such groups? Who would provide leadership for "house" churches and "family" churches? God, through the Holy Spirit, raises up and equips leaders for His church in such circumstances, as He always has in the past. Members of a home fellowship must be prepared to accept the leadership of the Spirit and the leadership of those through whom He chooses to minister.

Look again at the examples of the New Testament churches in the book of Acts, and the pattern outlined by Paul in his epistles. The leadership of the Holy Spirit in any small church fellowship will probably be the quiet interrelated leadership of several who comfort, encourage, and exhort.

Believers in a fellowship will begin to function in proper relationship to Christ once they realize the following three things:

- They are priests before God. (1 Peter 2:5)
- They do not need any mediator but Jesus. (1 Timothy 2:5)
- The Holy Spirit is functioning in them daily.

As believers in a fellowship realize these truths, they will begin to function in proper relationship to Christ. The Bible teaches that Jesus is the head, and we are the members of His body. (Ephesians 1:22-23)

When lay Christians begin to understand that they can pray directly to the Lord; and when, under the direction of the Holy Spirit, they can understand a passage of written or memorized Scripture, they are equipped to walk victoriously in hostile circumstances.

One exciting discovery will lead to another. These Christians will begin to let the Holy Spirit use them to touch the lives of others and minister to their needs. No authority on earth can destroy this kind of spiritual church!

C. INDIVIDUAL GIFTS FOR THE GOOD OF ALL

Let's review some of the basic things we know about the Holy Spirit.

- He is God. (Genesis 1:2)
- He is eternal. (Hebrews 9:14)
- He lives inside the believer. (1 Corinthians 3:16; Romans 8:9)
- He will never leave a believer. (John 14:16)
- His presence is demonstrated in fruit. (Galatians 5:22-23)
- He gives power to stand against the enemy. (Luke 9:1-2; James 4:7)

With these facts firmly in mind, believers are prepared to carry on as Christians in any situation. The individual believer will understand what Peter meant when he said, *"You also, like living stones, are being built into a spiritual house to be a holy priesthood, offering spiritual sacrifices acceptable to God through Jesus Christ."* (1 Peter 2:5) And later he added, *"You are a chosen people, a royal priesthood, a holy nation, a people belonging to God."* (1 Peter 2:9)

The implications of these teachings are tremendous to Christians in a hostile environment. Even when cut off from the traditional forms of the institutional church, they can continue to fulfill all the functions of the church in their own family or small fellowship. This includes witnessing, leading unbelievers to salvation in Christ, baptizing new believers, and sharing the Lord's Supper.

But the Holy Spirit will not be able to use believers who feel that they are not spiritually mature enough or deserve to be spiritual leaders. God doesn't use us on the basis of what we *feel* or *deserve.*

We must stand boldly on the teachings of the Bible. Jesus Christ is the head of the church—and He has not relinquished that position to any person or organization. The kind of problem that can develop due to a misunderstanding of this point was graphically illustrated when a Chinese Christian told a visitor that he had not been able to worship God in more than ten years.

When the shocked visitor inquired how *anything* could keep a believer from quietly worshipping the Lord for so long, the Chinese man explained that he had not been able to worship since the authorities had arrested his priest. It is sad that this man did not understand that he has complete access to the throne of God through Jesus Christ.

As the head of His church, Jesus has continued to empower the church by the Holy Spirit (Acts 2:33). The Holy Spirit can be trusted to meet the needs of each group of believers. He will give spiritual gifts to the members to strengthen the whole group (Romans 12:3-8). It is highly unlikely that one person will possess all of the gifts needed in any fellowship. Usually, each member has a spiritual gift that can help the whole group when it is used properly.

You should be familiar with the key passages teaching the gifts of the Holy Spirit and be prepared to have the Holy Spirit use them in your group. Paul told the Ephesian church, *"But to each one of us grace has been given as Christ apportioned it.... It was he who gave some to be apostles, some to be prophets, some to be evangelists, and some to be pastors and teachers, to prepare God's people for works of service, so that the body of Christ may be built up...."* (Ephesians 4:7, 11-12)

To the Corinthians he explained, *"Now about spiritual gifts, brothers, I do not want you to be ignorant.... Now to each one the manifestation of the Spirit is given for the common good. To one there is given through the Spirit the message of wisdom, to another the message of knowledge by means of the same Spirit, to another faith by the same Spirit, to another gifts of healing by that one Spirit, to another miraculous powers, to another prophecy, to another distinguishing between spirits, to another speaking in different kinds of tongues, and to still another the interpretation of tongues. All these are the work of one and the same Spirit, and he gives them to each one, just as he determines."* (1 Corinthians 12:1, 7-11)

If we are unwilling to let the Holy Spirit work freely in our midst, He will not provide the leadership we need. Peter strongly urges, *"Each one should use whatever gift he has received to serve others, faithfully administering God's grace in its various forms."* (1 Peter 4:10)

D. THE FRUIT OF THE SPIRIT

In the process of Spirit-led teaching by both word and example, the fruit of the Spirit is also important. In Galatians 5:22-23 we read, *"But the fruit of the Spirit is love, joy, peace, patience, kindness, goodness, faithfulness, gentleness and self-control."*

Building Christian character must always take precedence over displaying special abilities. Paul begins with "love" because all of the fruit of the Spirit is truly an outgrowth of love.

The first grouping of the three fruit—love, joy, peace—expresses the *Godward* aspect of the Christian life. The second set of three—patience, kindness, goodness—expresses the *manward* aspect of the Christian life. The third set—faithfulness, gentleness, self-control—expresses the *selfward* aspect.

It is impossible for the flesh to produce the fruit of the Spirit. When the Holy Spirit produces fruit in the lives of Christians, they may not be conscious of their spirituality, because God gets the glory.

Fruit grows in a climate blessed with an abundance of the Spirit and the Word. *"Walk in the Spirit..."* means keeping in step—neither running ahead nor lagging behind. This is the essence of godly living—a living relationship with the Holy Spirit. (see Galatians 5:16-18)

The fruit of the Spirit has to do with character. These are the fruit, or graces, of the Spirit–distinct from the gifts of the Spirit.

The list of the fruit of the Spirit is summarized elsewhere in Ephesians 5:9 as *"...all goodness, righteousness and truth."* If our lives bear this fruit, and we allow the Holy Spirit to work through us, using the gifts He provides, our Christian testimony will do more than survive—it will be triumphant.

STUDY GUIDE/DISCUSSION QUESTIONS

PASTOR FOCUS

You and your fellowship of believers are reviewing the functions of the Holy Spirit and sharing examples of His fulfilling these functions in your everyday lives. Read the list of the Holy Spirit's functions to the group. Then ask how many have been aware of the Holy Spirit comforting them in the past few days. Read the second, third and so on, asking for a show of hands on each point. After all the functions have been reviewed in this way, see if anyone would like to share the specific experience they had in mind when responding to an item on the list. Discuss why your group may not have experienced all the functions of the Holy Spirit. Then spend time praying for openness to the Spirit's control over every area of life.

WOMEN'S FOCUS

Re-read the story of the Chinese sister who sounded the alarm at the coal mine when prompted by the Holy Spirit. Describe an occasion when the Holy Spirit clearly empowered you to make a wise decision.

YOUTH FOCUS

1. Jesus said He would not leave us alone but would give us a Helper to be with us forever (John 14:16-18). He taught us that the Holy Spirit would be our Counselor (John 14:26).

Jesus also called Him the Spirit of Truth (John 14:17). The work of the Holy Spirit is so practical to us that it will be useful to begin by listing His functions or attributes.
(Fill in the function or attribute)

Function or attribute	Reference
• A_______________ us	Ephesians 1:14
• C_______________	John 14:16
• C_______________	John 16:18
• T_______________	John 14:26
• R_______________	John 14:26
• T_______________ of Christ	John 15:26
• G_______________	John 16:13; Romans 8:14
• R_______________	John 16:14; Luke 2:26
• G_______________ Christ	John 16:14
• Supplying p__________	Acts 1:8
• S__________ through us	Acts 4:31
• ____________ to us	John 16:13
• Bearing w ________ in us	Romans 8:16
• H_______________	Romans 8:26
• I_______________	Romans 8:26
• Giving spiritual g______	1 Corinthians 12:4-11
• R_______________	Titus 3:5
• Confirming our s________	Ephesians 1:13
• Producing His f________ in us	Galatians 5:22

2. In the above list of the work of the Holy Spirit, circle the activity or activities of the Holy Spirit in a restricted country where Christians are forced to meet without a building or sanctioned denominational leader.

MEN'S FOCUS

1. What do you know about the Holy Spirit from the following Scriptures?
   - He is ___________ (Genesis 1:2)
   - He is ____________ (Hebrews 9:14)
   - He lives _________________ (1 Corinthians 3:16; Romans 8:9)
   - He will never leave ______ _______ (John 14:16)
   - His presence is demonstrated _____ _______ (Galatians 5:22-23)
   - He gives power to stand ________ ______ (James 4:7; Luke 9:1-2)

   And from these four passages:
   - Ephesians 4:7, 11-12—____________________________
   - 1 Corinthians 12:1, 7-11—________________________
   - 1 Peter 4:10—________________________________
   - Romans 12:6-8—______________________________

2. The existence of a personal God, who has revealed Himself as three persons, is bitterly opposed by Satan. What particular resistance to this teaching is found in your area? How can you help both opponents and fellow-believers understand it?

3. What functions of the Holy Spirit seem especially important to you?

4. Review the gifts of the Holy Spirit. Are you aware of members of your fellowship who have received some of these gifts? Have you received such a gift?

5. Review the fruit of the Holy Spirit. Are they evident in you? In your fellowship group? How can we tell if we exhibit the fruit of the Spirit?

SECTION THREE

Training in Righteousness

Developing a Servant Spirit

9

TRAINING IN RIGHTEOUSNESS

Everyone who competes in the games goes into strict training. They do it to get a crown that will not last; but we do it to get a crown that will last forever.
1 CORINTHIANS 9:25

A young Romanian Christian was called in to the secret police for interrogation. He had dreaded this moment. Fear gripped him. He was unable to give a definite rejection to the police offer of good treatment and security if he would inform on his fellow-believers. He did not accept the offer, but his inability to reject it unquestioningly caused him great pain.

He could not sleep that night because of his fear and guilt. The next morning, an older Christian, led by the Holy Spirit, came to visit the family. He was unaware of the young man's problem. Being a former prisoner for his faith, he was able to counsel the young man from Scripture. He built up the young man in fellowship, training him for the next ordeal.

The young man was called for another interrogation, and the same thing happened. He was once again upset at not being able to give a definite rejection to the policemen's offer. Once again the older believer came to encourage him.

He was called and interrogated three more times. Eventually, the young man was able to reject the police offer completely. When the police realized he definitely would not inform on his fellow-believers, they stopped calling him in for interrogation.

Counsel, prayer and patient caring had brought him through and trained him in righteousness.

A. INTRODUCTION

The Oxford Universal Dictionary defines "training" as "to instruct, discipline so as to make obedient to orders."

In free societies, training is defined most often as the sharing of knowledge. The idea of discipline is almost non-existent. In Scripture, the term "training," as well as the related words "instruct" and "teach," suggest the idea of *discipline* rather than just the sharing of knowledge. This is seen repeatedly in the book of Proverbs as well as in the following references:

- *"...training in righteousness...."* (2 Timothy 3:16)
- *"For the grace of God that brings salvation has appeared to all men. It teaches us...."* (Titus 2:11-12)
- *"...because the Lord disciplines those he loves...."* (Hebrews 12:6)

In Romans 5:3-5, the Apostle Paul stresses that going through persecution is an essential element of a person's training:

> *Not only so, but we also rejoice in our sufferings, because we know that suffering produces perseverance; perseverance, character; and character, hope. And hope does not disappoint us, because God has poured out his love into our hearts by the Holy Spirit, whom he has given us.*

To maintain biblical integrity, let us consider training as a prescribed course in righteousness in which each individual is disciplined through practice to be obedient to God's direction for mankind and able to withstand the schemes of the devil.

People who are called, enlisted, or volunteer to commit themselves for a cause have a right to expect training in the job for which they have been selected. In some of the trades, this is called "apprenticeship." In medicine, it is known as "internship." In the military, it is referred to as "basic training." In Scripture, it is referred to as "discipleship." However, in our modern day, training is often bypassed due to the pressures of time, need and a low value placed on the office to be filled. This was not the case with Jesus in His selection and training of His disciples.

After calling His men to be *with Him,* He challenged them to commit themselves to following after Him—to be *fishers of men.* Jesus then began to train them to become His kind of *fishers of men.*

B. "BEING" IS THE RESULT OF "BECOMING"

In order to *be* a servant of God's kingdom of righteousness, one must first *become* a servant.

Becoming is the object of training that emphasizes the importance of one's deliberate and initial commitment to become a disciple of Jesus Christ. Commitment without training leads either to heroic disappointments or holy dissatisfaction.

In dealing with the attitudes of becoming a servant and the behaviors of being a soldier of the Kingdom of God, we turn to the Beatitudes in the "Sermon on the Mount" found in Matthew 5:3-12.

The message in the Beatitudes has particular relevance for Christians suffering unjustly and denied many basic rights we still have in free societies. The stories of all who are persecuted are similar though the *extent* of suffering varies. The message in the Beatitudes is for *all* who suffer persecution.

It is important to remember that each of the eight Beatitudes has a two-fold nature: a "knowing" and a "doing" response. We must not only *know* them, we must also *respond* to what we learn from them. Some Christians think they are just philosophical statements to be debated. Others think they are only pleasant-sounding sentences to be memorized.

Eight times in the Beatitudes it says, *"Blessed are...."* To understand the Beatitudes, we need to know the meaning of those words. *Blessed are* refers to Jesus' evaluation of the kind of person He names in each Beatitude. Jesus was referring to *His esteem for that kind of person.* His meaning is, "I esteem highly any person who...." He was urging us to have that kind of attitude. His deeper meaning is, "All you who hear Me, choose to become like these kinds of people."

We must never interpret the words "blessed are" to be a benediction. We must never consider that Jesus was promising happy conditions, as though He meant, "The one who is poor in spirit will feel good and be joyful."

C. DEVELOPMENT OF SERVANT ATTITUDES

The first four Beatitudes focus internally—that is, they speak to the heart of the one who wants to obey God. They can be viewed as four stepping stones to becoming an obedient servant of the Lord Jesus Christ.

HUNGER FOR RIGHTEOUSNESS
MEEKNESS
MOURNING
HUMILITY

1. Humility

"Blessed are the poor in spirit, for theirs is the kingdom of heaven." (Matthew 5:3)

Humility means acknowledging our poverty in spirit. It occurs when a man realizes his own utter lack of resources to meet life and finds his strength in God. Such an attitude leads him away from attachment to things to attachment to God and heaven.

The word for *poor* here means absolute, abject poverty. We can thus paraphrase the Beatitude this way:

Blessed are those who have realised their own utter helplessness and inadequacy and who have put their whole trust in God. Such a person will humbly accept the will of God and thus become a citizen of the kingdom.

An Asian woman, a leader in her church, was arrested and put in prison. Led of the Lord, she volunteered to do hard labor cleaning the filthy prison cells. This humble work gave her opportunity to sing and share Jesus with the prisoners in each cell. Through her words and actions many prisoners came to know the Lord.

2. Mourning

"Blessed are those who mourn, for they will be comforted." (Matthew 5:4)

This mourning is the kind of grief that cannot be hidden. It can be a deep sorrow for our own unworthiness that leads us to trust the Lord as our total Provider, seeking His presence and counsel (authority). Such action is rewarded by the Father's gracious comfort.

It can also be for grief over the sorrow and suffering of this world. Blessed is the man who cares intensely for the sufferings, sorrows and needs of others. And so again we can paraphrase this Beatitude thus:

Blessed are those whose hearts are broken for the world's suffering and are deeply sorry for their sin and unworthiness, for they will find the joy and comfort of God.

As we meditate on this, what comes to mind is the need to mourn for the state of the church and Christians generally. In many countries, churches are weak and nominal, or are split by internal conflicts. There is need to mourn. There is need to mourn also for believers who have quit the struggle and crossed to the other side.

Mourn for the poor quality of preaching, the lack of prayer and the deficiency of spiritual power. Mourn for those who come to the church only to find they are unwelcome. Mourn for Christians unwilling to introduce the light of Christ to them. Mourn for a church hiding its light, too scared to let it shine. Yes, there is much to mourn for. Yet, the promise says if we mourn, comfort will come.

3. Meekness

"Blessed are the meek, for they will inherit the earth." (Matthew 5:5)

Meekness is not to be confused with weakness. In Scripture, meekness means "power under control." In this context, the contrite, praying person is blessed with the indwelling control of the Holy Spirit and the inheritance promised to the believer even in conflict.

History shows that it is the people who have learned this, people with their passions, instincts and impulses under disciplined control, who have been great. (see Numbers 12:3 and Proverbs 16:32) Thus:

> *Blessed are those whose every instinct, every impulse, and every passion is under the control of God's Spirit! They will be right with God, self and others and enter the life which God alone can give.*

Pray for this meekness when entering into dialogue with those of opposing positions. There will be times when patience and self-control will be sorely tested. There may also be times when the Spirit will suggest a change of direction in the dialogue or a strategic retreat that looks suspiciously like defeat. To be meek is to be able to willingly accept temporary defeat in order that there may later be victory in the Spirit.

4. Hunger and thirst for righteousness

"Blessed are those who hunger and thirst for righteousness, for they will be filled." (Matthew 5:6)

This attitude portrays a maturity of belief that shows a servant is ready for service. When completeness or wholeness is achieved, the servant receives the satisfaction of being used of God for that which they have been called, trained and equipped.

In ancient times, wages were very low and men often could not earn enough for the family to eat well. Water was also a precious commodity. The emphasis in this Beatitude is the passionate desire for the whole, for complete righteousness as a matter of life and death. Blessed indeed is the one whose most passionate desire is to love God and to love others as they ought. Thus:

> *Blessed are those who long for total righteousness as a starving person longs for food and as a person perishing of thirst longs for water, for they will be truly satisfied.*

People of other faiths are impressed with those who take their faith seriously. They do not respect people whose religion is merely outward form, who are just *"weekend Christians."* Much of what they see is materialistic, that is, "carnal" or "worldly" (see 1 Corinthians 3). Christianity turns them off—the low regard for moral purity, the hedonism, the wishy-washiness, the unwillingness to suffer or make sacrifices, the fear of making a stand.

As Brother Andrew says, "How can Muslims respect a church that is in hiding?" Christians need to acknowledge their beliefs and be willing to suffer for their faith and convictions. A more complete righteousness will definitely have great impact. It will earn respect for our preaching the Gospel.

D. DEVELOPMENT OF SERVANT BEHAVIOR

The final four Beatitudes focus on the external behavior of the servant. Being a servant means being:

PERSECUTED
PEACEMAKERS
PURE
MERCIFUL

1. Merciful

"Blessed are the merciful, for they will be shown mercy." (Matthew 5:7)

As we in humility recognize our "poverty of spirit," God in His mercy forgives and equips us. Having received mercy, we are expected to show it to others.

The biblical term *merciful* is related to the word for empathy, which means the ability to get right inside another person's skin until we see things with his eyes, think things with his mind and feel things with his feelings. This is what Jesus did for us in His incarnation. Thus:

> *Blessed are those who empathize with others until they are able to see with the eyes of others, think with their thoughts and feel with their feelings.*

How do we see our non-Christian friends? Can we see Muslims, for example, as real people groping in the semi-darkness, under the mere glimmer of light that a crescent moon provides, thinking that is all the light there is?

As we see them, mercy would be an appropriate word to describe our feeling and attitude as well as actions toward them. Just as we would go to the aid of a blind man heading in the wrong direction, so mercy should similarly drive us to go after them and show those who are willing to listen, the way to more complete light. If we are secure in the knowledge that Christ is the Sun of Righteousness, then we do not need to prove anything but patiently and gently show others the way.

2. Pure

"Blessed are the pure in heart, for they will see God." (Matthew 5:8)

As our mourning to God begins the transforming process of our new life in Christ, so our lifestyle of purity amid the impure can become the beginning of reconciliation.

This Beatitude necessitates the strictest and most honest self-examination. We are to do everything with pure, unmixed motives. This demands the death of self and the springing to life of Christ within the heart.

So, blessed are those whose motives are unmixed and who operate in purity. They shall be given a vision of God Himself. As we draw closer to Him through purity, we shall see Him more clearly, love Him more dearly and follow Him more nearly. Thus:

> *Blessed are those whose motives are absolutely pure and whose life is characterized by purity, for they will be able to see God.*

The area of moral purity is one major concern of Muslims. Great stress is laid on modesty in dressing and purity of relationships between the sexes. But Christians seem so nonchalant about such issues. Is it because we do not care about purity? No. The difference is in our starting points. In the Muslim view, purity is from the "outside in." For the servant-soldier it must be from the "inside out."

Thus, Muslims seek to cleanse themselves knowing they are in need of cleansing, whereas we know Christ has already cleansed us. But we tend to disregard the danger that dirt can pose to us and we become careless. What is important to realize is that a careless disregard for even the "appearance of evil" will lead people to wrong conclusions and cause them to stumble. It is not enough to say we are pure. We must be seen to be pure.

3. Peacemakers

"Blessed are the peacemakers, for they will be called sons of God." (Matthew 5:9)

With the possession of a meek spirit, we are equipped to step into the midst of conflict and be ambassadors *"waging peace"* that passes all understanding.

The richness of the New Testament word "peace" describes a condition of perfect and complete positive well-being. It also describes right relationships—intimate fellowship and goodwill between human beings. Peace comes not from avoiding issues but from facing them, making peace even when the way is through trouble. Thus:

> *Blessed are those peacemakers who produce right relationships in every sphere of life, for they are doing a God-like work.*

Such actions may involve laying down one's life, like Jesus did, in order to reconcile men with God and break down barriers among men (Galatians 3:26-29). Are we willing to pay the price so that others might find peace with God? Are we willing to insist that all should hear the Gospel and believe? In some conflict areas of the world, Christians call this *"waging peace."*

Our brothers and sisters in Israel—where "peace" is sought but very evasive—remind us that Jesus' high moral teaching is that we should not resist evil with evil (Matthew 5:39). Jesus is calling His followers not to respond in kind to the acts of injustice and dehumanization directed against them, but rather to respond with transforming initiatives. This unique perspective that He teaches contrasts with the "fight or flight" responses so deeply conditioned in human beings.

When Jesus teaches here about "*turning the other cheek,*" it was an offensive—not a defensive—act of peace using a culturally relevant example of His day. A person who slapped another on the cheek normally used the back of the right hand as an act of insult by a superior to an inferior. Thus, by turning the "other" cheek, the one hit (the perceived powerless person) takes an initiative to force the aggressor to now return the swing and hit his face a second time. This time the "hit" must be with an aggressive open palm or fist thereby transforming the nature of the relationship.

The Christ-like response of turning the other cheek says the person does not assume the inferior place of humiliation the striker had in mind but views himself as an equal. The supposedly powerless person has redefined the relationship and forced the oppressor into a moral choice: escalate the violence or respond with repentance and reconciliation.

"Waging peace" involves: promoting love not hate, fostering unity among brethren, being a witness of a higher kingdom, following the example of Jesus.

Other transforming initiatives are to give your cloak when sued for your tunic (Matthew 5:40) and to carry a load for two miles for a person who can legally demand that you carry it for only one mile (Matthew 5:41). We must seek transforming initiatives within our own particular context.

4. Persecuted

"Blessed are those who are persecuted because of righteousness, for theirs is the kingdom of heaven." (Matthew 5:10)

With our hunger and thirst for righteousness comes the promise of persecution for those who take a stand for God. We have not been called to safety and comfort but to serve in the midst of conflict.

Persecution is not to be strenuously avoided, for it is the result of righteous living. To avoid it, one would have to cease living righteously. The passage in Matthew goes on to say:

> *Blessed are you when people insult you, persecute you and falsely say all kinds of evil against you because of me. Rejoice and be glad, because great is your reward in heaven, for in the same way they persecuted the prophets who were before you. (Matthew 5:11-12)*

We could cite many other circumstances that induce persecution. But as we see in other chapters, our thesis for the primary reason for persecution of Christians was stated by Jesus here in Matthew 5 and also in John 15:20.

> *Remember the words I spoke to you: "No servant is greater than his master." If they persecuted me, they will persecute you also.*

The master's lot is the servant's lot. Disciples follow the same path as their teachers. Persecution is, therefore, inevitable for the Christian. It is also noble.

The early church went through much persecution for their faith in Christ. It affected their livelihood. They had to ask themselves, *Should a Christian craftsman create idols for the temples? Or should a tailor sew robes for heathen priests?*

Persecution affected social life. Most feasts were held in the temple of some god. A common invitation would be dining at the table of such a god. Even an ordinary meal in a home began with a cup of wine poured out in honor of the gods, like grace before a meal. Could a Christian share in such a meal like that?

Persecution also touched their home life, when one member converted and the others became hostile. It split the home. As Jesus foretold, Christianity was often a sword that divided, causing much pain and internal struggles. (see Mark 13:12-13)

Serious persecution meant being flung to the lions, burned at the stake, or being wrapped in pitch and set alight to provide light for Nero's palace gardens. Or it meant being sewn in animal skins and set upon by Nero's hunting dogs.

Christians were tortured on the rack; scraped with pincers; had molten lead poured on them; had red-hot brass plates fixed to the most tender parts of their bodies; had eyes torn out; had limbs cut off and roasted before their eyes; had hands and feet burned while cold water was poured over other parts to prolong agony.

Most of us have never in our lives made a real sacrifice for Jesus. To have to suffer persecution is to walk along the same road as the prophets, the saints, and the martyrs. To suffer persecution is to make things easier for those who are to follow. To suffer persecution is to experience the fellowship of Christ, as Shadrach, Meshach and Abednego did in the furnace (Daniel 3:19-25). It is not always so dramatic, but it is nevertheless real. Most of us enjoy the blessing of liberty today because men and women in the past were willing to buy it for us at the cost of their own blood, sweat and tears.

E. CONCLUSION

Brother Andrew likes to tell the following parable he heard in his travels to the Middle East:

> *A certain man had two sons. One was rich and the other was poor. The rich son had no children while the poor son was blessed with many sons and many daughters. In time, the father of the two sons fell ill. He was sure he would not live through the week, so on Saturday he called his sons to his side and gave each of them half of his land for their inheritance. Then he died. Before sundown the sons buried their father with respect.*
>
> *That night the rich son could not sleep. He said to himself, "What my father did was not just. I am rich and my brother is*

poor. I have plenty of bread while my brother's children eat one day and trust God for the next. I must move the landmark which our father has set in the middle of the land so that my brother will have the greater share. Ah—but he must not see me; if he sees me, he will be shamed. I must arise early in the morning before it is dawn and move the landmark!" With this he fell asleep and his sleep was secure and peaceful.

Meanwhile, the poor brother could not sleep. As he lay restless on his bed, he said to himself, "What my father did was not just. Here I am surrounded by the joy of many sons and daughters while my brother daily faces the shame of having no sons to carry on his name and no daughters to comfort him in his old age. He should have the land of our fathers. Perhaps this will, in part, compensate him for his indescribable poverty. Ah, but if I give it to him, he will be shamed. I must awake early in the morning before it is dawn and move the landmark which our father has set!" With this he went to sleep and his sleep was secure and peaceful.

On the first day of the week, very early in the morning, a long time before it was day, the two brothers met at the ancient land marker.

They fell with tears into each other's arms.

And on that spot was built the New Jerusalem.[1]

STUDY GUIDE/DISCUSSION QUESTIONS

PASTOR FOCUS

What is the easiest—and the most difficult—Beatitude for **you** to live out? Why?

WOMEN'S FOCUS

Discuss the elements of the peace prayer attributed to Saint Francis of Assisi:

The Peace Prayer

Lord, make me an instrument of Thy peace;
Where there is hatred, let me sow love;
Where there is injury, pardon;
Where there is error, truth;
Where there is doubt, faith;
Where there is despair, hope;
Where there is darkness, light; and
Where there is sadness, joy.

O, Divine Master,
Grant that I may not so much seek to be consoled,
as to console;
To be understood as to understand;
To be loved as to love;
For it is in giving that we receive;
It is in pardoning that we are pardoned;
And it is in dying to ourselves that we are born
to eternal life.
Amen.

a. What are the practical difficulties in living this prayer? What parts are harder to apply to **your** life?

b. Together, pray the prayer aloud. Pray together for continued peace and harmony between the different races and religious groups in your country and any problem areas.

YOUTH FOCUS

Believers in North Korea's underground church recite five principles, along with the Lord's Prayer, at their secret gatherings:

- Our persecution and suffering are our joy and honor.
- We want to accept ridicule, scorn and disadvantages with joy in Jesus' name.
- We want to wipe others' tears away and comfort the suffering.
- We want to be ready to risk our lives because of our love for our neighbor, so that they also become Christians.
- We want to live our lives according to the standards set in God's Word.

Discuss how these believers are being trained in righteousness.

MEN'S FOCUS

Each of the eight Beatitudes have a two-fold nature in that they exhibit a "knowing" and a "doing" response. Beside each Beatitude list what God wants **you** to *know* and to *do.*

- *"Blessed are the poor in spirit, for theirs is the kingdom of heaven."* (Matthew 5:3)

- *"Blessed are those who mourn, for they will be comforted."* (Matthew 5:4)

- *Blessed are the meek, for they will inherit the earth.* (Matthew 5:5)

- *Blessed are those who hunger and thirst for righteousness, for they will be filled.* (Matthew 5:6)

- *Blessed are the merciful, for they will be shown mercy.* (Matthew 5:7)

- *Blessed are the pure in heart, for they will see God.* (Matthew 5:8)

- *Blessed are the peacemakers, for they will be called sons of God.* (Matthew 5:9)

- *Blessed are those who are persecuted because of righteousness, for theirs is the kingdom of heaven.* (Matthew 5:10)

10

LOVE SHOWN IN COMMUNITY

Dear children, let us not love with words or tongue but with actions and in truth.

1 John 3:18

"Dear Ruth, I'm going to be in your neighborhood Saturday afternoon and I'd like to stop by for a visit. Love Always, Jesus"

Her hands were shaking as she placed the letter on the table. *Why would the Lord want to visit me? I'm nobody special. I don't have anything to offer.* With that thought, Ruth remembered her empty kitchen cabinets. *I really don't have anything to offer. I'll have to run down to the store and buy something for dinner.* She reached for her purse and counted out its contents: $5.40. *Well, I can at least get some bread and cold cuts.*

She threw on her coat and hurried out the door. A loaf of French bread, a half-pound of sliced turkey, and a carton of milk left Ruth with a grand total of twelve cents to last her until Monday.

Nonetheless, she felt satisfied as she headed home, her meager offerings tucked under her arm.

"Hey lady, can you help us?" Ruth had been so absorbed in her dinner plans she hadn't even noticed two figures huddled in the alley. A man and a woman, both of them dressed in little more than rags. "Look lady, I ain't got no job, ya know, and my wife and I have been livin' out here on the street, and, well, now it's gettin' cold and we're gettin' kinda hungry and, well, if you could help us, lady, we'd really appreciate it."

Ruth looked at them both. They were dirty, they smelled bad and, frankly, she was certain that they could get some kind of work if they really wanted to.

"Sir, I'd like to help you, but I'm a poor woman myself. All I have is a few cold cuts and some bread, and I'm having an important guest for dinner tonight and I was planning on serving that to Him."

"Yeah, well, okay lady, I understand. Thanks anyway." The man put his arm around the woman's shoulders, turned and headed back into the alley. As she watched them leave, Ruth felt a familiar twinge in her heart.

"Sir, wait!" The couple stopped and turned as she ran down the alley after them. "Look, why don't you take this food. I'll figure out something else to serve my guest." She handed the man her grocery bag.

"Thank you, lady. Thank you very much!"

"Yes, thank you!" It was the man's wife, and Ruth could see now that she was shivering.

"You know, I've got another coat at home. Here, why don't you take this one?" Ruth unbuttoned her jacket and slipped it over the woman's shoulders. Then smiling, she turned and walked back to the street without her coat and with nothing to serve her guest.

"Thank you, lady! Thank you very much!"

Ruth was chilled by the time she reached her front door, and worried too. The Lord was coming to visit and she didn't have anything to offer Him. She fumbled through her purse for the door key. But as she did, she noticed another envelope in her mailbox. *That's odd. The mailman doesn't usually come twice in one day.* She took the envelope out of the box and opened it.

"Dear Ruth, It was so good to see you again. Thank you for the lovely meal. And thank you, too, for the beautiful coat. Love Always, Jesus"

The air was still cold, but even without her coat, Ruth no longer noticed.[1]

A. INTRODUCTION

In his book *The Upside Down Church,* Pastor Greg Laurie says, "The first Christians didn't out-argue pagans—they outlived them…. Christianity made no attempts to conquer paganism and dead Judaism by reacting blow by blow. Instead, the Christians of the first century outthought, out prayed and outlived the unbelievers.

"Their weapons were positive not negative. As far as we know, they did not hold protests or conduct boycotts. They did not put on campaigns to try to unseat the emperor. Instead, they prayed and preached and proclaimed the message of Christ, put to death on the cross, risen from the dead, and ready to change lives. And they backed up their message with actions: giving, loving."[2]

We live in a world that is rapidly changing. Rapid advances are being made in science and technology. In politics and economics, we are seeing the coming together of nations and business conglomerates for greater control and mutual survival.

And the age-old problems of poverty, hunger, famine, wars, crime and disease show no signs of going away. What is our response as Christians living in today's world?

B. BEING SALT AND LIGHT IN COMMUNITY

At the end of the Beatitudes which we discussed in the last chapter, we have these words of our Lord:

> *"You are the salt of the earth. But if the salt loses its saltiness, how can it be made salty again? It is no longer good for anything, except to be thrown out and trampled by men.*
>
> *You are the light of the world. A city on a hill cannot be*

hidden. Neither do people light a lamp and put it under a bowl. Instead they put it on its stand, and it gives light to everyone in the house. In the same way, let your light shine before men, that they may see your good deeds and praise your Father in heaven." (Matthew 5:13-16)

Here Jesus uses two strong metaphors, or pictures, clearly understood by his original listeners—that of being salt and light. The church is to exercise these twin roles in the society where God has planted it. It requires courage, moral and spiritual strength, love and compassion. Such an influence is felt when Christians by their presence and influence hinder the spread of evil in their circumstances.

Either individually or as a group, by making a stand or expressing their views, by public demonstration or working in committees, by letters or phone calls to leaders or the press, it is possible to address the issues of injustice, oppression, cruelty, indifference, corruption or moral evil. Sometimes it does not take much. At other times, one must be prepared for imprisonment or even the loss of one's life. Are we prepared to do what is necessary?

1. The Salt of the Earth

Jesus is making a statement of fact when He says in Matthew 5:13, *"You are the salt of the earth."* His statement is not a command or a wish list. Christians being "salt" in their world is reality here and now. The implication is that we are to be *now* what God has already made us to be.

The context here is believers facing persecution. There were few believers at that time and the people around them considered them insignificant. The value of salt may vary in different places, yet it has unusual properties that far exceed its value. We have the saying that *"a man is worth his weight in salt."*

That is as it should be when Christians take their stand for God in society—they can be said to be *"worth their weight."* Their stand for good causes society to be infertile for the growth of evil and ungodly influences. When England went through revival under the ministry of the Wesleys and George Whitefield in the eighteenth century, a possible revolution with much bloodshed, such as the French experienced, was averted. Usually the influence of Christians affects society on a more moderate scale—conversations are moderated, consciences are pricked, respect for others is heightened.

Those who follow Christ must not remain silent about their faith. They must not hide themselves, but live and work in places where their influence can be felt. The light that is in them can then be most fully manifested so others may see the light of real Christian goodness. It is a light not from this world. It comes from God. That light is Jesus and it will therefore give honor and praise to its Giver.

Salt was highly valued in the ancient world for four special qualities:

a. Salt was pure.

Coming from the sea and made glistering white by the sun, it was the most primitive of all offerings to the gods. If the Christian is to be salt, he must be *an example of purity.* In the world, efforts to lower standards of honesty, diligence in work, conscientiousness and morality are going on all the time.

If Christians only compare themselves to others—and regard themselves to be 5% *better* than the world—the devil can lower the world to hell in a bucket of immorality and Christians will ride down with them, still feeling they are 5% better than the world. (see 2 Corinthians 10:12)

Christians must compare their lifestyle to the teachings of Jesus—the one who holds high the standard of purity in speech, conduct and thought. Words cannot be effective unless backed up by pure living.

b. Salt was inexpensive—but exceedingly precious.

Christians may seem few, insignificant and of no consequence to society. In 1 Corinthians 1:26-31, Paul addressed the early Christians in this way:

> *Brothers, think of what you were when you were called. Not many of you were wise by human standards; not many were influential; not many were of noble birth. But God chose the foolish things of the world to shame the wise; God chose the weak things of the world to shame the strong. He chose the lowly things of this world and the despised things—and the things that are not—to nullify the things that are, so that no one may boast before him. It is because of him that you are in Christ Jesus, who has become for us wisdom from God—that is, our righteousness, holiness and redemption. Therefore, as it is written: "Let him who boasts boast in the Lord."*

Though it may appear they are few in numbers, lowly and unimportant, Christians are exceedingly precious to God and are called by Him to exercise godly influence over the whole of society. (see 1 Peter 2:9)

c. Salt was a preservative to keep meat from going bad.

Salt rubbed into meat slows the rotting process. Christians whose lives exhibit *blessedness* will have a preserving impact upon a society that, if left to itself, will rot and deteriorate. The Christian makes society—whether that society consists of his friends in school, his fellow students at college, his co-workers, or those with whom he plays sports—less subject to decaying and ungodly influences.

Our witness can have a preserving effect on our society that is going wrong, if we will pay the price.

d. Salt seasoned food.

Salt brings out the distinctive flavor of food. The increase of God's people should increase the "flavor of life" in many different ways. By His very presence, Jesus raised the spirits of people. There was a quality about His life that could not be explained in natural terms. The Apostle Paul reminds us that our speech should always be *"seasoned with salt"*:

> *Let your conversation be always full of grace, seasoned with salt, so that you may know how to answer everyone. (Colossians 4:6)*

> *Do not let any unwholesome talk come out of your mouths, but only what is helpful for building others up according to their needs, that it may benefit those who listen. (Ephesians 4:29)*

In this context Paul also talks about not grieving the Holy Spirit. Since speech is linked to a person's spiritual state and has tremendous potential for building up or tearing down (James 3:3-12), the constant reminder is to watch not only *what* we say but also *how* we say it.

By our presence, participation and penetration of society, in our daily contacts in our neighborhood and community, we are to bring the flavor of Christ to an unbelieving world.

2. The Light of the World

> *Let your light shine before men, that they may see your good deeds, and praise your Father in heaven. (Matthew 5:16)*

Jesus is also the great Light of the world (John 8:12). He brings those of us who believe in Him out of darkness into His light

(Colossians 1:12-13) and makes us become lights. In essence, we live the Beatitudes. What does light do?

a. Light exposes dirt.

If Christians live holy and righteous lives, it will show up the unrighteous deeds of others (Ephesians 5:8-14). For example, people who take bribes feel very vulnerable if there are others that don't. Christians who work in government offices can, by their uprightness and integrity, diminish the amount of corruption just by their very presence and principles.

b. Light brightens the way so that we do not stumble.

> *Your word is a lamp to my feet and a light for my path. (Psalm 119:105)*

If Christians walk by the principles of the Word of God, their lives take on a higher purpose and direction than that of serving self. The light manifested by such a life will not fail to attract the attention of a watching world. The world then is faced with a choice—to accept or reject such a model. That light becomes darkness to those who reject it. But it illuminates the lives of those who accept it, and they will not consistently make wrong choices.

c. Light discourages works of darkness.

More crimes are committed at night rather than in the daytime.

> *This is the verdict: Light has come into the world, but men loved darkness instead of light because their deeds were evil. Everyone who does evil hates the light, and will not come into the light for fear that his deeds will be exposed. But whoever lives by the truth comes into the light, so that it may be seen plainly*

that what he has done has been done through God. (John 3:19-21)

d. Light drives out fear.

When light shines, the fears of the night fade away. People who are afraid of the dark prefer to sleep with the light on.

e. Light has other functions.

Light enables one to discern between friend and foe and between truth and counterfeit. It enables work to be done. *"As long as it is day, we must do the work of him who sent me. Night is coming, when no one can work."* (John 9:4)

Light causes plants to grow. Used in modern technology, it aids in telecommunications (fiber optics), helps to heal (lasers), aids in publishing books, and so on.

The light of the Gospel blesses in many ways. Christians who walk in the light can in turn bless others by sharing the knowledge they have concerning life, death, sin, salvation, God, the devil, heaven and hell. For these are the issues that plague people on a wide scale and for which they strive to find adequate answers.

The light will be recognized, not just in words, but in *"good deeds,"* which others will see and praise our Father in heaven. (see Matthew 5:16)

In Kumasi, Ghana, African Enterprise has city-cleaning teams. Before an evangelistic campaign, Christians often ask government leaders if they can clean up the city. Then they send out teams of people with makeshift straw brooms and pails of soapy water to sweep and scrub. Christian workers have cleaned hospitals, city parks, and government grounds before major outreaches.

Some Christians demonstrated a similar creative approach during the Gay Games in Amsterdam. They wanted to share their faith with the crowds at the international homosexual festival, which drew an estimated 100,000 participants, spectators and tourists. Instead of a confrontational approach, they distributed 5,000 yellow roses with a note proclaiming God's love. Although some rejected the gifts, the approach led to serious conversations for others happy to take the flower and surprised to hear more about God's love for homosexuals and less about His disapproval of their lifestyle. Nearly one hundred Christians from eight countries took part in the three-week outreach. Besides giving the flowers, they played music, presented dances at key venues, ran a daily coffee bar, and offered free shoe shines outside Amsterdam's Central Railway Station.

3. A Warning

Can the Church of Jesus Christ in these times rise up to meet these challenges? Our ability to make an impact on the world depends on our being different. There's no need to try and be different or advertise the fact. We ***are*** different. What is required is merely that we not be ashamed of it.

If our standard of morality is no different from that of the people of the world, then we are no longer "salt" in the world.

If our lives do not shine with the qualities of Christ, we will not be able to lead people to Him. This is in line with the prayer of Jesus for His disciples in John 17:15-19. Impacting the world through compassion and a different lifestyle in order to draw men and women to Him is the church's big challenge today!

In Indonesia, rampaging mobs rioted, looting and destroying Chinese-owned shops and Christian churches. As the angry people were about to burn down one church building, they were astonished to see Muslim neighbors surrounding the building. "Don't torch this church," they begged.

Dumbfounded, the mob asked the group, "Why are you doing this? That's a Christian church and it has no place in this community!"

The group replied, "Yes, it is a Christian church, but these

Christians are not ordinary people. They are good people. They respect us and have done so much good for this community. We won't allow you to touch them or their building."

The mob disappeared.

Impacting society and the world through love, compassion and a different lifestyle draws the respect of people and even authorities. Such a testimony draws people to Jesus.

C. GIVING HUMANITARIAN AID

Other words for "humanitarian" include: caring or looking after; charitable or loving; compassionate or kind. In James 1:27 we are told that *"Religion that God our Father accepts as pure and faultless is this: to look after orphans and widows in their distress...."*

God's love compels us to feed the hungry, empower the poor, defend the weak and help those suffering from floods, earthquakes, epidemic and war. When we do these things, it includes encouraging and strengthening those persecuted for their faith in Christ. The church has often led the way in education and medical services in developing countries until governments or other local agencies were able to take over.

It is wise to do humanitarian work in areas of our world that still need this kind of help. And we often do not have to look very far to see this need. The slum areas of our cities or the countryside are places where needy people live who need our help. How aware are we of such places and people? What are we going to do about them?

As we look at the needs of the world, we feel totally inadequate. World population is growing at ninety million annually. Food production can hardly keep up with demand. Natural calamities continue to generate famine and hunger in many regions.

Rich nations, in order to protect their own economies, sometimes deny poorer nations the opportunity to develop their economies. For example: giving aid by dumping food-surplus in developing countries damages local agriculture in the long term.

Diseases such as AIDS and tuberculosis, as well as environmental pollution, will steadily degrade world health, especially in poorer countries.

What can Christians do? Pray that funds received may be wisely used by Christian relief agencies and that the Lord will guide donors as to how to give. It is not always food or money that is most needed. Rather it is training that is most needed—training farmers so they can grow more food; training widows in a business so they can support their children; and most important, training spiritual leaders in the Word of God.

Brother Andrew says that giving humanitarian aid is a picture of Jesus knocking at the door of our hearts (our lives) in Revelation chapter 3. The doors of many hearts in the church are closed to acts of mercy and love in action. Therefore, Jesus stands knocking at the door of our hearts asking that we open that door and let Him in. His coming into our lives enables us to do acts of love.

D. SHOWING LOVE TO OTHERS

Back in Chapter Eight, we noted that Paul began his list of the fruit of the Spirit with "love" since all of the fruit of the Spirit is an outgrowth of love.

In the New Testament, the apostles used two words that have been translated "love." The first word—*agape*—means to "actively seek the best for others." It is action, not emotion. God wants that for us. He wants good things to happen to us! The second word—*philos*—means "feeling friendly towards" a person. As Christians, we should have *agape* love and also *philos* love for others. Jesus commanded us to love even those we might consider not worthy of our love. We must love them as they are. We must not pressure them to change or even expect them to change before we show love to them.

When we love someone, we should love them "unconditionally"—we should not love them so they will give us something or even return our love.

In other words, we Christians should be people who are known for their great love for others. First Corinthians 13 gives us an overview of what *"agape"* love is and how it is exhibited.

Agape love should be shown to everyone—even to those who appear to be unlovely and therefore do not seem to deserve it. Agape love is given unconditionally—it does not seek anything in return. It is not dependent on a good response.

1. Love for God

We are commanded first to love God and then to love others. As we study the teaching on love in Scriptures—particularly in the New Testament—we can see a continuing outflow of love:

- Love for God above all else, above all others
- Love for our spouse, children and family
- Love for our brothers and sisters in Christ
- Love for our neighbors
- Love for our enemies

2. Love for family

It is not difficult to understand commands of Scripture to love your wife and children. Although, it *is* a challenge to love your wife as Christ loved the church and gave His life for her (see Ephesians 5:25-29). Christian love begins in the home. This is often the true test of our love because it is in the family where we reveal what we are like in our inner being. Love in the family cannot be "faked."

3. Love for extended Christian family

In John 13:35, Jesus pointed out that the true mark of His disciples is showing love (*agape*) to fellow believers. He said that love for one another would be how non-believers identify us as His disciples.

4. Love for neighbors

The second part of the Great Commandment (Luke 10:27) is *"Love your neighbor as yourself."* Jesus then told the story of the Good Samaritan to define "your neighbor" as anyone in need of help. This kind of love is very practical.

It was the middle of winter and the elderly Christian in prison had a badly infected ear. He thanked God that he had been able to keep his fur hat that afforded him some protection from the biting cold. And he had a "pillow" at night.

One day one of his cellmates asked him for his fur hat. The Christian had been willing to share food with his colleagues, but felt he could not give up his hat. After all, he had an infected ear. He needed that hat.

Through the night he wrestled with his conscience. He was haunted by Scriptures like, *"Give to the one who asks you, and do not turn away from the one who wants to borrow from you"* (Matthew 5:42). After a night of prayer, he sought forgiveness before God and was ready to hand over his hat. In the morning he learned that during the night the guards had taken the cellmate to another cell with more severe climate.

That same morning, guards held a routine check of the cells and among the personal objects confiscated was the believer's fur hat.

He had tried to keep something that he was about to lose, and God wanted to see the hat used for continued good with the other prisoner. Many years later, this believer remembered that lesson in Christian maturity that the Holy Spirit taught him.

5. Love for enemies

Perhaps the most difficult of all the commands of Jesus is to love our enemies (Matthew 5:44). Christians should always seek the best for others—even those who mistreat them.

Romanian pastor Dr. Paul Negrut visited Trian Dors, one of his old friends in Romania. As Paul entered his friend's humble home, he noted that Trian was bleeding from open wounds. "What happened?" he asked.

"The secret police just left. They confiscated my manuscripts, then they beat me," Trian calmly replied.

Paul says, "I began to complain about the heavy tactics of the secret police. But Trian stopped me. 'Brother Paul,' he said, 'it is so sweet to suffer for Jesus. God didn't bring us together tonight to complain but to praise Him. Let's kneel down and pray.'

"He knelt and began praying for the secret police. He asked God to bless them and save them. He told God how much he loved them. He said, 'God, if they come back in the next few days, I pray that You will prepare me to minister to them.' "

Paul continued, "By this time I was ashamed. I thought I had been living the most difficult life in Romania for the Lord. And I was bitter about that."

The Christian's only method of destroying his enemies is to love them into becoming his friends.

Trian Dors then told Paul how the secret police had come to his home regularly for several years. They beat him twice every week. They confiscated all his papers. After each beating, Trian would always talk to the officer in charge. He would look into his eyes and say, "Mister, I love you. And I want you to know that if our next meeting is before the judgement throne of God, you will not go to hell because I hate you but because you rejected love." Trian would repeat these words after every beating.

Years later, one night that officer came alone to his home. Trian prepared himself for another beating. But the officer spoke kindly and said, "Mr. Dors, the next time we meet will be before the judgement throne of God. I came tonight to apologize for what I did to you and to tell you that your love moved my heart. I have asked Christ to save me. But two days ago the doctor discovered that I have a very severe case of cancer and I have only a few weeks to live before I go to be with God. I came tonight to tell you that we will be together on the other side."[3]

When Christians function collectively as salt and light and individually show true agape love to everyone, victory is assured.
Matthew 5

STUDY GUIDE/DISCUSSION QUESTIONS

PASTOR FOCUS

Discuss the positive challenges listed in this lesson. List some accomplishments and some failures that you as an individual and/or as a local church have experienced with respect to each of the challenges. What will you seek to concentrate on as soon as you can?

WOMEN'S FOCUS

1. Jesus said, *"You are the salt of the earth. . . ."* What is the meaning and the power of this illustration?

2. In James 1:27 we are told that *"Religion that God our Father accepts as pure and faultless is this: to look after orphans and widows in their distress...."* Explain this verse as you would to a new believer.

3. Open Doors International provides assistance to widows, pastors, excommunicated believers, and others in need. This is done through socio-economic recovery projects in restricted countries to help believers (many from a Muslim background) sustain themselves and their family financially. However, if it is true that only two things are eternal—the Word of God and the souls of people—how does Christian humanitarian aid advance the Kingdom of God?

YOUTH FOCUS

1. Jesus also likened Christians to light. Light exposes dirt; lights up the way so that we do not stumble; discourages works of darkness; drives out fear; enables work to be done.... Light enables one to know the difference between friend and foe and between truth and counterfeit. How are Christians like light?

2. Read 1 Peter 2:12—*"Live such good lives among the pagans that, though they accuse you of doing wrong, they may see your* **good deeds** *and glorify God on the day that he visits us."* (emphasis added) Compare this to Ephesians 2:10—*"For we are God's workmanship, created in Christ Jesus to do* **good works,** *which God prepared in advance for us to do."* (emphasis added) How are *"good deeds"* (providing food, water, clothing, shelter, and medical help) related to, yet different from, *"good works"* (witnessing and prayer)?

MEN'S FOCUS

1. Identify ways *you* can be salt and light to each of the following
   - God
   - Family
   - Extended Christian family
   - Neighbors
   - Enemies

2. What area of showing true *agape* love to others is the most difficult for you?

3. Loving one's enemies seems almost impossible. What power is available to the Christian to practice this kind of love? Can you love your enemy and fight with him too?

11

PERSEVERANCE AND ENCOURAGEMENT

Let us not give up meeting together, as some are in the habit of doing, but let us encourage one another—and all the more as you see the Day approaching.

HEBREWS 10:25

A Chinese brother spent twenty-one years and eight months in prison for his faith. When he was imprisoned his wife was left alone with the care of six children and her mother-in-law. Here is her story:

> When my husband—who was a pastor—was imprisoned in April 1958, I was told I would never see him again. It was a very heavy burden to provide for my children and mother-in-law. My heart was full of frustration and I argued with God about my situation. The future seemed so dark.
>
> One night God spoke to me and said, "These things have come from me." I told Him, "If they are from you, please protect my family and me. Do not allow me to disgrace your Name. I want to follow you and glorify you!" Then I had peace in my heart.
>
> People failed me but through those difficult years

God never forsook me. But He did test me. The first test was *the pressures of life.* I earned only 80 cents a day. How could my family and I live on such a small income? God provided for us as He did for Elijah. He promised to be my Shepherd and Provider.

But one night my mother-in-law announced that there was no food left for breakfast. She decided that the next morning she would go visit her daughter to ask for food. That night I asked God why He had not provided for the next day. After my prayer, I heard Him say, "If I can provide for the birds, I can provide for you." I slept peacefully.

The next morning at 5:55 a.m. there was a knock at the door. I opened it to see a lady about sixty years old that I didn't know. She said, "Are you Sister Alice? It was so difficult to find you. The Spirit moved me to give you this." And she placed a parcel on the table and started to leave.

I asked her name and she replied, "I have no name. Just thank the Lord!"

She walked out and disappeared so I opened the parcel. Among some food items, it contained an envelope with $50. God is never late. We didn't even miss one meal. My mother-in-law said, "Now I don't have to visit my daughter today."

Over the months, many similar experiences occurred. People regularly sent money in the mail with no return address.

The second test was *political pressure* from the party. Because my husband had been arrested for refusing to submit to the Chinese government's religious policies, I was also considered to be a counter-revolutionary. Authorities pressured me to criticize my religious beliefs and divorce my husband.

Many days I was subjected to six hours of pressure in these struggle sessions. If I didn't know the Lord, I would have committed suicide. Two other women I knew went insane and committed suicide under these circumstances. I hung on with the help of God. My strategy was to close my eyes and pray to endure the struggle sessions.

The third test was the *pressure of work*. Because of the accusations against me, I was not allowed to work in a factory or an office. Thus, after the six-hour struggle sessions, I was still required to do my eight hours of hard labour. I pulled wagon loads of construction bricks, stones and cement for 80 cents a day. Every load was *extremely* heavy.

This work made me so exhausted that I was tired out before I began. Perspiration flowed down my body. In the winter it was even more difficult to pull the wagons over frozen mud. Sometimes I had to shovel cement over my head to the second floor. I survived by constantly praying and asking God to help me. He was merciful and gave me strength.

The fourth test was *the lust of the flesh*. I was 39 years old when my husband was taken. The government officials tried to persuade me to marry another man. If only I would submit to the officials, I would be permitted to move into new living quarters. My records would all be changed to look brand-new and I would no longer have to bear the heavy burdens.

Some men came to me with gifts of money and clothes and one even prepared a divorce declaration for me. They'd quietly knock at my door at midnight.

I'd tell them, "I'm a Christian. I cannot divorce and remarry." God loved me so much that He gave me the strength to overcome all these temptations for a comfortable life. Whenever I prayed, He provided all that I needed...even more abundantly than I had asked.

After twenty-one years and eight months my husband was released from prison. Twenty-one years of separation is a long time. But God led us through.[1]

A. PERSEVERANCE

If the offensive disciplines of spiritual warfare are the Word and prayer, the central attitude for those in the battle is faithful obedience.

In Romans 5:3, the Apostle Paul says it is suffering that produces perseverance which in turn produces character. Later in Romans, Paul also adds that we have hope because of perseverance and the encouragement of the Scriptures (Romans 15:4). James concludes that perseverance brings maturity and completeness. (James 1:4)

To continuously walk in the Spirit and produce the fruit of the Spirit we must have that quality called perseverance.

And in Revelation 3:10, Jesus commends the church in Philadelphia because they kept His command to *endure patiently*—that is, persevere. It is not a call to just "hang in there" and do nothing. Rather, it is to "work deliberately, knowing with certainty that God will never be defeated." The winner will always be the one who does not give up.

The enemy's attempt to counter this quality is to create spiritual battle fatigue followed by spiritual lethargy—a general attitude we simply call "giving up" or "quitting." Too many Christians quit minutes before the victory.

A frail sister in China who was severely persecuted commented, "A ship cannot stop just because there is a storm. It just has to make sure it stays on the right course. Without times like these, we may not know how to serve the Lord." Life is also like that. During those terrible storms, members of the Persecuted Church testify that all you can do is tie yourself to the helm and hold fast to your confidence in God's faithfulness and His everlasting love in Christ Jesus.

Hebrews 10:19-39 is a great passage to study on this topic. The key verse is verse 36: *"You need to persevere so that when you have done the will of God, you will receive what he has promised."* Note that this verse stands in the context of suffering, insults, persecution, imprisonment and confiscation of property.

A pastor in Cuba who was experiencing severe hardship and difficulties was asked, "With all these problems, don't you ever want to give up?" The pastor smiled and simply replied, "If there were no battles, there would be no victory." Someone else once said, "Whatever does not kill me strengthens me."

The Chinese people would not have had the Bible in their language as early as they did without this quality in the lives of pioneer missionaries. Robert Morrison grew up in a poverty-stricken area of a Scotland manufacturing town. A Sunday school teacher did not give up on him and after much perseverance by that teacher, young Morrison became a follower of Jesus.

Sometimes the Lord calms the storm. Sometimes He lets the storm rage... and quiets His child.—A sign hanging on the wall in a Christian's home

He went on to become the pioneer Protestant missionary who translated the Bible into the Chinese language in the early 1800s. But he was tested by many difficulties. It took him sixteen years under terrible working conditions. His Chinese assistant, Ako, carried poison to take as suicide rather than endure the treatment he knew he would receive if discovered. Later Morrison was rewarded when Ako became his first convert.

Robert Morrison lost his son and then his wife, but he persevered. He was buried beside his son and wife in the old Protestant cemetery in Macao. Today his gravestone can be seen there: a monument to his perseverance. Today there are many brothers and sisters in China who are also persevering despite many difficulties.

B. ENCOURAGEMENT

If perseverance is the grace God gives us to endure and press on, then encouragement is the parallel gift of helping *others* endure and press on.

A parable is told of a group of frogs traveling through the woods. Two of them fell into a deep pit. All the other frogs gathered around the pit. When they saw how deep the pit was, they told the two frogs that they were as good as dead. The two frogs ignored the comments and tried to jump up out of the pit with all of their might. The other frogs kept telling them to stop, that they were as good as dead. Finally, one of the frogs took heed to what the other frogs were saying and gave up. He fell down and died. The other frog continued to jump as hard as he could. Once again, the crowd of frogs yelled at him to stop the pain and just die. He jumped even harder and finally made it out.

When he got out, the other frogs said, "Did you not hear us?" The frog explained to them that he was deaf. He thought they were encouraging him the entire time!

An encouraging word to someone who is down can lift them up and help them make it through the day. On the other hand, a destructive word to those who are down can be what it takes to kill them. Be careful of what you say.

Speak *life* to those who cross your path. It is sometimes hard to understand that an encouraging word can go such a long way. Anyone can speak words that tend to rob another of the spirit to continue in difficult times. One who will take the time to encourage another is a special individual.

Several years ago, former American prisoners of war were interviewed to determine what methods used by the enemy had been most effective in breaking their spirit. Researchers learned that the prisoners didn't break down from physical deprivation and torture as quickly as they did from solitary confinement or from being frequently moved around and separated from friends. It was further learned that the soldiers drew their greatest strength from the close attachments they had formed to the small military units to which they belonged.

These observations give us insight into why Christians need the group experience of fellowship with other believers to help them remain loyal to the Lord. Our own personal relationship to God, vital as that is, is not sufficient to produce spiritual maturity and endurance. Relationships within unified, Spirit-filled bodies of believers are essential for growth and for maintaining our individual faithfulness to the Savior. (Hebrews 10:23-25)

Throughout the Scriptures there are repeated requests to encourage others in the family of God. Romans 12 lists encouragement as a spiritual gift. Later, Paul writes in 1 Thessalonians 5:11, *"Therefore encourage one another and build each other up, just as in fact you are doing."*

Our word *encouragement* has derived from an old English word *incouragement,* which literally meant "to put courage in." It's the act of inspiring others with renewed courage and hope. And in humility each of us must come to the point where we acknowledge we need massive doses of it regularly. Hope is the oxygen of the human spirit.

Chuck Swindoll points out that the root word for *encourage* in Hebrews 10:25 is the same word—Counselor—that John uses to refer to the Holy Spirit in chapters fourteen and sixteen of his Gospel. He concludes, "In fact, when we encourage others, we come as close to the work of the Holy Spirit as anything we can do in God's family."[2]

A significant biblical language scholar also concludes, "One of the highest of human duties is the duty of encouragement.... It is easy to discourage people in their enthusiasm... The world is full of discouragers. We have a Christian duty to encourage one another. Many times a word of praise or thanks or appreciation or cheer has kept a person from complete discouragement."[3]

Brother Andrew learned early in his ministry the importance of encouragement when he fellowshipped with Christians in restricted situations in Eastern Europe. They told him, "Andrew, just your being here is worth ten of your best sermons!" Today as he travels in Muslim-dominated areas of the world, he receives the same comment. Indeed, Brother Andrew often defines the generic ministry of Open Doors as encouragement—a ministry that is expanded by people returning for further fellowship and by Open Doors providing requested material or training assistance.

Couriers visited a pastor in the southern part of Vietnam. They could not speak Vietnamese and he was very suspicious of them. So they did what the Spirit prompted. They knelt on the floor of the sanctuary and began to pray out loud in English. Soon the pastor joined them with tears flowing down his face. That pastor later wrote them a letter as to the importance of their visit that was translated as follows:

> *It was deeply moving that you and I could pray and praise the name of Jesus together. Although we have different languages, we can understand each other in the love of the Lord and through the Holy Spirit.*
>
> *We know that you want to give our church the Bible. We praise the Lord that He revealed our need to you...and He will help you bring the Bibles in. We have told Him about this need and we are awaiting His answer.*

Encouragement repeatedly comes up when analyzing the stories of Christians in prison. A report by a prisoner meeting another brother or sister in the prison camp is given with great joy. And when the two were able to spend time together, the language is one of absolute rapture. (see Matthew 25:36)

Valentina Saveleva spent five years in the harsh Soviet camps because she had transported Christian literature. She found the camp very depressing and shares how God answered her prayers:

> *The Lord saw my need and in his mercy sent me a Christian sister named Natasha.... The Lord sent her to give me relief in my critical moment of need. We prayed together a lot and always tried to support one another in prayer. I remember how we often met outside at night under the open heavens. We couldn't stay there long, because the temperature was often below -40° Fahrenheit and our work boots didn't keep our feet very warm. We would sing and pray for a few minutes, go back to our separate barracks to warm up a little, and then meet outside again. Sometimes we stood silently, just gazing together toward heaven....*
>
> *Sometimes my only desire was that the Lord would hurry up and take me home to be with him. But Natasha refreshed me very much. She had such a solid influence for good on my life. Often I thought that the Lord sent her to that camp just for my sake.*[4]

Richard Wurmbrand tells the story of eighteen elderly men confined in a Bucharest prison. It was "a windowless underground room with water dripping from the roof. To avoid freezing to death, the men formed themselves into a human snake, each one clinging to the man in front for warmth, as they stamped around in an endless circle. Often a man collapsed, but the others always dragged him up from the water and forced him on. Warmth and encouragement and life—all this we gain from one another."[5]

C. CONCLUSION

READ ALOUD AS A DECLARATION OF FAITH:

(Together if in a group: **leader reads bold;** group declares the Scripture response)

With God's enabling:

Never again will I confess fear, for *"God did not give us a spirit of timidity, but a spirit of power, of love and of self-discipline."* (2 Timothy 1:7)

Never again will I confess supremacy of Satan over my life, for *"...the one who is in you is greater than the one who is in the world."* (1 John 4:4)

Never again will I confess lack of wisdom, for I am in *"...Christ Jesus, who has become for us wisdom from God."* (1 Corinthians 1:30)

Never again will I confess "I can't," for *"I can do everything through him who gives me strength."* (Philippians 4:13)

Never again will I confess defeat, for *"God...always leads us in triumphal procession in Christ."* (2 Corinthians 2:14)

Never again will I confess unworthiness, for *"God made him who had no sin to be sin for us, so that in him we might become the righteousness of God."* (2 Corinthians 5:21)

Never again will I confess failure, for *"...in all these things we are more than conquerors through him who loved us."* (Romans 8:37).

Never again will I confess frustration, for *"You will keep him in perfect peace him whose mind is steadfast, because he trusts in you."* (Isaiah 26:3)

Never again will I confess troubles, for Jesus said, *"In this world you will have trouble. But take heart! I have overcome the world."* (John 16:33)

Never again will I confess confusion, for *"God is not a God of disorder but of peace"* (1 Corinthians 14:33) and *"We have not* *received the spirit of the world but the Spirit who is from God, that we may understand what God has freely given us."* (1 Corinthians 2:12)

Never again will I confess insecurity, for *"When you lie down, you will not be afraid; when you lie down, your sleep will be sweet...for the LORD will be your confidence and will keep your foot from being snared."* (Proverbs 3:24, 26)

Never again will I confess discontent, for *"I have learned to be content whatever the circumstances."* (Philippians 4:11)

Never again will I confess loneliness, for Jesus said, *"Surely I am with you always, to the very end of the age"* (Matthew 28:20) and *"Never will I leave you; never will I forsake you."* (Hebrews 13:5)

Never again will I confess bondage, for "*...where the Spirit of the Lord is, there is freedom.*" (2 Corinthians 3:17)

Never again will I confess worries and frustration, for the Bible says, *"Cast all your anxiety on him because he cares for you."* (1 Peter 5:7)

Never again will I confess curses or bad luck, for *"Christ redeemed us from the curse of the law by becoming a curse for us...that the blessing given to Abraham might come to the Gentiles through Christ Jesus, so that by faith we might receive the promise of the Spirit."* (Galatians 3:13-14)

Never again will I confess weakness, for *"The LORD is the stronghold of my life."* (Psalm 27:1)

Never again will I confess condemnation, for "*... there is now no condemnation for those who are in Christ Jesus.*" (Romans 8:1) I am in Christ. Therefore I am free from condemnation.

Never again will I confess lack, for "*...my God will meet all your needs according to his glorious riches in Christ Jesus.*" (Philippians 4:19)

Never again will I confess fear of the future, for *"As it is written: NO eye has seen, no ear has heard, no mind has conceived what God has prepared for those who love him—but God has revealed it to us by his Spirit."* (1 Corinthians 2:9-10)[6]

STUDY GUIDE/DISCUSSION QUESTIONS

PASTOR FOCUS

1. Have you ever been tempted to give up? What characteristics help you to persevere in your faith?

2. Read Hebrews 10:25 and discuss how this works in practice.

WOMEN'S FOCUS

1. Why is encouragement so vital in the Christian life?

2. How do you act as an encourager to others?

3. Think of a Christian living outside your region and write them a letter of encouragement.

YOUTH FOCUS

In order to continuously walk in the Spirit and produce the fruit of the Spirit, we must have that quality which we call perseverance. From the life story of Robert Morrison earlier in the chapter, highlight the situations through which Morrison developed perseverance.

MEN'S FOCUS

Tell how someone by word, deed or unknown action has encouraged you in the past or is encouraging you now.

12

FORGIVENESS AND GRACE

For if you forgive men when they sin against you, your heavenly Father will also forgive you. But if you do not forgive men their sins, your Father will not forgive your sins.

MATTHEW 6:14-15

On January 23, 1999, fifty-eight-year-old Australian Baptist missionary Graham Staines and his two sons were burned to death when the vehicle they were sleeping in was doused with gasoline and set on fire. Allegedly, members of a Hindu fundamentalist group in the Indian state of Orissa did this terrible crime. Graham Staines had been working with leprosy patients for thirty-four years.

Hundreds of millions witnessed Gladys Staines, Graham Staines' widow, forgive her family's murderers in the name of the Gospel on Indian television. The scene moved many to tears "and may have achieved more for the Gospel in India than many years of missionary work," according to an Indian evangelist.

Describing her prompt forgiveness of the killers as a "spontaneous act," Gladys Staines said that forgiving them took away the bitterness, which otherwise would have remained in her heart. Since the incident, people have been coming to her door asking how they can become Christians.

The media once described Ciudad Juarez, Mexico, as the "City of Tears" and the "Killing Fields." But in May 1999 it was transformed into a "City of Peace and Hope" by a unique "Festival of Life 99."

One of the street-witnessing teams became involved in an extraordinary situation. A young Mexican called Samuel would walk for two hours each day to join them and act as an interpreter. They discovered that Samuel's mother and sister had been murdered and that he witnessed the killings. And despite his having tried to intervene, he was unable to stop the murder. He said he knew the man who did it.

He had a desire to go and avenge the killings, but then became a Christian and his whole attitude changed. He began a Bible study group now attended by twenty people. On the final night of the "Festival of Life 99," he saw the man who had murdered his mother and sister go forward to receive Jesus Christ as his Savior. Samuel made his way through the throng of people and shook his hand and welcomed him into the kingdom. Samuel was able to forgive him.

A. FORGIVENESS DEFINED

The world does not understand a person's ability or reasons to forgive. Forgiveness is most unnatural in a world where people are self-centered and try to use any means to get ahead of others. There is also pain to be overcome because behind every act of forgiveness lies the wound of betrayal; but there is far more pain and emotional, social and physical damage done when we do not forgive.

Forgiveness is one of the most powerful actions that Christians can perform.

An Asian Christian apologist says,

"If I am asked, 'What separates Christianity from other religions?' or 'What's different about Christianity? Aren't all religions the same when you get down to it?' One of the first things I would say is one beautiful word: *forgiveness.*"

Forgiveness is a key component of victorious, overcoming Christians who are recovering from the loss, abuse and trauma of persecution. See Luke 23:34; Colossians 3:13

Forgiveness is to be given even when it is not asked for. On the cross, some of the final words of Jesus were: *"Father, forgive them, for they do not know what they are doing"* (Luke 23:34). The soldiers crucifying Him had not asked for forgiveness, but Jesus realized they needed to be forgiven.

Forgiveness can only be truly accomplished by the power of the Holy Spirit. When given, it communicates most powerfully the love of God. And we are called to be like God, who is love, to bear God's family resemblance.

Forgiveness is a personal transaction that releases the one offended from the offense.

To understand forgiveness we must realize what forgiveness is ***not.*** (see Figure 8)

The forgiveness required by the Scriptures is more than detached or limited forgiveness. It is full and complete forgiveness in which there is a total cessation of negative feelings toward the offender and the relationship is restored and grows.

B. BENEFITS OF FORGIVENESS

The benefits of forgiveness to the one who forgives as taught in Scripture are:

1. Forgive because God has been gracious to you and forgiven you.

Only God can forgive sins. Throughout the Old Testament we read of what a person needs to do to receive His forgiveness. We hear David exclaim, *"He forgives all my sins…"* (Psalm 103:3, KJV). We also see examples of human forgiveness—even in pain—such as Joseph forgiving his brothers for selling him into slavery. By this act, Joseph gains his true freedom. He then names his son Manasseh, *"one who causes to be forgotten."*

In the New Testament we see Jesus, the Lamb of God, come into the world to die for our sins. Through His blood that He shed on the cross, we can once and for all receive the ultimate forgiveness of our sins. This is the pure *"gospel of God's grace"* (Acts 20:24). This

Figure 8: What Forgiveness Is Not

Forgiveness is not forgetting.
Deep hurts can rarely be wiped out of one's awareness.

Forgiveness is not pardoning.
Forgiveness is not the same as "a pardon," which is a legal transaction that releases an offender from punishment for an action.

Forgiveness is not reconciliation.
Reconciliation takes two persons, but an injured party can forgive an offender without reconciliation.

Forgiveness is not condoning.
Forgiveness does not necessarily excuse bad or hurtful behavior.

Forgiveness is not dismissing.
Forgiveness does not pass off an offense as unimportant or insignificant. Rather, it takes the offense seriously.

Forgiveness is not a vague notion of "tolerance."
Forgiveness does not stand by and just tolerate an offense. To tolerate an offense is a low-grade distortion of forgiveness that sweeps the real issues in life under the carpet. It can mask or hide feelings that may later erupt into sickness or taking vengeance.

forgiveness is a gift. We do not deserve it but God, in His grace, reached out to provide forgiveness to a dying world.

The challenge of forgiveness is equal to the challenge of the commands to *"love your enemies"* and *"pray for those who persecute you."*

> *Bear with each other and forgive whatever grievances you may have against one another. Forgive as the Lord forgave you. (Colossians 3:13)*

In the final analysis, forgiveness is an act of faith. By forgiving another, I am trusting God to be a better justice-maker than I am. By forgiving, I release my own right to get even and leave all issues of fairness for God to work out. I leave in God's hands the scales that must balance justice and mercy.[1]

2. Forgive because your own forgiveness in the future depends on it.

Not only are we commanded to forgive others, but our being forgiven in the future depends on our actually doing that.

In the disciple's prayer—which we often refer to as the Lord's Prayer—Jesus taught His disciples to pray to their heavenly Father for forgiveness in a similar manner to the way they forgave others. Then Jesus continues after the prayer with this teaching:

> *For if you forgive men when they sin against you, your heavenly Father will also forgive you. But if you do not forgive men their sins, your Father will not forgive your sins. (Matthew 6:14-15)*

This is a very direct statement not open to much variation of opinion in interpretation. Our ongoing forgiveness is directly related to our forgiving those who have hurt us.

Later, Peter asks Jesus how many times he should forgive a brother who sins against him. He thinks he is magnanimous and suggests seven times! Jesus makes His famous reply, *"…not seven times, but seventy-seven times."* (Matthew 18:22)

Jesus then tells a parable about a man who, after much pleading for mercy, was released from the huge debt he owed. But then he went out and would not release another person who owed him only a very small debt. In the parable, the master throws the man into jail to be tortured until he pays back his large debt. Then comes the conclusion: *"This is how my heavenly Father will treat each of you unless you forgive your brother from your heart."* (Matthew 18:35)

3. Forgive because it brings healing and restoration.

In Jesus' teaching, there is little doubt that, as a Christian, I *must* forgive those who have wronged me. Then our human, time-bound minds cry out with the loud inquiry, "Why?"

Philip Yancey gives three practical reasons why we must forgive that are foundational for healing and restoration.

a. Forgiveness alone can stop the cycle of blame, pain, vengeance and violence.

The meaning of the New Testament word "forgive" literally means *"to release, to throw or send away, to free from an obligation."* When we learn to "free" those who have offended us, that is, *forgive* them, we break the chain or cycle of blame, pain, vengeance and violence.

One reviewer of this section noted: "The Bible does not tell us to go to someone and ask them to forgive us. That is an artifact from our nominal Christian worldview. The Bible *does* teach that we are to (1) forgive others and (2) go and actively try to reconcile with them. If doing this includes asking forgiveness (because of the other person's worldview), then we do so. Forgiving the person and bringing about reconciliation—not just asking for forgiveness—is what actually breaks the chain."[2]

The Russian writer Solzhenitsyn believed that the ability to forgive is what truly makes us different from animals. Only humans can perform that most unnatural act of forgiveness that transcends the relentless law of nature.

A teacher once told each of her students to bring a clear plastic bag and a sack of potatoes to school. For every person they refused to forgive, they chose a potato, wrote on it the name of the person and the date, and put the potato in the plastic bag. Some of their bags became quite heavy.

The only thing harder than forgiveness is the alternative: to not forgive.

They were then told to carry this bag with them everywhere for one week, putting it beside their bed at night, on the seat beside them when riding in a vehicle, and next to their chair whenever they sat down.

The hassle of lugging this around with them made it clear what a weight they were carrying spiritually, and how they had to pay attention to it all the time to not forget and keep leaving it in embarrassing places.

Naturally, the condition of the potatoes deteriorated to a nasty, smelly slime. What the teacher had the children do was a "picture" of what we pay for not forgiving those who offend us—a heaviness or "rottenness" in our spirits; shame and embarrassment; lack of freedom....

Too often we think of forgiveness as a gift to the other person, but it clearly is for ourselves as well.

b. It can loosen the stranglehold of guilt in the person who did wrong.

Forgiveness, though undeserved and unearned, can cut the cords and let the oppressive burden of guilt roll away. The resurrected Jesus led Peter through a process of forgiveness that allowed him to go through the rest of his life without the guilt of having betrayed the Son of God. (John 21:15-17)

c. It places the one who forgives on the same side as the one who did the wrong.

Through the process of forgiveness, we realize we are not as different from the wrongdoer as we would like to think. And we end up linked on the same side.

In essence, God linked Himself with us humans in the Incarnation. Somehow, God had to come to terms with these creatures He desperately wanted to love. On earth, living among us, He learned what it was like to be human—yet without sin. But He put Himself on our side. God made Him who had no sin to be sin for us.[3]

Forgiveness is a key component of "the way of the cross" that makes us "more than conquerors."

Corrie ten Boom often remembered the horrors of Ravensbruck and how the Nazis had abused and killed her sister. Now she found it almost impossible to show the true Christian attitude by forgiving the guards. Where was love, acceptance and forgiveness in a horror camp where it was reported that more than 95,000 women died? How could she ever forget the horrible cruelty of the guards and the smoke constantly coming from the chimney of the crematorium?

Then in 1947, Corrie was speaking in a church in Munich. When the meeting was over, she saw one of the cruelest male guards of Ravensbruck coming forward to speak to her. He had his hand outstretched. "I have become a Christian," he explained. "I know that God has forgiven me for the cruel things I did, but I would like to hear it from your lips as well. Fraulein, will you forgive me?"

Conflict raged in Corrie's heart. The Spirit of God urged her to forgive. The spirit of bitterness and coldness urged her to turn away. *"Jesus, help me. I can lift my hand. I can do that much."*

As their hands met it was as if warmth and healing broke forth with tears and joy. "I forgive you, brother, with all my heart." Later Corrie testified that "it was the power of the Holy Spirit" who had poured the love of God into her heart that day. Once again the Holy Spirit had triumphed.

C. GRACE

We have left to the end a very important characteristic in the training of a servant of Jesus Christ. This is the quality of living the Christian life with grace.

We use the word *"grace"* to describe many things in life:

- A well-coordinated athlete or dancer
- Good manners and being considerate of others
- Beautiful, well-chosen words
- Consideration and care of other people
- Various expressions of kindness and mercy

To show grace is to extend favor or kindness to one who doesn't deserve it and can never earn it. Receiving God's acceptance by grace always stands in sharp contrast to earning it on the basis of works. Every time the thought of grace appears, there is the idea of its being undeserved. In no way is the recipient getting what they deserve. Favor is being extended simply out of the goodness of the heart of the giver.

Also, grace is absolutely and totally free. You will never be asked to pay it back. You couldn't, even if you tried. Grace comes to us free with no strings attached. It is shown by an act of unmerited favor—most often to the down and out.

Christ came down from heaven and He reminds us that the greatest in the kingdom is the one who serves. Those on the ladder of power reach up. Those on the ladder of grace reach down.

One famous preacher said: "Love that goes upward is worship; love that goes outward is affection; love that stoops is grace."

Jesus Himself never used the word "grace." He just taught it and lived it. The Apostle John describes Jesus' glory as *"full of grace and truth"* (John 1:14). In a world of darkness and demands, rules and regulations, edicts and expectations demanded by hypocritical religious leaders, Jesus came and ministered in a new and different way.

After commenting on His glory, John goes on to add, *"From the fullness of his grace we have all received one blessing after another"* (John

1:16). John and the other disciples became marked men. Jesus' style became theirs. They absorbed His tolerance, acceptance, love, warmth and compassion so that it ultimately transformed their lives.

Thus, grace is Christianity's best gift to the world. It's a force stronger than vengeance, stronger than racism, stronger than hate. But sadly, to a world desperate for this grace the church sometimes presents one more form of what Philip Yancey refers to as "ungrace."

Charles Swindoll powerfully lists these enemies of grace as:

- *From without:* legalism, expectations, traditionalism, manipulation, demands, negativism, control, comparison, perfectionism, competition, criticism, pettiness and a host of others.
- *From within:* pride, fear, resentment, bitterness, an unforgiving spirit, insecurity, fleshly effort, guilt, shame, gossip, hypocrisy, and many more.[4]

1. The practical outworking of grace

Nothing has the power to change us from within like the freedom that comes through grace. And grace has a very practical outworking in our lives.

a. A greater appreciation for God's gifts

Those who claim the freedom God offers gain an appreciation for the gifts that come with life: salvation, life, laughter, music, beauty, friendship, forgiveness...

b. Less time and energy being critical of others' choices

When you begin to operate in the context of grace and freedom, you let small, insignificant things bother you less and less. You will allow others to make their own decisions in life, even though you might choose to do a different thing than they do. A grace-full Christian is one who looks at the world and others through glasses with "grace-tinted lenses."

c. More tolerant and less judgmental

When you are seriously involved in your own pursuit of grace, you'll no longer lay guilt trips on those with whom you disagree.

d. A giant step toward maturity

As your world expands, thanks to an awakening of your understanding of grace, your maturity will enlarge. You will never be the same![5]

2. Grace in an unresponsive society

How can Christians show grace in a society that is, or seems to be, veering away from God? Although Elijah worked outside the system opposing the evil actions of rulers, Obadiah worked within the system. He ran Ahab's palace while sheltering God's prophets on the side. Esther and Daniel were also employed by heathen empires. Jesus submitted to the judgment of a Roman governor. Paul appealed his case all the way to Caesar.

a. Dispensing God's grace is the Christian's main contribution

The most important thing that the church does that is different from the world is to show grace.

Jesus did not let any institution interfere with His love for individuals. Here is where the fruit of the Spirit are so important in our lives. Jesus said we are to have one distinguishing mark—not political correctness nor moral superiority, but love. In 1 Corinthians 13, Paul explains that without love we are nothing.

b. Commitment to grace does not mean Christians will always live in perfect harmony with their government

Kenneth Kaunda, the former President of Zambia, was once heard to say: "…what a nation needs more than anything else is not a Christian ruler in the palace but a Christian prophet within earshot."

Jesus warned us that the world who hated Him would hate us also. As the early church spread throughout the Roman Empire, the slogan "Jesus is Lord" was a direct affront to the Roman authorities. When conflict came, brave Christians stood up against the state, appealing to a higher authority.

Through the years, this same energy continued. It was Christianity that brought an end to slavery. The same energy drove the early labor movement, women's right to vote, as well as human rights and civil rights campaigns.

In all of this, we are to be *"wise as serpents and harmless as doves"* (Matthew 10:16, KJV). All our actions—and even counteractions—are to be seasoned with grace. When we show just the opposite, then we must consider the wisdom of our choices.

c. Too close a connection between church and state is good for the state and bad for the church

Herein lies the chief danger to grace. The state, which runs by rules of "ungrace"—as does the entire world system—gradually drowns out the church's sublime message of grace.

The church works best as a force of resistance, a counterbalance to the consuming power of the state. The closer connection the church has with the government, the more watered down its message becomes. Can you imagine any government making a set of laws based on Jesus' Sermon on the Mount in Matthew 5–7?

A state government can shut down stores and theatres on Sunday, but it cannot compel worship. It can arrest and punish murderers, but cannot cure their hatred or teach them love. It can pass laws making divorce more difficult, but cannot force husbands to love their wives, and wives to love their husbands. It can give subsidies to the poor, but cannot force the rich to show them compassion and justice. It can ban adultery but not lust, theft but not covetousness, cheating but not pride. It can encourage virtue but not holiness.

So let the church be the church. Let it operate as the church should—with love, truth, unity and grace.

Love, truth, unity and grace should also be the operating mandate for every individual Christian.[6]

3. How to develop grace

How do we become so permeated with grace that we enable others to enter into its glorious freedoms? There are two phases in developing grace:

First, it takes an admission of humanity. In other words, an attitude that says in authentic honesty, "I am only human. I won't try to impress you." Grace begins within people like that.

Second, it takes an attitude of humility. Nothing is so welcomed by the God of Grace as true humility. No person can operate in the flesh and produce any good thing, so our ego seeks to prevent us from trying.

It is in accepting grace that we can begin to model amazing grace. Only then do we realize how good grace really is.[7]

STUDY GUIDE/DISCUSSION QUESTIONS

PASTOR FOCUS

1. Philip Yancey describes three practical reasons why we must forgive that are foundational for healing and restoration. Why does forgiveness, when properly done, bring healing and restoration?

2. Identify the primary biblical principles that distinguish Christianity and make it unlike any "religion" on earth.

3. "Too close a connection between church and state is good for the state and bad for the church." Why is this true from your observations?

WOMEN'S FOCUS

1. *"Grace is Christianity's best gift to the world."* Explain why you agree or disagree with this statement.

2. Identify and discuss the four primary ways grace enhances our lives.
   - A greater appreciation of God's _________.
   - Less time and energy being _____________ about others' choices.
   - More _________________ and less __________________.
   - A greater step toward ________________.

3. Identify the biblical difference(s) between grace and mercy. Consider how to apply each in our relationships with those who experience pressure and persecution.

4. One of the most difficult areas to deal with in persecution can be summed up in one word—loss. This may include a loss of employment, career, reputation, health, virginity (abused), mobility, freedom, possessions, homeland (refugee) or family member (kidnapped, killed). Tell how you would encourage someone who has experienced one of the above losses.

YOUTH FOCUS

1. The central features of Christianity are love and forgiveness. Muslims are taught to *"fight and slay"* the enemies of Islam (Sura 2:190-191). Judaism teaches *"An eye for an eye and a tooth for a tooth"* (see Deuteronomy 19:21). Jesus Christ says: *"Love your enemies and pray for those who persecute you…"* (Matthew 5:44). Identify what forgiveness is NOT.
   Fill in the blanks with one of the following words:

   dismissing, reconciliation, forgetting, pardoning, tolerance, condoning

   - Forgiveness is not ______________________. Deep hurts can rarely be wiped out of one's awareness.
   - Forgiveness is not ______________________. This takes two persons, but an injured party can forgive an offender without reconciliation.
   - Forgiveness is not ______________________. Forgiveness does not necessarily excuse bad or hurtful behavior.
   - Forgiveness is not ____________________. It involves taking the offense seriously, not passing it off as inconsequential or insignificant.

- Forgiveness is not a vague notion of "________________". This is, at best, a low-grade parody of forgiveness. At worst, it's a way of sweeping the real issues in life under the carpet.
- Forgiveness is not _________________. A pardon is a legal transaction that releases an offender from the consequences of an action, such as a penalty.

2. Identify the primary reasons why we must forgive others (see text for answers):
   - Psalm 103:3; Colossians 3:13—God has _____________ us.
   - Matthew 6:14-15; 18:22, 35—Our own ________________ depends on it.
   - Forgiveness brings _____________ and _______________.
   - Forgiveness alone can stop the cycle of _______________ and the pain as well as __________________ and violence.
   - Forgiveness can loosen the ________________ of guilt in the __________________.
   - Forgiveness places the ____________________ on the same side as the one who did the ________________.

MEN'S FOCUS

1. Why is forgiveness such a hard action to implement?

2. What is the real blessing of forgiveness?

3. Why is grace so important to Christian living? What elements of "ungrace" do you see in your Christian community?

4. How are you committed to show and reveal grace in your world today?

5. Christians are taught to have both an attitude and a readiness to forgive as we all live by grace. Ideally, there should be repentance on the side of the offender (Luke 17:3-4; Matthew 18:15-18). If there is no repentance what should be our position? (see 1 Peter 2:23)

SECTION FOUR

The Way of the Cross Today

Toward an Understanding of Persecution

13

OUR UNIQUE SAVIOR

Who Is Jesus?

Jesus Christ is the same yesterday and today and forever.

HEBREWS 13:8

Louis Pasteur's co-worker in the demonstration of what used to be called the germ theory was Dr. Felix Ruh, a Jewish doctor in Paris. Dr. Ruh's granddaughter had died of black diphtheria. Vowing he would find out what had killed his granddaughter, he locked himself in his laboratory for days. He came out with a fierce determination to prove, with his colleague Louis Pasteur, that the germ theory was more than a theory.

Previously, the medical association had disapproved of Pasteur and had succeeded in getting him exiled, but he did not go far from Paris. He hid in the forest and erected a laboratory in which to continue his forbidden research.

Twenty horses were led out into the forest to the improvised laboratory. Scientists, doctors, and nurses came to watch the experiment. Ruh opened a steel vault and took out a large pail filled with black diphtheria germs, which he had cultured carefully for months. There were enough germs in that pail to kill everyone in France.

The scientist went to each horse and swabbed its nostrils, tongue, throat, and eyes with the deadly germs. Every horse except one developed a terrific fever and died. Most of the doctors and scientists wearied of the experiment and did not remain for what they thought would be the death of the remaining horse.

For several more days this final horse lingered, lying pathetically on the ground. While Ruh, Pasteur, and several others were sleeping on cots in the stables, the orderly on duty had been instructed to awaken the scientists should there be any change in the animal's temperature during the night.

About two a.m., the temperature showed a half degree decrease, and the orderly wakened Dr. Ruh. By morning the thermometer had dropped two more degrees. By night the fever was entirely gone, and the horse was able to stand, eat and drink.

Then, with a sledgehammer, Dr. Ruh struck the beautiful horse a deathblow between the eyes. The scientist drew blood from the veins of this animal that had developed the black diphtheria but had overcome it. The scientists drove as fast as they could to the municipal hospital in Paris. They forced their way past the superintendent and the guards and went into the ward where three hundred babies lay, segregated to die from black diphtheria. With the blood of the horse, they forcibly inoculated every one of the babies. All but three lived and recovered completely.

The blood of an overcomer saved them. The blood of an *Overcomer* has also spiritually saved many people. He too had to die to bring life to others.[1]

A. INTRODUCTION

We are about to study what Christians in free societies would often consider the "heaviest" or most difficult portions of this book. The materials that follow on "Who is Jesus?" "The way of the Cross" and "Responding to Persecution" were originally written to meet the needs of Christians living in restricted and threatened nations. The principles of this material are in essence a gift from persecuted Christians back to Christians living in free societies. Try to read the material with the spirit of one who is about to experience persecution.

B. WHO IS JESUS?

Jesus Christ is the central figure of history, the Bible and the church. As such, He is unique and unlike any other individual who ever walked on this earth. Though He was God, *he became flesh and blood and moved into the neighborhood* (John 1:14, The Message). He was and is fully man and fully God. (see Philippians 2:6-11)

Jesus is the centerpiece of civilization. He is the central person in all of history. Jesus of Nazareth is both the One from whom all our theology comes, and the One on whom all our theology focuses. He is the person who outshines all other persons, and His is the name that surpasses all other names. If "history" could be likened to a door, we would say that He is the hinge on which the door of history swings. He is the point where eternity intersects with time. He is the Savior who redeems us by *drawing all things to himself.* (Colossians 1:15-17)

Jesus Christ is the full revelation of God. He is the absolute Word and God incarnate. He is the powerful Son of God and loving Savior of mankind (John 1:1-18). He is our role model and our guide in all we do. He is our gentle master and wise mentor, compassionate counselor and healer, reliable Savior and our only Redeemer. He is our close friend and faithful companion, our holy and yet merciful Lord.

He is the fulfillment of all three of the Old Testament roles of Prophet, Priest and King (Hebrews 10:19-23; Revelation 17:14). In everything, He is *supreme.* (Colossians 1:15-20; Hebrews 1:1-3)

An anonymous author concludes his summary of the impact of Jesus' life with these words:

> *All the armies that have ever marched, all the navies that have ever sailed, all the kings that have ever reigned and all the governments that have ever ruled, combined, have not influenced the life of man upon this earth nearly as much as that one solitary life!*[2]

In summary, Jesus is the King of Kings and the Lord of Lords!

Though He is indeed a King, Jesus Christ's purpose for coming to earth was not to enjoy life and live like a king but to demonstrate His servanthood. He was born in humble circumstances, and all His life He identified with the poor and with those whom society scorned, such as Zacchaeus and Mary Magdalene. Though a King, He came to suffer at the hands of men—to endure the shame of the cross—in order to defeat Satan so God might be glorified and mankind redeemed.

Hundreds of years before Jesus' birth, a prophet predicted the coming of a special child who would be born of a virgin and called *Immanuel*—"God With Us" (Isaiah 7:14). The prophet added a list of His titles that are also unique: *Wonderful Counselor, Mighty God, Everlasting Father, Prince of Peace* (Isaiah 9:6). But the prophet's most detailed prophecy later reveals a picture of a suffering Jesus.

C. JESUS IS THE SUFFERING SERVANT

1. Proof that Jesus is the Suffering Servant

a. Jesus modeled servanthood for us.

Jesus said that He did not come into the world to be served like royalty—to which He was entitled—but He came to be a *servant* (Mark 10:45). In His teachings He also taught some significant paradoxes: to die is to live (John 12:24); to lose is to gain (Mark 8:35); and to lead is to serve. (Mark 10:42-45)

b. Isaiah presents Jesus as the Suffering Servant.

As early as six hundred years before Jesus' birth, Isaiah predicted His coming and the atoning significance of His coming. In his writings, Isaiah portrays four "Servant Songs." The best known and the climactic one is the fourth song and each phrase and every word demands thoughtful attention. Like the others, it is written in symmetrical Hebrew poetry. It is found in Isaiah 52:13 to 53:12 in five paragraphs of three verses each. Isaiah 53:5 is the central verse and theme:

> *But he was pierced for our transgressions, he was crushed for our iniquities; the punishment that brought us peace was upon him, and by his wounds we are healed.*

Again and again the writers of the New Testament refer directly and indirectly to this passage in Isaiah when describing the Lord Jesus and His atoning work on Calvary's cross.

The Apostle Paul clearly says that it was Jesus who, though He was God, humbled Himself, gave Himself to be crucified and on the cross died for us all (see Philippians 2:6-8). But He rose from the dead! Paul goes on to say that *"God exalted him to the highest place and gave him the name that is above every name, that at the name of Jesus every knee should bow...and every tongue confess that Jesus is Lord...."* (Philippians 2:9-11)

We can only faintly understand the mystery of what our Savior endured. But we trust and rejoice in the assurance that He paid the full penalty for all our sins. Christ's deepest pain opened the door to our greatest joy.

2. What Jesus' suffering servanthood means to us today

a. The secret of victory is always the cross.

This is God's way: the Lamb who was slain is placed upon the throne, as we see pictured in the Revelation of Jesus Christ. (17:14; 19:7-10; 5:6)

Though the details of Isaiah 53 apply directly to Jesus Christ, the chapter also implies that obedience to God's will is also for the disciples of Jesus. The disciple of Jesus *takes up his cross daily,* whatever the cost. (see Luke 9:23)

The Apostle Paul often spoke of the cross, especially in his letter to the Galatians. First he made the incredible statement, *"I have been crucified with Christ and I no longer live, but Christ lives in me. The life I live in the body, I live by faith in the Son of God, who loved me and gave himself for me."* (Galatians 2:20)

Suffering is the very heart of the Gospel. Without crucifixion there can be no resurrection. But resurrection always follows the cross. 1 Peter 2:19; 1 Peter 3:17-19; 1 Corinthians 15:19

Then at the end of the letter, he concludes, *"May I never boast except in the cross of our Lord Jesus Christ, through which the world has been crucified to me, and I to the world."* (Galatians 6:14)

In 2 Corinthians 1:9, Paul speaks of the *sentence of death* in himself as his way of overcoming death. Only as we are able to give to God our possessions, our future, our loved ones, even our own life, are we free to be more than conquerors.

The emphasis in Luke 9:23-25 is not only on sacrifice, but on the truth that only the one who truly follows Jesus can fulfill His command to *deny himself and take up his cross daily.* Why? Because crucifixion is God's invitation to resurrection.

D. JESUS IS THE RISEN LORD

1. Proof that Jesus is the risen Lord

The good news is that Jesus Christ was a pioneer not only of true servanthood and suffering but also of eternal and resurrected life.

The resurrection of Jesus Christ from the dead enables us to now understand the full meaning of Isaiah's Suffering Servant. *"He is not here; he has risen, just as he said…"* (Matthew 28:6). Just as Jesus predicted His suffering, He also predicted His resurrection and the defeat over Satan, the curse of sin, and even death.

2. What Jesus as our risen Lord means to us today

This resurrection power He now makes available to you and me. But resurrection can only follow the cross.

Jesus Christ, the crucified and risen one, is the cross-bearer, and all our "crosses" derive from His.

In 1 Corinthians 15 the Apostle Paul places our whole lives in the context of the resurrection. He writes that if the resurrection did not happen, we Christians are of all people most to be pitied (verse 19). Why? Because, if Jesus did not rise from the dead, we have by faith placed our eternal destiny in a falsehood; our faith is *futile* (verse 17). If Jesus did not rise from the dead, we have renounced this world's prospects and resisted this life's temptations all for nothing. But, we know that Jesus Christ *is* the risen Messiah. *"Christ has indeed been raised from the dead"* (verse 20)—and He is alive today!

Many of us would not be able to agree with Paul, for our standards and style of living today are not determined by Christ's resurrection. And if the resurrection had not occurred, we would still live a very "good life." We have not risked all to follow Him. Yet our ultimate freedom is to deny ourselves, take up our cross daily and follow Jesus. (see Luke 9:23)

Jesus empowered us with His resurrection power when He sent the Holy Spirit on the Day of Pentecost (Acts 2:1-41). His disciples, previously known more for their cowardice and fear, now filled with the Holy Spirit, became men of spiritual power and authority.

Through participation in His death and resurrection, we become a "cell" in the body of Jesus (Ephesians 1:22-23). Jesus shines into us and through us by His Holy Spirit. Martin Luther reportedly said, "I am a victorious Christian as long as I think of Jesus and me as one person…."

E. JESUS' CALL AND COMMISSION TO US

1. Jesus' Call to Commitment

The Gospel is both an invitation to the blessings of God as well as a challenge to completely commit our will to the will of God. Jesus, in His call to the disciples, requires three elements of commitment as recorded in Luke 9:23.

> *Then he said to them all: "If anyone would come after me, he must deny himself and take up his cross daily and follow me."*

a. Relational aspect of commitment

The relational aspect of commitment is found in the phrase *"If anyone would come after me...."* There is a desire on our part that causes us to want to come to Jesus to be His follower. It is a relationship that we seek to establish with Him. But what is the origin of this relationship? We do not have anything in us that is good enough to be offered to God. It is God Himself who has committed Himself to us. It is He who has taken the initiative that makes it possible for me to respond and commit myself to Him.

b. Entrusting aspect of commitment

The word *entrusting* is a banking term referring to depositing for safekeeping. It means giving or turning something over to another for them to keep safe.

When a person commits himself to another person, a relationship has been established between the two people. Now there must be evidence to prove that one has made that commitment. What is this "proof"? This proof is the aspect of entrusting one's self to that second party. In our Luke text, we see two phrases that reflect this aspect of commitment, *"deny yourself"* and *"take up your cross daily."*

• ***Deny yourself.***

When we make a commitment it costs us something. The biblical concept of commitment calls us to "deny ourselves." It is not self-denial; it is not to deny *something*. Rather it is a complete and total denial of one's self so that we no longer seek for what pleases self.

This is in direct contrast to the typical way of life where people try to get what they can for themselves. The basic sinful nature of the world, whether communist, capitalist or revolutionary, is the same. It desires to promote self at the expense of others. Jesus says His followers will be known as those who deny themselves.

• ***Take up your cross daily.***

The second part of commitment is even more extreme than denying one's self. Commitment also calls for "taking up the cross." When you commit yourself to Jesus, you deny yourself and become willing to go to your own execution! We only commit ourselves to being willing to die when we understand that the present life ends in death anyway, and the One who has promised us forgiveness and eternal life can really deliver it.

A young man who had recently become a Christian was returning home to a country where the punishment for conversion to Christ was death. He was asked whether or not he was afraid to go back. He replied, *"I have already died in Christ!"*

c. Commissioning aspect of commitment

The personal and trusting relationship between God and His followers now leads the believer to a commissioning—Jesus said, *"Follow me."* This commitment is not to a task but to a person. To be a follower of Jesus is to be a disciple of Jesus.

What is the task to which He has called us? The task is none other than what we call "The Great Commission":

> *Then Jesus came to them and said, "All authority in heaven and on earth has been given to me. Therefore go and make disciples of all*

nations, baptizing them in the name of the Father and of the Son and of the Holy Spirit, and teaching them to obey everything I have commanded you...." (Matthew 28:18-20)

2. Jesus' Commission

Jesus gave His commission for global evangelism to His disciples as His last command just before His ascension to heaven. After His command to go to every people group in the world and make disciples on the basis of His authority (Matthew 28:18-20), Jesus reassured them—and us—with these comforting words, *"And surely I am with you always, to the very end of the age."*

Dutch theologian Abraham Kuyper is credited for the statement, "There is not one square inch of the entire creation about which Jesus Christ does not cry out, 'This is mine!' "

Brother Andrew says, "By the assertion of His authority, Jesus defined the battlefield for us and set the goals of spiritual conflict. He has sent His followers into enemy territory to claim people who are held in sin by Satan, behind whatever barrier—whether it is cultural, linguistic, or even governmental."[3]

3. Obedience to Jesus' Commission: The "Way of the Cross" Today

Members of the Persecuted Church around the world have long understood the true significance of the cross of Christ.

- Pastor Allen Yuan in China, who spent almost twenty-two years away from his large family in prison for his faith, often talks about his sufferings over those years. But he invariably concludes with the statement, *"They are nothing compared with the Cross!"*
- The well-known and loved pastor in China, Watchman Nee, was martyred in the early 1970s. One of his elderly co-workers said recently, "If we call ourselves Christians—

people following Christ—we should know what road we are taking. Christ went the way of the Cross. We must be prepared to do likewise."

- A Christian aid worker was overwhelmed at the enormous need among the believers of southern Sudan. He recalls children in a village wearing nothing but hand-carved bone crosses fashioned in necklaces around their necks. He pointed to the cross of one emaciated child and questioned her with hand motions. She smiled broadly, took off the necklace and handed it to him. His thoughtful analysis is this: "That little act symbolises the state of the suffering church in Sudan. With absolutely nothing in the way of material possessions, they still have the cross of Jesus Christ. They are prepared to share its hope—even though it means death."[4]

It is easy to die for Christ. It is hard to live for him. Dying takes only an hour or two but to live for Christ means to die daily to self.
From the journal of Indian missionary and martyr Sadhu Sundar Singh (1889-1929)

- A thirty-two-year-old pastor works in Upper Egypt, an area of intense persecution of Christians. He runs a day care centre, a medical clinic, and a literacy training program, as well as caring for the families of those in prison. He has been beaten twice by Muslim extremists and is threatened daily with death. He knows they are trying to kill him—but he continues to bear his cross daily.
- A leading pastor in Egypt told about a parishioner who tearfully came for counseling. Young people she had trained at her work were recently promoted to be her supervisors. She was passed over solely because she was a

Christian. The pastor concluded, *"That's the cross we must bear here in Egypt!"*

- A Methodist pastor in Cuba, whose father spent five years in prison for political subversion, tells how his father wanted the family to escape to Miami. But the pastor decided that staying in Cuba was a cross he must bear. His father assured him he would pay a high price for that decision. He goes on to tell how his seminary education was interrupted for compulsory service in a primitive work camp where most of the men were hardened criminals. He and seven other Christians met secretly at night in the sugar cane fields to pray, read the Bible and encourage one another. *"I became a pastor in that work camp, not in seminary."*[5]

The essence of these examples is that instead of exercising and asserting my will, I learn to follow "the way of the cross" to comply with His will.

My King

Jesus Christ is the greatest person to ever cross the horizons
of this world.
He's God's Son.
He's the sinner's Savior.
He's the centerpiece of civilization.
He stands in the solitude of Himself.
He's august and He's unique.

He supplies strength for the weak.
He's available for the tempted and the tried.
He sympathizes and He saves.
He guards and He guides.

He heals the sick.
He cleanses the lepers.
He forgives sinners.
He discharges debtors.
He delivers the captives.
He defends the feeble.
He blesses the young.
He serves the unfortunate.
He regards the aged.
He rewards the diligent and
He beautifies the meek.

He is the key to knowledge.
He's the wellspring of wisdom.
He's the doorway of deliverance.
He's the pathway of peace.
He's the roadway of righteousness.
He's the highway of holiness.[6]

(Read Hebrews 10:19-25 aloud together, if in a group.)

Therefore, brothers, since we have confidence to enter the Most Holy Place by the blood of Jesus, by a new and living way opened for us through the curtain, that is, his body, and since we have a great priest over the house of God, let us draw near to God with a sincere heart in full assurance of faith, having our hearts sprinkled to cleanse us from a guilty conscience and having our bodies washed with pure water. Let us hold unswervingly to the hope we profess, for he who promised is faithful. And let us consider how we may spur one another on toward love and good deeds. Let us not give up meeting together, as some are in the habit of doing, but let us encourage one another—and all the more as you see the Day approaching. (Hebrews 10:19-25)

STUDY GUIDE/DISCUSSION QUESTIONS

PASTOR FOCUS

1. Explain the difference between *"The Way of the Cross"* and what might be called *"The Way of the Culture."*

2. Philippians 3:10-11 says: *"I want to know Christ and the power of his resurrection and the fellowship of sharing in his sufferings, becoming like him in his death, and so, somehow, to attain to the resurrection from the dead."* Explain this verse to a new believer.

3. Christians in free societies like to quote Romans 8:28: *"And we know that in all things God works for the good of those who love him, who have been called according to his purpose."* Vietnamese Christians living under extreme pressure and persecution prefer to recite Romans 8:36: *"For your sake we face death all day long; we are considered as sheep to be slaughtered."* What is the significant difference between these approaches to suffering and persecution?

4. The Apostle Paul quotes Isaiah 54:1 in his letter to the Galatians (4:25-27) applying it to the New Testament church. Patrick Johnstone says: "Just as the full meaning of the Suffering Servant of Isaiah 53 could only be seen after the resurrection of Jesus, so the joyous harvest of Isaiah 54 could only be seen after the birth of the Church at Pentecost. The rejoicing is therefore over a spiritual harvest—a gospel promise in which the world-wide Church is gathered through the preaching of the gospel."[7] What is the connection between suffering and glory?

WOMEN'S FOCUS

1. From Isaiah 52:13–53:12 describe five characteristics of Jesus of Nazareth that show Him to be qualified as a "servant":
   -
   -
   -
   -
   -

2. From the above passage (and Philippians 3:10), explain the meaning of Jesus' death and resurrection.

3. Allen Yuan, who spent twenty-one years and eight months in prison, said about his sufferings, "They are nothing compared with the cross." Some feel he means that his suffering was very little compared to what Christ suffered on the cross. Others think he means his suffering was insignificant compared to the benefits of Christ's cross he experienced. Discuss what you think he means.

YOUTH FOCUS

1. What does it mean to you to (a) deny yourself, (b) take up your cross daily, and (c) follow Jesus? (Luke 9:23) How do you walk the way of the cross in your area of the world?

2. How do sufferings, pressure, trials or persecution bring reassurance to you of God's forgiveness and love?

3. How would you explain Galatians 2:20 and 6:14 to a new Christian friend?

MEN'S FOCUS

1. How can we draw constantly on the available resurrection power of the Holy Spirit?

2. How should Christ's authority and promised presence impact our obedience to His last command?

3. The Bible alludes to "three crucifixions." Explain each in:
   - Revelation 17:14; 19:7-10; 5:6
   - Galatians 2:20
   - Galatians 6:14

14

OUR UNIQUE CALLING

Do We Really Have to Suffer?

To this you were called, because Christ suffered for you, leaving you an example, that you should follow in his steps.

1 PETER 2:21

During the Cold War era, visitors to the old Museum of Atheism and Religion in Leningrad were first subjected to a major display of pro-evolution propaganda. Then one entered the religion section dominated by displays of the sordid history of Christianity, such as the Inquisition and the Crusades.

Towering over that display area was a huge crucifix. The museum guides would explain it this way: "Christians love to suffer. Ever since their leader Jesus Christ was crucified on a cross like this one, they have had a persecution complex!"

A. SUFFERING AND PERSECUTION

While we are definitely not called upon to have a persecution complex, as Christians we are repeatedly reminded in Scripture that our lot is to follow in the footsteps of our Lord and Master.

When Jesus gave the last major teaching session to His disciples, He included a serious prediction about the reactions of the world. Jesus told His closest followers they were to remain in Him as a branch in the vineyard is connected to the vine. (John 15-17)

He then reminded them again of His command that they were to love each other as He had loved them and was willing to lay down His life for them—the highest form of love. They did not understand Jesus' remark, nor did they realize it would be fulfilled the very next day.

Then He contrasts the love of the brethren with the reaction of hatred from the world:

> *"If the world hates you, keep in mind that it hated me first…for they do not know the One who sent me."* (John 15:18, 21)

A little further down in the discourse, He says, *"…in fact, a time is coming when anyone who kills you will think he is offering a service to God."* (John 16:2b)

Jesus was indicating that as He suffered, so would His disciples. Every human being endures some suffering in his lifetime. It may be the physical suffering of sickness or injury. It may be the inner suffering caused by the death of a loved one, rejection by friends, or simply loneliness. Whatever the cause may be, we all seek to avoid it as much as possible.

That may be one reason Christians often avoid the subject of suffering, although it is clearly presented in the Bible. Some Christians seem to think that since we belong to the Lord, He will protect us from any and all suffering.

But, the Scripture makes it very plain that Christians are subject to all the causes of suffering common to men, plus the added persecution that comes with taking a clear stand for Christ. The book of 1 Peter is especially valuable to study in this regard. We will refer to it often in this chapter, as well as to other passages.

As we see in Figure 9, it is very important to remember that when Jesus sent out His disciples on their own to minister, He warned them that He was sending them out as sheep among wolves (Matthew 10:16; Luke 10:3). Sheep are not known for their ability to win a fight against wolves. For these sheep, persecution and suffering is the norm. But Jesus promised to be the Great Shepherd who would be with His sheep in every experience.

Consider the Christian's place in the world. Satan is the prince of this world. We are strangers and refugees here looking forward to a better land (Hebrews 11:8-16). The concept of being a "refugee" is useful (see 1 Peter 2:11). There are millions of political refugees in the world today. They are scattered in "camps" in many places in the world. They cannot return to the places they have left, and they are not yet at the places they hope to reach. Their present conditions are often "miserable" by the standards of the world, yet they have chosen it above what they had before. They live hoping for a better future.

The situation of Christians is very similar. They have left the world of sin and set out as pilgrims toward the heavenly kingdom. They have rejected the old life and should not be surprised that those still in the old life reject them. Christians live in the blessed hope of the glorious appearing of Jesus Christ.

Any Christian who has not faced the fact that Jesus warned us that the world will hate us will be easily discouraged and rendered impotent by Satan when suffering comes. Consider 2 Timothy 3:12, *"In fact, everyone who wants to live a godly life in Christ Jesus will be persecuted."* On the surface, this verse seems to imply that every Christian should be experiencing persecution and if not, there is a question as to whether the believer is really living a godly life.

But we must note the context. The preceding verses talk about the lack of godliness that will exist in the last days. It is worth rereading these warnings:

"But mark this: There will be terrible times in the last days. People

Figure 9: Sheep Do Not Carry AK-47s

Christians might respond to Jesus' comment that we are like sheep among wolves (Matthew 10:16) in one of the following four ways:

1. **No contact with wolves** (Isolationists)
   The first group says, "Jesus, You can't really mean I'm supposed to go out there where those vicious wolves are! So I'm just going to stay right in the middle of this big flock of sheep where it is safest. I want no contact with wolves."

2. **Super-sheep on steroids** (Triumphalists)
   The second group says, "OK, if I have to go out there where those wolves are, I'm going to be prepared." They work at trying to become a "Super-sheep on steroids." They pack their special "wolf-zapper" gun and try to blow the wolves off the face of the earth.

3. **Sheep in wolves clothing** (Conformists)
   The third group is much more sophisticated. They say, "Well, if you can't fight 'em, join 'em!" So they make themselves look so much like a wolf they aren't noticed. They become the opposite of what the Bible warns about "Sheep in wolves clothing"!

4. **Sheep who go—whatever the cost** (Literalists)
   The fourth group obey Jesus…and GO, knowing they are walking into a pack of wolves! They say, "I will go whatever the cost!" But they also know that their Master walks with them and they have constant communication with Him. And they have the directions He commanded: "Be shrewd as snakes and as innocent as doves" (Matthew 10:16). *The Message* paraphrases that: "Be cunning as snakes and inoffensive as doves!" It is these followers of Jesus who accomplish great things for God.

Sheep among wolves do not carry AK-47s to protect themselves—or their lambs.
Sheep have only one defense—they stay close to the Shepherd.

will be lovers of themselves, lovers of money, boastful, proud, abusive, disobedient to their parents, ungrateful, unholy, without love, unforgiving, slanderous, without self-control, brutal, not lovers of the good, treacherous, rash, conceited, lovers of pleasure rather than lovers of God—having a form of godliness but denying its power. Have nothing to do with them." (2 Timothy 3:1-5)

The list of words and phrases in the preceding paragraph sound like they came from the daily newspaper. Paul goes on to show how these kinds of people will even be deceitful and get into the church to do harm.

And then he gives a three-point charge to Timothy, his protégé. First he tells Timothy to follow his example—an example of patiently enduring many persecutions and sufferings. Then he challenges Timothy to continue in the faith that he had learned from his family ever since he was born (verses 14-15). Finally, he exhorts Timothy to base his life on the God-inspired Holy Scriptures.

B. MYTHS ABOUT SUFFERING—AND WHAT THE BIBLE REALLY SAYS

As we consider suffering and persecution, we first point out several myths that are common in Christian thinking today.

Myth #1. All suffering is punishment for sin.

Many people assume that suffering is always punishment for sin. Sometimes suffering *is* a punishment for sin. The Bible teaches that a person will reap what he sows (Galatians 6:7-8). Trouble may come as a natural consequence of sin. God may also use suffering to draw back to Himself one of His children who has sinned. (Hebrews 12:3-12)

If we behave lawlessly, we can expect to suffer for it, for the ruler *"does not bear the sword for nothing."* (Romans 13:4)

Our suffering may be self-inflicted. We should not invite

persecution by doing culturally insensitive things in the community where we live. Christians show insensitivity when they do such things as set up loudspeakers outside their churches; conduct loud services in sensitive areas; or use unethical methods of evangelism. When they make disrespectful comments about or make fun of other religions, they show insensitivity to the people who belong to those religions. When Christians do any of these things, they invite hostility against the church and bring unnecessary suffering on themselves.

However, sin is not the only explanation for suffering. The book of Job gives us a classic example of a man who suffered in spite of his righteousness, and his friends completely misjudged the situation. Job's trouble was not God's punishment.

First John 3:18-21 tells us, *"Dear children, let us not love with words or tongue but with actions and in truth. This then is how we know that we belong to the truth, and how we set our hearts at rest in his presence whenever our hearts condemn us. For God is greater than our hearts, and he knows everything. Dear friends, if our hearts do not condemn us, we have confidence before God...."*

Peter also makes it very plain that we may be called upon to face undeserved suffering. First Peter 2:19 says, *"For it is commendable if a man bears up under the pain of unjust suffering because he is conscious of God."*

Myth #2. Sufferers should not be sad or sorrowful.

We must dispel the idea that a believer should not be sad or sorrowful when suffering comes. The idea that a believer should show joy in all circumstances is neither biblical nor realistic. Jesus wept when His friend Lazarus died, although it was probably more for the sorrow of Mary and Martha than for Lazarus (John 11:33-35). Paul tells us to *"mourn with those who mourn"* (Romans 12:15). Peter recognizes that suffering causes sadness (1 Peter 1:6), but he encourages believers to rejoice in spite of their suffering because it is a blessed privilege to suffer for Christ (1 Peter 3:12-18). We should not assume that this kind of inner rejoicing in the glory of God will always take away the human pain we feel.

Myth #3. Suffering comes only to the holiest Christians.

Another misconception (aka: "myth"-conception) is the assumption that suffering for Jesus comes only to the "holiest" Christians. This mistake opens the door to pride for those who are suffering and spiritual defeat for those who are not yet called upon to suffer. Note that James and Peter were both arrested by Herod. James was beheaded and Peter was not. God has a personal and specific plan for every believer. As we walk with Him by the Holy Spirit, we will see great variety among the brethren. We are to praise the Lord for His personal interest. (see John 21:22)

Myth #4. Suffering is glamorous.

Those with the mistaken idea that suffering is glamorous put believers who have suffered "on a pedestal" and think that they are special, holy people. We are all laborers together with God. As each of us fulfills God's will for us, let us rejoice together and avoid "hero worship."

We must be careful not to glory in suffering nor seek persecution. We do not seek to be a martyr, but we are not surprised if that happens.

Myth #5. Persecution should be feared.

Some Christians make the mistake of allowing Satan to give them a morbid fear of persecution. This does not mean we take the prospect of persecution lightly, but we need to realize that God will not ask more of us than He gives us the strength to endure. Often Christians suffer more from the fear of coming persecution than from the persecution itself. Satan tries to make us worry about the past or the future. Christ provides grace for the present.

A church leader in Vietnam had worked closely with foreign

missionaries and it was assumed that he would leave before the communist takeover. When the departure day came, he said, "I cannot leave now, my people need me." He and his family were included in another evacuation list a few days later, but he said, "Take these, they are more fearful than my wife and I." A third and final opportunity came up the next day, but he said, "We cannot leave. God's will be done." This man has suffered since that time, but he has stood faithful to his Lord.

If we are confident that our suffering comes as God's will for us, we can accept whatever may come without fear, *"So do not fear, for I am with you; do not be dismayed, for I am your God. I will strengthen you and help you...."* (Isaiah 41:10)

Myth #6. Suffering is a mark of defeat.

Christians who view suffering negatively would rather talk about blessings and prosperity than the cost of discipleship and concentrate more on what they can get out of Christianity rather than what they can put into it.

A parallel false teaching stresses that if you only have enough faith, you can avoid suffering and persecution. A close look at the "heroes of faith" in Hebrews chapter 11 quickly dispels this myth as *"All these people were still living by faith when they died. They did not receive the things promised; they only saw them and welcomed them from a distance."* (Hebrews 11:13)

We are told in the Bible that suffering for Christ is not a mark of defeat but a mark of victory (see Luke 6:22-23). Note that we do not seek persecution in order to have this blessedness and victory, but when persecution comes we can expect this blessedness to accompany it.

Myth #7. Christians never suffer.

The Bible makes it clear that Christians will suffer. Some preachers have the idea that teaching this fact will drive away new believers.

Note that when Paul traveled throughout Asia Minor, he told the new believers, *"We must go through many hardships to enter the kingdom of God"* (Acts 14:22). He was preparing them for the future as well as explaining their present situation. We should prepare for the same.

Paul showed us an example of this when he prayed three times for the removal of his *"thorn in the flesh."* Then he saw that it was God's will for him, and he accepted it. (2 Corinthians 12:7-10)

When suffering Christians are not sure they are in the will of God they will be unsure if their suffering is really God's will. However, our great God *"works for the good of those who love him..."* (Romans 8:28). If we consciously submit to His will, He will give His divine direction. Our suffering and persecution can be placed in His hands by an act of our will. No believer needs to suffer alone and in doubt. Commit it all to the Lord. (Proverbs 16:3)

C. SUFFERING IN THE WILL OF GOD HAS MEANING AND PURPOSE

When we suffer in the will of God, suffering always has meaning and purpose. Often those who are suffering cannot at the time understand this. But they must by faith accept that this *is* true.

Biblical reasons why God allows suffering are:

- *Suffering proves and purifies our faith.* (1 Peter 1:6-7; 5:10; Romans 5:3-4; James 1:2-4)
- *Suffering burns away pride, as it did in Paul's life.* (2 Corinthians 12:7-10)
- *Suffering makes our lives more holy.* (Hebrews 12:3-10)
- *Suffering contributes to the spiritual strength of others.* (Philippians 1:14)
- *Suffering accomplishes purposes unknown to us now.* (1 Corinthians 13:12)
- *Suffering brings us together in unity,* (John 17:23) and this unity brings spiritual power. (Acts 2:42-47)

In several countries, including Iran, Christians tell us that before the persecution, they were divided. Under persecution they were forced to become united, and as a result, their faith was strengthened and their numbers grew. In some regions persecution has regrettably brought splits between Christians over how to respond to persecution.

• *Suffering often brings about a greater harvest of souls.* (Acts 8:1-4)

Again and again we see that in many countries, right before persecution comes, the church grows rapidly. It is helpful to remember this theme from the book of Acts: persecution does not necessarily cause church growth but church growth appears to cause persecution!

• *Suffering blesses us.* (Matthew 5:10-11)

Jesus specifies that we are blessed if we suffer for righteousness and for His name's sake.

• *Suffering causes what we really believe to become evident to others.*

James, in his letter to the early Christians, lists the qualities that trials of many kinds develop in us. (James 1:2-3)

• *Suffering points to the glory of heaven.*

Suffering and persecution turn our hearts and minds to the glory that will be ours in heaven. Jesus promises a great reward in heaven to those who suffer (Matthew 5:12). Paul said that the sufferings of the present are not worthy to be compared with the glory of the future (Romans 8:17-18), and Peter agreed (1 Peter 1:6-7; 4:13; 5:1-10). A Christian song says, "It will be worth it all, when we see Jesus." Those that are living today as "spiritual refugees" look longingly toward their eternal home in heaven.

• *Suffering causes those who suffer to share in the suffering of Jesus.*

In suffering, the Christian is following the example of Jesus (1 Peter 2:21-25). We also participate with Him in suffering (Romans 8:17; Philippians 3:10; 1 Peter 4:13). His suffering was prophesied (as ours has been). He was rejected by the world (as we are). He was insulted, and suffered physical pain and physical death. Can we expect any better treatment from a lost world?

One pastor who had escaped from China told an interviewer that the Red Guards had treated him "all right." But his face was covered with scars. When pressed with questions about his scars, he said, "They treated me as I expected. After all, they killed my Lord."

• *Suffering can bring victory.*

We must be convinced of this vital point. The key to this victory is *faith*. Think about the story of Job in the Old Testament. He was convinced that his suffering was unjust. All his questioning and debating with his friends offered no help. By faith, he finally placed his hope in God (Job 19:23-27). He then went on to consider the meaning of suffering in the world. Again he could find no answer except to submit by faith to an all-wise and all-powerful God. (Job 42:1-6)

Peter advised those who are suffering to *commit themselves* to God (1 Peter 4:19). Our trust is not in a God who uses His power without a plan or at His whim. Rather, our trust is in a loving, purposeful God who promises that all things work together for good for those who love Him (Romans 8:28). God has a plan and purpose for our life, and through our obedience to His teaching, He is going to work in us and through us that which will ultimately bring glory to God. With this kind of faith, we will see victory.

Jesus warned us of suffering, and promised us victory at the same time (John 16:33). He also promised us a *Comforter*, the Holy Spirit. The testimonies of those who have weathered severe persecution show why Jesus called the Holy Spirit the *Comforter*. But remember, faith is built on the Word of God. We need to know the promises of God in His Word if we are going to call on them in time of need. If our faith is strong, we can expect to know victory in suffering.

Accepting persecution is the secret of victory, rather than the absence of trouble or the presence of prosperity and affluence.
1 Corinthians 4; 2 Corinthians 4 and 11

In 1 Corinthians 4 and also in

2 Corinthians 4, Paul gives a record of his life in Christ. It is not a story of peace and harmony, comfort and popularity. Rather, it is a story of rejection and hardship, even despair. And yet Paul comes through victorious because he shows that the heavenly treasure of Jesus Christ and His message is carried in *jars of clay.* (2 Corinthians 4:7)

Just as jars made from clay were used in New Testament times to carry water, God's children are His *"jars of clay"* made to carry the water of life. This shows that the power in our lives that enables us to be victorious comes from God. The sooner we can realize that, the sooner we can see God's victory in our lives. The sooner we see ourselves as a channel for God's power, the sooner we will become *more than conquerors.* (Romans 8:37)

The earthen vessel is always the means of God's victory. The sooner we realize the truth of that, the sooner we can apply it to our lives. Also, the sooner we learn to treat one another not as "in the flesh," but rather, as "in Christ"—new clay vessels meant to bear heavenly treasures—the sooner we will be victorious.

As we look over these truths about suffering that are taught in the Bible, two of them seem to be most basic for the Christian to understand.

First, let us be certain that suffering comes as God's will for us. If we are confident of this, we can accept whatever may come. (Romans 8:12-25)

Second, even though we are weak creatures, we can know victory over these circumstances.

Encourage your heart on these two points, and nothing the enemy throws against you can conquer your faith. Always remember that Jesus lives within His people!

D. SUFFERING AND PERSECUTION TODAY

Today, Christians around the world face all kinds of severe suffering and persecution. In countries such as Sudan where war has been a part of life for years and years, believers are suffering from planned starvation programs and physical attacks. And many have been captured and/or sold into slavery.

Countries and regions such as Iran, southern Sudan, and northern Iraq have tried to eliminate Christian leadership by martyrdom. In Saudi Arabia and North Korea, Christians have been imprisoned, tortured and publicly executed.

In Chiapas, southern Mexico, more than 35,000 Christians have been unjustly and forcibly driven from their homes just because they are evangelical Christians. Thousands have also been murdered and viciously mistreated. Many homes have been burned to the ground.

In Peru, China, Sudan, Cuba, Vietnam, Laos and numerous other countries, Christians unjustly spend time in prison for their activities, which often includes going to secret, unregistered worship meetings.

Across the nation of Indonesia, hundreds of churches have been burned and many Christians martyred by Muslim extremists.

Nepali Christians are facing threats from a Maoist insurgency group. They are also concerned by petitions organized by Hindu militants asking the government to deal more strictly with churches in the country, which are rapidly growing. The president of the National Christian Fellowship of Nepal has called on believers around the world to pray this move against Christians will not succeed.

Five churches were destroyed in the eastern part of Nepal after local Hindus and Buddhists became angered by the number of people becoming Christians. Although there were no known Christians in the country in the 1950s, through a sovereign move of the Holy Spirit, there are now about 500,000.

Nepali authorities have largely ignored laws that prohibit evangelism or conversion, but the window of opportunity could close at any time. Christians have been arrested and held in jail from time to time for witnessing. Many Christians face social and economic persecution, finding it hard to get work.

Often, in areas such as the southern Philippines, Pakistan and Peru, children from Christian families are abducted. Perhaps this is the worst form of persecution to bear.

Often, a Christian's own family turns against them. At public meetings, Christians may be criticized or even attacked by their neighbors and former friends—and also by members of their families. Only a strong commitment to the Lord can resist this kind of psychological weapon used by the enemy. In the Old Testament book of Job, Job's own wife advised him to *"curse God and die."* (Job 2:9)

Remember that none of this catches God by surprise. The coming storm clouds of persecution are quickly moving toward many societies that are currently free societies.

When preparing this material, we received stories from more than two hundred evaluators living in Australia, Brazil, Canada, Germany, Holland, Italy, New Zealand, the Philippines, South Africa, the United Kingdom, and the United States. Their illustrations included: harassment, classifying the Bible as "hate literature," job losses for being a public Christian, legislated acceptance of gay marriages, accusations of being "intolerant" because of one's faith in Jesus Christ.... These types of incidents are on the rise in most free societies.

In the twentieth century, probably more Christians were killed for their faith than in all of church history. Various sources indicate that Christianity has the most martyrs of all religions. It would be impossible to give a pattern that Christians could use to meet each kind of persecution they encounter. Even if we could provide such a pattern, it would be useless, for in our own strength, we are no match for the enemy. The guidelines given us in the Bible are still the most reliable words.

E. HOW CAN WE BE PREPARED FOR PERSECUTION?

Our preparation must be in:

- knowing God's Word

- an abiding faith *in* Him that results in communication *with* Him
- submitting daily to the Holy Spirit and
- knowing that other believers are praying for us

The expressions *"by faith"* and *"through faith"* are found twenty-four times in Hebrews 11. Faith opens to us the resources Paul mentioned in Philippians 4:13, *"I can do everything through him who gives me strength."*

God uses problems and persecution in our lives in the following ways:

- God uses problems and persecution to DIRECT you.

Sometimes it seems as though God lights a fire under us to get us moving. Problems and pressures often point us in a new direction and motivate us to change. Is God trying to get your attention? *"Sometimes it takes a painful situation to make us change our ways."* (Proverbs 20:30, TEV)

- God uses problems and persecution to INSPECT you.

People are like tea—if you want to know what's inside them, just drop them in hot water! Has God ever tested your faith with a problem? What do problems reveal about you? *"When you have many kinds of troubles, you should be full of joy, because you know that these troubles test your faith, and this will give you patience."* (James 1:2-3, NCV)

- God uses problems and persecution to CORRECT you.

Some lessons we learn only through pain and failure. Perhaps when you were a child, your parents told you not to touch a hot stove. But you probably learned by touching the stove and getting burned.

David says that the punishment God gave him *"was the best thing that could have happened to me, for it taught me to pay attention to your laws."* (Psalm 119:71-72, LB)

- God uses problems and persecution to PROTECT you.

A problem can be a blessing in disguise if it prevents you from being harmed by something more serious. Last year, a friend was fired from his job for refusing to do something that was wrong that his boss had asked him to do. His unemployment was a problem—but it saved him from being convicted and sent to prison a year later when management's actions were eventually discovered. *"You intended to harm me, but God intended it for good...."* (Genesis 50:20)

God is at work in your life—even when you do not recognize it or understand it. But it's much easier and more profitable when you cooperate with Him. This is the way to victory![1]

• God uses problems and persecution to PERFECT you.[1]

Problems, when responded to correctly, are character builders. God is far more interested in your character than your comfort. Your relationship to God and your character are two things you are going to take with you into eternity. *"We can rejoice when we run into problems...they help us learn to be patient. And patience develops strength of character in us and helps us trust God more each time we use it until finally our hope and faith are strong and steady."* (Romans 5:3-4, LB)

STUDY GUIDE/DISCUSSION QUESTIONS

PASTOR FOCUS

1. You are a committed Christian living in a hostile community. In spite of your attempts to show love, many in your community hate you passionately because of your faith, which is different from their faith. Also, your home is quietly used for secret house church meetings.

   Early one morning, a mob of neighbors begins to violently attack your home. Soon the police arrive and listen to both sides of the issue. The police give you a choice of going to the police station (where you know you'll receive a beating) or face a local hearing of your neighborhood committee. Which would you choose? Why?

2. Tertullian reportedly said, "The man who is afraid to suffer cannot belong to Him who suffered." Explain why you agree or disagree.

3. Look again at Hebrews 11 and review what believers have faced in the past. Pay special attention to verses 35-38 to be reminded that while some were delivered (verses 33-34), others were not.

WOMEN'S FOCUS

From your experience, describe an example where someone invited "*persecution*" by being culturally insensitive to the community around them. How would **you** counsel these people if you could say three things to them?

YOUTH FOCUS

1. Review and identify common myths about suffering.

Choose from one of the following options:

feared, defeat, glamorous, holiest, punishment, sorrowful

- Suffering is ____________________ for sin.
- Sufferers should not be _________________.
- Suffering comes only to the _________________ Christians.
- Suffering is ____________________.
- Suffering should be ________________.
- Suffering is a mark of _________________.

2. Which one of the above misconceptions do you think is most common? Explain why you chose the one you chose.

3. The Bible identifies purposes for suffering. Check each reference and explain the meaning and purpose:

Choose from the following options:

purposes, holy, pride, purify, encouragement, unity, harvest

- 1 Peter 1:6-7; 5:10—to ______________ our faith.
- 2 Corinthians 12:7-10—to burn away _________________.
- Hebrews 12:3-10—to make our lives more _____________.
- Philippians 1:14—to contribute to the _________________ of others.
- 2 Corinthians 3:12—to accomplish __________________ unknown to us now.
- John 17:23 and Acts 2:42-47—to bring us together in _________.
- Acts 8:1-4—to bring about a greater _______________.

MEN'S FOCUS

1. Choose one of the following options about suffering:

   allows, heaven, victory, suffer, suffering, evil deeds, meaning, persecution, glory

   - Christians will ____________________.
   - God ____________________ suffering.
   - Suffering in the will of God has ________________.
   - We should never suffer for _____________ _____________.
   - There is blessing in __________________ for what is right.
   - Suffering points to the _________________ of ________________.
   - Sufferers share in the _________________ of Jesus.
   - There can be __________________ in suffering.

2. *"Accepting persecution is the secret of our victory rather than the absence of trouble or the presence of prosperity and affluence."* Review what the Bible says about suffering and explain why you agree or disagree with the above statement.

3. In 2 Corinthians 11:13–12:10 underline/circle phrases that identify "pressure" or "persecution" to you. How did Paul handle pressure and persecution?

4. Should Christians expect more suffering and difficulties than their non-believing neighbors, or less?

5. Of the above things the Bible teaches about suffering, which have you never thought about before?

6. How does this teaching about suffering relate to the Bible teaching that God loves us and allows only what is good for us to come to our lives?

7. What is your response to Brother Andrew's comment on persecution being "that which comes after trying every way to be friends"?

8. How can we encourage those Christians in difficult parts of the world who experience severe suffering? What can we learn from them?

Figure 10: Open Doors "World Watch"
10 Countries Where Persecution Is Most Severe
(See Appendix A—page 373)

1. North Korea
2. Saudi Arabia
3. Laos
4. Vietnam
5. Iran
6. Turkmenistan
7. Maldives
8. Bhutan
9. Myanmar (Burma)
10. China

See Endnote[2]

15

RESPONDING TO PERSECUTION

Not "If" but "When"!

Do not repay evil with evil or insult with insult, but with blessing, because to this you were called so that you may inherit a blessing.

1 PETER 3:9

Abdul, born into a middle-class Sunni Muslim family, began practicing his Islamic faith at the age of ten. He remained very religious until he was twenty-three years old.

As a teenager, he began asking questions that are normal for any teenager to ask himself: *Who am I? Why was I born? Who created me? Why am I Muslim?* However, one question occupied his mind more than all the others: *When I die, will I go to be with God?*

He had been taught that Christians believe in three gods, and that the Bible had been corrupted. A missionary asked him to prove that. For nine months he tried to find the proof, but failed. During that time, God spoke to him. He submitted to God and received Jesus Christ as his Lord and Savior!

For three years he kept his new faith a secret. He knew that what he had done was against Islam and that he could be killed if he didn't return to his Islamic beliefs.

After Abdul was discipled, he was invited to go to Spain to serve as a host in The Pavilion of Promise in Seville as part of EXPO '92. This was more than just a job to him—it was an opportunity to serve God. He went and was greatly blessed.

When he returned to his home country, he had problems at the airport. Airport security took his passport from him. Two inspectors questioned him and asked if he had converted. He admitted that he *had* converted. He was then handcuffed and shipped downtown to security headquarters. There, he was blindfolded and led away for interrogation. During the interrogation, they called him names and threatened to put him behind bars for the rest of his life. They beat his hands and feet, spat on him, and slapped him in the face. He was refused even a sip of water.

After more interrogation—with more threats and beating and an order to report to their office later—they let him go. But not before a stern warning was given to him: "Unless you return to Islam, you will pay a costly price. And it will involve your family!"

In the following months of more harassment, Abdul stayed away from all church meetings. He didn't want to be the cause of his family suffering if they found out that he had converted. He also did not want to be the cause of harm coming to his Christian friends.

Eventually, he decided to tell his oldest sister since he had a close relationship with her and knew that she would listen to him. She listened and cried, then encouraged him to leave the country so their family would not suffer because of him.

The authorities bugged Abdul's home and his phone, opened his mail, watched his bank account, and put surveillance on him at work. He never knew what would be done to him after threats made to him. The stress and anxiety of the unknown was almost unbearable. So, after eight months of harassment, surveillance, and illegal house searches, Abdul decided to leave his country.

Today Abdul and his wife have resettled in the free world.

A. APPROPRIATE BIBLICAL RESPONSES WHEN PERSECUTION COMES

A Christian who is ready will stand strong and grow in times of crisis. The Bible gives us several examples of responses to persecution. The appropriateness of a given response depends on divine guidance, as such responses may differ greatly, even in similar circumstances.

The appropriate biblical response when persecution comes is always one that is in the center of God's will. Matthew 13:13-14; Luke 22:41-52; Psalm 43:1; Proverbs 25:21-22

1. Fleeing–when it is clearly the will of God

In the New Testament, to avoid Herod's death orders, Joseph and Mary took the baby Jesus and fled to Egypt. (Matthew 2:13-14)

Jesus told His disciples to leave a town and flee to the next one if they were persecuted (Matthew 10:23; Luke 9:5). We cannot say that Jesus Himself ever "fled" from persecution. But when a group of angry people wanted to throw Him off a cliff, He *"walked right through the crowd and went on his way"* (Luke 4:30). Again, when a group *"picked up stones to stone him,* He *"hid himself, slipping away…."* (John 8:59)

The Apostle Paul, who endured so much persecution, resorted to flight several times in his missionary work (Acts 9:25; 9:30; 17:10). In these flights, friends and followers assisted Paul. People mobilized to save his life and ministry. Yet he did not try to avoid persecution as a lifestyle practice.

2. Staying and enduring

In Luke 22:41-52, in His darkest hour—in the Garden of Gethsemane—Jesus knelt down and prayed, *"'Father, if you are willing, take this cup from me; yet not my will, but yours be done.'...a crowd came up, and...Jesus' followers...said, 'Lord, should we strike with our swords?'... But Jesus answered, 'No more of this!'"* In that hour *"when darkness reigns"* Jesus was obedient to the will of the Father. He chose to neither *flee* nor *fight.* He persevered, endured and stood strong through the storm!

The Bible gives us numerous examples of believers who stayed and endured persecution—even to the point of death—rather than seeking to run from it.

a. By hiding

In Joshua 2, we read that Rahab hid the Israeli spies. Many Christians are led of God to go into hiding or to hide others. Corrie ten Boom became well-known because of her "hiding place" for Jews during the Nazi occupation of Holland in World War II. Persecuted Christians in Indonesia have hidden in the tops of coconut trees and stayed there for many weeks, waiting until it was safe to return to their homes.

b. By boldly being "salt and light"

In Matthew 5, when talking to His disciples Jesus used illustrations of salt and light. *"You are the salt of the earth,"* and *"You are the light of the world,"* He said (verses 13 and 14). Salt preserves and seasons. Light does away with darkness. Jesus used the imagery of salt and light in Matthew 5 for those who were His followers. When Christians flee from a place, the preserving and seasoning effect of their righteous living departs with them. The effect of their light goes with them, leaving the darkness to become even darker.

Today, many people question how "correct" it is for persecuted Christians to leave their homeland. Those who choose to leave must be sure that God has directed them to leave. A person who wants to flee should first ask, *If all Christians flee, what witness for the Lord is left in my community?* Next he should ask, *Is God directing* **me** *to leave my country?*

c. By responding with non-violence

The response of non-violence and non-retaliation by most Christians to persecution has been based on the following significant biblical truths:

- Praying—God hears the prayer of the oppressed.

"Vindicate me, O God, and plead my cause against an ungodly nation; rescue me from deceitful and wicked men." (Psalm 43:1)

- Not taking vengeance or retaliating—God alone is the judge and the sovereign Lord.

He alone knows the hearts of people and how to deal with them. Thus if we take vengeance into our own hands, we are assuming God's role.

"It is mine to avenge; I will repay. In due time their foot will slip; their day of disaster is near and their doom rushes upon them." (Deuteronomy 32:35; see also Romans 12:17-21)

"If your enemy is hungry, give him food to eat; if he is thirsty, give him water to drink. In doing this, you will heap burning coals on his head, and the LORD will reward you." (Proverbs 25:21-22)

The Hebrew word for "reward" also means "completion." God completes the process initiated by the one who shows compassion to his enemy.

d. By giving one's life

Martyrdom may be the end result of those who endure. In addition to Jesus, three martyrs are named in the New Testament—John the Baptist, Stephen and James. Some of the unnamed heroes of the faith mentioned in Hebrews 11:37 were also martyred.

Martyrdom is described as a legitimate response to persecution.

This is not easily understood in our day and in our culture that specializes in personal "rights" and the avoidance of suffering. But a special crown is awaiting those who lay down their lives for their faith. (Revelation 2:10)

The appropriate response to persecution that one chooses depends on that person's intimate relationship with God the Holy Spirit and openness to His direction.

3. Exercising legal privileges

Paul was a master of this. In Acts 22, he sees no benefit in getting beaten up, so he uses his Roman citizenship to protect himself. In Acts 25, he appealed to Caesar, again using his right of citizenship, and escapes almost certain death from religious Jewish leaders.

Dealing with injustice is also part of the Christian calling. Today in some countries where Christians are persecuted, especially in Latin America, lawyers are "exercising legal privileges" to help those who are suffering. As these men speak out against injustice, they need to be careful. They risk persecution along with those they are helping.

Brother Abdias Tovilla studied law in order to help his indigenous people of Chiapas in southern Mexico. There, many people have been expelled from their homes simply because of their evangelical faith.

In Peru, a Christian council was established to make legal appeals on behalf of the hundreds of Christians who have been unjustly incarcerated on subversion charges.

The church in Sri Lanka—a threatened minority—is an example of how Christians come to the aid of a church that has been attacked. The Evangelical Alliance of Sri Lanka in cooperation with the Religious Liberties Commission of the World Evangelical Alliance adopted the following guidelines when a church or home of a believer is attacked:

a. Making our presence known

Leaders visit the church to provide encouragement to the pastor and the church members.

b. Documenting the incident and letting the worldwide Body of Christ know

This is often done via the Internet. It has resulted in more prayer for those Christians who are suffering.

c. Providing material support

Churches join to provide material support—food, clothes, and so on—to the victims and the homeless.

d. Serving as an advocate

An advocate is a person who intervenes in support of a person or cause. Christian leaders may ask that justice be done for the persecuted. Thus, they serve as "advocates" for the persecuted by speaking or writing to government officials about incidences of persecution.

e. Educating the pastor and members about their legal privileges with guidelines on reporting

Christian leaders can use the legal system to gain favorable public opinion to restrain future incidents.

f. Providing a "Do" and "Don't Do" list for exercising religious freedom

The following list has practical suggestions on how the church carries out its programs in a hostile environment so as not to invite trouble:

- Be sensitive to the sound levels during meetings.
- Integrate into the village without alienating the community.

- Be culturally sensitive to your community in matters of conduct—especially the youth.
- Avoid high publicity programs on special religious holidays.
- Do not use relief or social programs as "bait" for evangelism but rather for relationship and opportunity.
- Adopt a simple lifestyle consistent with that of the local people in the community.
- Encourage unity among Christian leaders in the area.
- Gather in smaller congregations if hostility persists.
- Avoid putting outsiders in a prominent role in the community.
- Always avoid disrespectful comments about other religions.
- Discuss and communicate with religious leaders before persecution takes hold.

All in the church and those in small group fellowships must consider the possibility that suffering *will* come, then consider how they should respond to it biblically. Then, as they respond the way God would have them respond, victory is assured.

B. BIBLICAL PRINCIPLES LEARNED FROM THE PERSECUTED CHURCH

The Bible clearly explains how Christians should act when they are persecuted. Our brothers and sisters currently "standing strong through the storm" offer us some specific encouragement. They say:

1. Don't be surprised!

Scripture has much to say about our attitudes and how we should act when testing, trials, suffering and persecutions come to us. In Peter's first letter in the New Testament, he tells us to not be surprised when such things happen to us. Peter teaches that when suffering and persecution come to us, our first reaction should not be one of surprise.

Dear friends, do not be surprised at the painful trial you are suffering, as though something strange were happening to you. But rejoice that you participate in the sufferings of Christ, so that you may be overjoyed when his glory is revealed. If you are insulted because of the name of Christ, you are blessed, for the Spirit of glory and of God rests on you. (1 Peter 4:12-14)

Peter here echoes instructions found elsewhere in the New Testament regarding suffering by persecution. (see John 15:18–16:4; 2 Timothy 3:12; 1 John 3:13)

We are not to be surprised that we suffer. Suffering is to be anticipated with an awareness that it does not interfere with God's plan for us.

2. Rejoice!

The Apostle Paul commands us to "*Rejoice!*" (Philippians 4:4). The verb construction in the original language is continuous, as in *"keep on rejoicing."* When we rejoice, our faith grows and our fears become less.

In 1 Peter 4:13 we are directed to rejoice in our trials. This is perhaps one of the most challenging directives in the Bible and parallels Jesus' teaching in the Beatitudes (Matthew 5:11-12) as well as that of James in his letter (James 1:2-3). *The Messsage* paraphrases James 1:2-3 this way: *"Consider it a sheer gift, friends, when tests and challenges come at you from all sides. You know that under pressure, your faith-life is forced into the open and shows its true colors."*

One of the most comforting promises of God is *"And we know that in all things God works together with those who love him to bring about what is good."* (Romans 8:28)

First Peter 4:14 indicates that the Holy Spirit rests upon us to equip and sustain us through pain and fear. He is the One who gives special grace to rejoice continually regardless of our circumstances.

3. Pray with thankfulness.

In Philippians 4:6, the Apostle Paul urges us, *"Do not be anxious about anything, but in everything, by prayer and petition, with thanksgiving, present your requests to God."* While it is assumed we will cry out to God for help when problems come, Paul does not expect us to doubt, blame or question God. Rather, we are to act with an attitude of thankfulness because God has a purpose for us and supplies us with His resurrection power. The next verse expresses the results of such a grateful heart: *"And the peace of God, which transcends all understanding, will guard your hearts and your minds in Christ Jesus."*

The Scriptures also teach us to pray for the sufferers (Acts 12:5; Hebrews 13:3; Colossians 4:18) as well as for the persecutors (Matthew 5:44; Romans 12:14). We should pray that those who suffer will have wisdom to know how to respond to persecution.

4. Evaluate the source of suffering.

In 1 Peter 4:15-19, we see two other necessary elements of proper response to suffering and persecution. One is to evaluate the suffering. Peter indicates that all suffering is not necessarily God's will. He shares four evils for which we should never suffer: *murder, theft, evil-doing* and *troublesome meddling.* We must evaluate the suffering's purpose and cause, and be sure we are suffering because it is God's will.

Peter also indicates in verse 17 that we must also be prepared for suffering. When we suffer, God is chastening, testing and purifying us as members of His church at the end of the age before His coming. This concept gives us another basis upon which to evaluate our circumstances.

When we have the attitude that we are preparing for the coming of Jesus, the sting of suffering and persecution is less severe. Peter also said, *"Therefore, since Christ suffered in his body, arm yourselves also with the same attitude…."* (1 Peter 4:1) The Chinese Bible translation is even more forceful for this verse, *"Make this willingness to suffer your weapon."* No wonder so many Chinese Christians have snatched the weapon from the enemy's hand and are using it for God's victory.

5. Refuse to be ashamed.

Believers should not allow Satan to make them feel ashamed when they are suffering. Often when we suffer isolation from other believers, Satan will try to discourage and dishearten us.

If believers realize that suffering for Jesus is not unusual, and that Christians all over the world are facing similar situations, they will be encouraged. Peter says, *"However, if you suffer as a Christian, do not be ashamed, but praise God that you bear that name."* (1 Peter 4:16)

6. Respond as Christ responded.

When we suffer, we should respond as Christ responded. He did not return insult for insult. He did not threaten. He did not ask for revenge on those who wronged Him. He loved them and prayed for them. We are told to bless those who curse us, love those who hate us and pray for those who persecute us (Matthew 5:38-48). If we respond in the flesh when we suffer, our suffering may lose its value as a witness to a lost world.

Christians often report that leaders of persecution against them became believers—because of *how* Christians took the abuse. (see 1 Peter 3:8-12)

7. Refuse to retaliate.

The Bible gives illustrations of several options how one might respond to persecution—from fleeing to staying and enduring. But the Bible *never* approves retaliation against or killing of someone who initiates abuse against us because we are followers of Jesus Christ.

8. Trust God.

Peter also indicates in 1 Peter 4:19 that a disciple's attitude and response should be that of "entrusting himself to God." As said in

Chapter Thirteen, the word *entrusting* is a banking term referring to depositing or giving something for safekeeping. Peter is saying that our faithful Creator is completely capable and trustworthy in taking care of all our needs. It is so much easier to deal with suffering if we have already purposed in our hearts to turn everything over to the Lord. If we have an attitude of submission, obedience and sacrificial service, we will not be overwhelmed about the trials and persecutions He may allow.

Two biblical points are important here:

- Nothing and no one can separate the believer from Christ (see Romans 8:31-39), not even persecution. (verse 35)
- God will never permit persecution to become unbearable, for he knows exactly how much the individual can endure (1 Corinthians 10:13). However, we may choose to let our "persecution" become unbearable.

9. Stand firm and stand together.

As members of the same family, it is our responsibility to help a member of our family who is suffering.

The Body of Christ is strong when each part is closely knit together. When one part suffers, all the other members suffer. (see 1 Corinthians 12:20-27)

Members of the Persecuted Church who have been helped by others around the world have made comments like those of young Salamat Masih in Pakistan. He was charged with *writing* blasphemies against the prophet Mohammed—even though Salamat was illiterate. He was on death row but he was finally found not guilty.

During this stressful time, Salamat received cards sent from all over the world. Each card assured him that people were praying for him. "I never realized that I had so many brothers and sisters around the world," Salamat said.

Figure 11: The Truth About Persecution: Four Responses

(Adapted from Matthew 13)

1. THE OPTIMIST—"It could never happen here"

The truth about persecution falls "beside the road"—and the birds eat the seed: the Evil One comes and snatches away the seed. He says, "Our country's constitution permits freedom of religion. Look at all the churches. It could never happen here!" The Optimist filled with pride wants to "feel good" about the good news of Jesus Christ but feels confused and "misunderstands" the truth about persecution.

2. THE PRAGMATIST—"It doesn't happen anymore"

The truth about persecution falls "in rocky places"—and in the dry soil it sprouts and withers: a temporary reasoned approach without a firm rooting. The Pragmatist with all naiveté wants to "stand strong" when the storms of persecution come but falls away and "denies" the truth about persecution.

3. THE HEDONIST—"No time to think about it"

The truth about persecution falls "among thorns"—and the thorns choke out the seed: the worries of this world and the deceitfulness of riches. The Hedonist in full denial desires to "give it all to Jesus" and avoid the deceit of materialism but gives up and "chokes" the truth about persecution.

4. THE REALIST—"Keep watch because we do not know the day or hour it comes"

The truth about persecution falls "on good soil"—and yields an abundant crop: phenomenal spiritual growth and good preparation to "stand strong through the storm." The Realist invites the Holy Spirit to live within—heart, mind and soul—in order to be able to hear, understand and apply the truth about persecution.

C. INAPPROPRIATE RESPONSES TO PERSECUTION

When believers are not prepared and persecution comes, they are tempted to fall into one of the following errors:

1. Renounce their faith and join hands with the enemy

The error of denial is obvious, but it is one that Christians who are unprepared often fall into. Peter denied Christ at the time of His trial because of fear. Judas inwardly renounced his faith in Jesus and betrayed Him into the hands of the enemy. All of us have been guilty of this sin to varying degrees at different times. Remember that even this sin can be forgiven.

2. Withdraw from other Christians

The error of this response is not always outwardly obvious. The believer may be proud inwardly that he has not denied the Lord. But if he totally cuts himself off from other Christians because he is afraid, the enemy will have him where he wants him and his spiritual life will wither away. Isolated in prison, even John the Baptist began doubting Jesus (Luke 7:20). Many Christians have taken this approach when first faced with persecution. Later after realizing their error, they contacted other Christians and were restored to Christian fellowship.

3. Rebel openly and retaliate

This response will have negative effects, which may last for a long time. When believers openly rebel, their actions may seem courageous at first. But such action almost always causes them to become proud—and it almost always causes the authorities to respond violently. They may put those who are rebelling in prison or they may even kill them.

Many pastors and church members, especially in several countries of Southeast Asia, struggle with an issue closely related to rebellion and retaliation. They ask themselves, *Is it right or wrong for us to carry weapons to defend ourselves and our Christian community?*

As we consider the biblical basis of bearing arms (carrying weapons), we see that soldiers and policemen fulfilling their "civic" (public) duty do carry weapons. However, from the life, testimony, witness and teaching of Jesus throughout the New Testament, we see that He did not retaliate or use force against His enemies. (The one exception is when He drove out the money changers and sellers from the temple.)

Also the Apostle Paul taught that we must never pay back evil for evil to anyone (see Romans 12:17-21). Therefore we conclude that fighting back is almost never a valid option. We must ensure that any action we take—whether we resist or submit—is guided by the Holy Spirit.

4. Flee

When they can possibly do so, Christians often relocate to places that they think are safer than where they are. They think that this is the only way the church will be able to worship and evangelize.

When Jesus was crucified, all the disciples were afraid and fled. Later they learned that *"the safest place in the world is in the center of God's will!"* The church can not only function, it can also flourish in a hostile environment.

D. THE CIRCLE OF FREEDOM

The circle below represents our current life in free societies. Every time our freedom is violated or infringed on, our *"circle of freedom"* becomes more clouded, congested and/or restricted. Persecution is comparative, that is, it ranges from minor discrimination to doing serious harm. That harm can include refusing to allow children to go to school; refusing jobs to people; beating, mutilating or killing people or their family members; destroying property—burning churches, schools, businesses and homes of people; and so on. Each person responds differently to similar pressures. The degree that Christians believe there is persecution in their lives varies person by person—depending on what each is experiencing and that individual's response to it.

In Open Doors we have concluded that there is no scale by which one can measure harm done to people and then say: "This is persecution!" As we have met with believers going through severe persecution, we have learned that even within a nation, Christians

Figure 12: The Circle of Freedom: A Suggested Model for Understanding Persecution in Free Societies

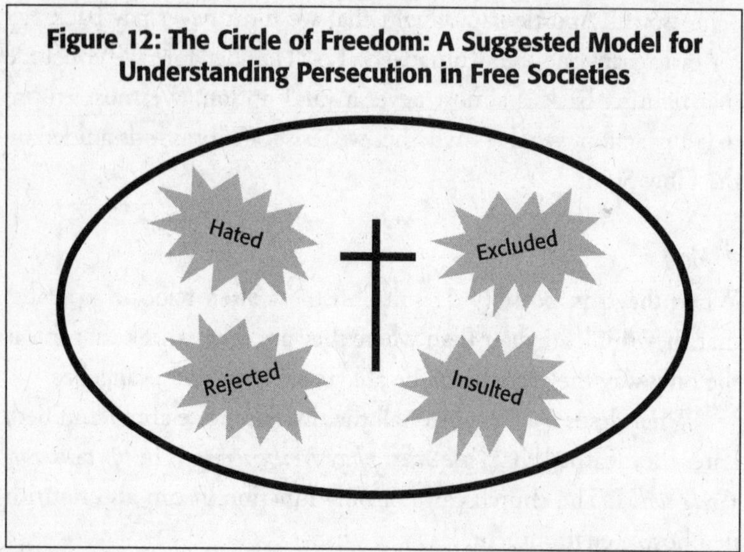

in different parts of the country may experience different degrees of hatred, exclusion, insults and rejection. In the same country, Christians may serve peacefully within government offices in one region, while others are abused and killed by religious extremists in another region.

E. CONCLUSION

Every experience God gives us, every person He puts in our path, is the perfect preparation that only He can see. But the problems and persecution you face will either defeat you or develop you—depending on how you respond to them. Unfortunately, most people fail to see how God wants to use problems and persecution for good in their lives. They respond foolishly and resent them, rather than pausing to consider what benefit they might bring.

A young woman went to her mother and told her that things were so hard for her. She did not know how she was going to make it and wanted to give up. She was tired of fighting and struggling. It seemed as soon as one problem was solved a new one arose.

Her mother took her to the kitchen. She filled three pots with water. In the first she placed carrots, in the second she placed eggs, and in the last she placed tea leaves. She let them sit and boil without saying a word. In about twenty minutes she turned off the burners. She fished the carrots out and placed them in a bowl. She pulled the eggs out and placed them in a bowl. Then she ladled the tea out into a bowl.

Turning to her daughter, she asked, "What do you see?"

"Carrots, eggs, and tea," she replied.

Her mother brought her closer and asked her to feel the carrots. She did and noted that they were soft. She then asked her to take an egg and break it. After pulling off the shell, she observed the hard-boiled egg. Finally, she asked her to sip the tea. The daughter smiled as she tasted its rich aroma.

The daughter then asked. "What does it mean, mother?"

Her mother explained that each of these objects had faced the same adversity—boiling water—but each reacted differently. The carrot went in strong, hard and unrelenting. However, after being subjected to the boiling water, it softened and became weak. The egg had been fragile. Its thin outer shell had protected its liquid interior. But, after sitting through the boiling water, its inside became hardened. The tea leaves were unique, however. After they were in the boiling water they had changed the water.

"Which are you?" she asked her daughter. "When adversity knocks on your door, how do you respond? Are you a carrot, an egg, or tea leaves?"

Think of this: *Which am I?*

Am I the carrot that seems strong, but with pain and adversity, do I wilt and become soft and lose my strength?

Am I the egg that starts with a malleable heart, but changes with the heat? Did I have a fluid spirit, but after a loved one's death, a relationship breakup, a financial hardship or some other trial, have

I become hardened and stiff? Does my shell look the same, but on the inside am I am bitter and tough with a stiff spirit and a hardened heart?

Or am I like the tea leaves? The tea leaves actually change the hot water, the very circumstance that brings the pain. When the water gets hot, it releases the fragrance and flavor. If I am like the tea leaves, when things are at their worst, I get better and change the situation around me through Christlikeness.[1]

STUDY GUIDE/DISCUSSION QUESTIONS

PASTOR FOCUS

1. (Read the story again about Abdul at the beginning of this chapter.) You live in a country like Abdul's with relative freedom, although Christians are a small minority and despised. A new regime of anti-Christian extremists comes to power and threatens to eliminate the Christian community. They begin by unofficially encouraging local extremists to burn down the church buildings. As well, Christians begin being laid off or fired from their jobs.

   a. How would you respond as a pastor of a church in the region? What are your options? What would be necessary to implement each option?

   b. Discuss Abdul's choices and whether he made the best, appropriate and biblical decision.

2. Does the Bible distinguish between a believer's civic duty and personal duty in bearing or not bearing arms? Discuss together with specific references. Is it ever right to use weapons to protect yourself or your family? What does the Bible teach? Discuss with the group Romans 12:17-21.

WOMEN'S FOCUS

What should your response be as a Christian to "encourage one another"?

a. How do **you** respond to strong opposition in a Christlike manner?

b. How does our suffering increase our communion with Christ and our understanding of what He suffered for us?

c. Should Christians ever hide or keep their faith secret to protect themselves and their families and jobs?

d. How do some Christians bring persecution on themselves needlessly? Are there examples in your area?

YOUTH FOCUS

1. Explain what each of the following verses means to you.

Choose from one of the following options:

surprised, stand, thankfulness, source, rejoice, ashamed, trust, respond

- Don't be ________________________. (1 Peter 4:12-13)
- ________________________. (Matthew 5:11-12)
- Pray with ________________________. (Philippians 4:6)
- Evaluate the ____________________ of suffering. (1 Peter 4:15-19)
- Don't be ____________________ of suffering. (1 Peter 4:16)
- ________________________ to suffering as Christ did. (Matthew 5:38-48)
- ________________ God. (1 Peter 4:19)
- __________________ firm and ______________together. (1 Corinthians 12:20-27)

2. How does Hebrews 11 dispel the myth that if you just have enough faith you can avoid suffering and persecution?

MEN'S FOCUS

What are primary responses believers who are unprepared for persecution tend to use when faced with persecution? What is the biblical concern with each response?

Choose from the following options:
join hands, rebellion, isolation, flee, carry, hide, withdraw

Deny: Renounce their faith and ___________ ___________ with the enemy.

Hide: Totally ___________ their faith and ___________ into ___________.

Rebel: In despair, strike out in ___________.

Retaliate: For protection, they ___________ arms or weapons—and use them!

Flee: ___________ (thinking it is the only option).

SECTION FIVE

The Victorious Church and Family

Essence, Function and Form

16

THE SIMPLICITY OF THE CHURCH

Essence, Function and Form

And he is the head of the body, the church; he is the beginning and the firstborn from among the dead, so that in everything he might have the supremacy.

COLOSSIANS 1:18

Rene looked carefully both ways as he turned the corner. No one seemed to be watching. Wiping the perspiration from his forehead, he glanced at his watch. He was five minutes early. He walked slowly around the block a second time to arrive at the large gate at exactly 7:14. He pressed the bell three times: short...long...short. It was the newly changed code to indicate he was a fellow believer. The gate opened and closed quickly as Rene slipped inside. In two hours time there would be several hundred believers gathered secretly in the basement for fellowship.

Rene sat quietly waiting for the others. He remembered reading in a magazine about a small group in China that gathered weekly in the back room of a small store to worship together. It was the era of the infamous Cultural Revolution. Since the believers could easily be overheard by anyone entering the store, they "sang" hymns together by someone first whispering the name of the song. Then they would silently move their lips and simply think of the words and music.

He chuckled out loud as he recalled Pastor Wally saying, "We are an underground church like the believers behind the Bamboo Curtain. The difference is that we can praise in full voice because the facilities are soundproofed. Not even our closest neighbour can hear us."

This is a description of a church group in Saudi Arabia—a country that has not had an official church in over 1,400 years. And yet many believers meet together secretly and at great risk all over the country.

What is the church? To understand its essence, function and form, consider the concept of "fishing." What is required to have fishing? Some may immediately think: a fishing pole and a hook. While helpful, these two items are not always necessary. Whatever is necessary every time in order to have "fishing" would be considered the *"essence."*

- *The Essence of Fishing* is whatever the minimum essentials are in order to achieve fishing: a person (or fisher) to do the fishing—and a fish. With no fisher there are only fish in the water, and with no fish there is no fishing, only a person spending time by the water. *Essence never changes.*
- *The Function of Fishing* is its purpose: "to catch fish." This is the same function every time whether the person is fishing for pleasure, for employment or to escape from other responsibilities. The function fulfills the purpose of the essence. *Function never changes.*
- *The Forms of Fishing* can be as varied as you wish as long as they do one thing: fulfill the function, which is to catch fish. Different countries permit different items and different methods: fishhooks, spears, nets, dynamite, drain the pond,

and so on. We are not concerned about laws for the moment, only principles: to fulfill the function and meet the essence. *Form, unlike essence and function, can always change.*

We can apply the same principles to the essence, function and form of the church.

- *The Essence of a church* is its minimum essentials: committed believers gathered in the name of Jesus Christ.
- *The Function of a church* is fivefold: to *evangelize* (Matthew 28:19); to *disciple* or train those who are evangelized (Matthew 28:20); to *minister to* or serve people showing God's love (Matthew 22:39; Ephesians 4:12); to *fellowship* together (Ephesians 2:19; Galatians 6:10); and to *worship.* (Matthew 4:10; John 4:23)
- *The Forms of a church* are as varied as you wish—meet in a building, in a field, in a home; meet on Sunday, Saturday or Monday afternoon…. We are not concerned about traditions for the moment, only principle: *Does the form fulfill the function and meet the essence?*

To understand the makeup of the church, we must also be able to clearly distinguish the essence, function and form of the church. Essence and function never change but the resulting forms can change regularly.

A. ESSENCE: BASIC REQUIREMENTS OF A CHURCH

The Scriptures give us three requirements that never change for the "essence" of a church. They are:

1. Personal faith in Christ

Individuals must trust in Jesus Christ as Lord and Savior. When they do, the result is the new birth: *"unless one is born again, he cannot see the Kingdom of God"* (see John 3:1-17; 2 Corinthians 5:17). By prayer, they can then go directly into God's holy presence.

2. Two or more sharing faith

One person cannot be a church, since a church is made up of *living stones* and is a body with *members*. (1 Peter 2:5; 1 Corinthians 12:12; Matthew 18:20)

3. Commitment to Jesus Christ and to each other

God draws certain believers together in a special relationship that the Bible calls being *built together* (Ephesians 2:22). Christ Himself brings Christians together in this relationship and directs them to care for each other (1 Corinthians 12:25-26). A church such as this is the work of God and is not merely a human organization.

Christ is the head of the church and we are the Body of Christ. Without commitment and submission to Him, there can be no church.

As we consider this teaching on the church, we can see that there are many misunderstandings about the church. It is not a building; it is not a human organization; it is not headed by a human being; and it does not require a particular group of "ordained" persons or "clergy."

This does not mean that the church should not "ordain" leaders, or "separate unto the Gospel" those who have God-given abilities to lead the church. Nor does it mean that people with no training or experience should be given responsibility in the church, though at times this may be necessary. When those who show evidence of spiritual gifts and who seriously study the Word of God are ordained, the church can greatly profit by their having been ordained. But when ordination becomes a badge of superiority or a religious "class" division, it is a hindrance to the church.

Ordained people are to be *"servants"* of the church. As servants, they are important and valuable, but they are not essential to the survival of the church in times of persecution. Such leaders, when recognized by the government, may be required to carry out activities normally found in institutional churches in free societies, for example, performing weddings and funerals. Many times these activities required by the government are not identified in the Bible as basic functions of the church.

The first thing we notice in the Scriptures about our lives as believers is that we are expected to "live" our faith. The miracle of the new birth and the presence of the Holy Spirit in our hearts should be evident in the way we live our everyday lives. Basic principles such as submission to Christ and commitment to well-being of other believers are not to be just ideas. They are to affect the way Christians live.

A women's group studying this material in Australia noted, "As the Body of Christ, all believers have a mandate to respond to God's calling and serve in the church accordingly, with or without the contribution of ordained leaders."[1]

B. FUNCTION: THE PURPOSES OF THE CHURCH

Jesus Christ ordained five functions for His church to accomplish in our work for Him. We are to *evangelize* (Matthew 28:19); to *disciple* or train those who are evangelized (Matthew 28:20); to *minister to* or serve people demonstrating God's love (Matthew 22:39; Ephesians 4:12); to *fellowship* together (Ephesians 2:19; Galatians 6:10); and to *worship* together (Matthew 4:10; John 4:23). In the Bible, there is not a priority order for these five purposes. They are all equally important.

1. Evangelism

Once we know Christ as Lord and Savior, we will want to share our wonderful experience with those we love. Sometimes we find it hard or embarrassing to share the Gospel with our relatives and friends. But since we believe that all who are without Christ will suffer for eternity separated from God, and because we love them, we must tell them. No matter how oppressive the culture or the political situation is, we must tell them.

People who are determined to do so can always find ways to share the Good News with their friends and loved ones in a loving, respectful way. Telling God's plan of salvation to others is an important evidence of our relationship with God. It is also a primary function of the church.

2. Discipleship

Once we have seen a person come to know Christ, we are responsible to make sure that person grows in the Lord. Many Christians expect that a new convert will learn from the regular preaching services. So they take no additional responsibility. In some cultures, if a person saves someone's life, that person becomes responsible for the one saved. This is a good concept for the Christian.

Since the Bible is so important to Christian growth, many Christians want to immediately give a Bible to anyone they lead to the Lord. In some countries, such as Russia or China, Christians have faithfully carried on for years without Bibles. But it has been very difficult for them. They have had to depend on Scripture verses that one of the church members memorized earlier, or heard on a Christian radio broadcast. The desperate hunger for the Bible among Christians who have been cut off from it for an extended period dramatically illustrates just how important the Bible is to the Christian life.

Once we have led someone into new life in Christ, we share a responsibility to make sure that person learns what the Bible teaches about the Christian life.

Believers in restricted countries find clever and creative ways to protect their Bibles. Some tear the binding apart so that each book of the Bible becomes a separate, small pamphlet. Those trying to destroy Bibles would not recognize these pamphlets as the Bible. This also makes it possible for many people to use one Bible at the same time. Whatever the circumstances, it is important that believers, whether new believers or those who've known Christ for many years, continue to read and study the Bible.

When the Holy Spirit brings a group of believers together as a church, the five basic functions of a church will be evident. Small informal churches often enjoy getting together to worship, minister and fellowship, but then find it difficult to teach and evangelize. But these churches must learn to teach and evangelize.

When formal training centers are closed by the authorities, it is especially imperative that local churches take seriously their responsibilities to teach (2 Timothy 2:2). This teaching may have to be done on a one-to-one basis when a mature Christian and a young Christian can get together.

The Bible gives many examples of leaders trained in this way. Besides the clear example of Christ teaching His disciples, Barnabas taught Mark (Acts 12:25; 15:39); Priscilla and Aquila helped Apollos (Acts 18:24-26); and Paul trained Timothy. (Acts 16:1-3)

Paul gives a detailed approach on how to "disciple" a young believer. He taught first by example (1 Corinthians 4:16), then lived with his disciples, sharing all he had with them (Acts 20:34). His relationship with them was not just "student-teacher." Rather, he became personally involved with them in ministry (1 Timothy 1:1-2). He gave them responsibilities while they were still in training, and also kept in close contact with them after they became leaders themselves. (1 and 2 Timothy, and Titus)

3. Ministry

When we *"minister"* or serve, we are showing or demonstrating God's love to others by helping to meet their needs and heal their hurts in the name of Jesus. Each time you reach out in love to others you are ministering to them. The church's job is *"for the equipping of the saints for the work of ministry"* (Ephesisans 4:12, NKJV), or as the NIV says, *"to prepare God's people for works of service."*

Jesus commanded us to preach the Gospel, heal the sick and cast out demons (see Mark16:15-18). One preacher said: "God does not want to be included in *our* plans. He wants us to be included in *His* plans." We need to be aware of the spiritual needs of both fellow believers and non-believers and try to help them at every opportunity. Saying something encouraging to or doing something kind for a struggling friend may be the deciding factor in whether or not that friend is able to stand against the enemy.

4. Fellowship

As Christians, we are called to belong, not just to believe. We are not meant to be loners but true members of His body—a real part of Jesus' family. Therefore, it is important for Christians to spend time together to talk about their spiritual lives, encourage each other and have fellowship.

Satan brings all his efforts to bear on Christians to prevent them from fellowshipping together. He realizes that believers need to help and strengthen each other, so he will try to prevent it by trying to cause Christians to be indifferent about meeting together (Hebrews 10:24-25). Or he may try to bring about difficult circumstances that would discourage them from meeting together.

The Lord can use even informal or casual meetings to strengthen Christians, especially when formal meetings and large group fellowships are forbidden. Though going to large meetings may be very encouraging, Christians can receive more help one-to-one in small "cell" groups where they can discuss their needs in depth.

5. Worship

It is a privilege and responsibility to worship God. Worship begins when the Holy Spirit enters our being and then takes more and more control of our lives. We worship the Lord because of who He is, because of His creation and because He has redeemed us and continued to be with us. Worship flows from the heart of a grateful and thankful person.

Worship is a matter of attitude. It is a way of life. *"Offer your bodies as living sacrifices, holy and pleasing to God—this is your spiritual act of worship"* (Romans 12:1). Every believer should worship the Lord privately, as well as, whenever possible, gather with other believers to worship. This may be expressed outwardly in prayer, various bodily positions (such as, standing with hands raised, kneeling or even lying), singing, clapping, and so on. For most believers, music is an important part of worship. The form of worship should reflect the believer's cultural methods of showing adoration as long as it does not conflict with biblical guidelines (for example, offering sacrifices).

The Bible makes it clear that believers should worship, and why they should worship. It is obvious that many practices used in pagan religions—bowing to images, self-inflicted punishment of the body, sacrifices of blood—have no place in the church.

Worship in Scripture revolves around praising God—an act of the will that should not be related to feelings or circumstances. In other words, we should praise God even when we feel sad and discouraged because things seem to be going wrong. When we do so, we are submitting to His divine will and we bring pleasure to Him. (Psalm 67:3; Hebrews 13:15; Isaiah 12:1)

C. THE EXAMPLE OF THE EARLY CHURCH

The early church, in spite of intense persecution, fulfilled the five basic functions of the church.

1. Evangelism

When the church first came into being, the authorities permitted believers to preach in public. Peter preached to thousands on the

Day of Pentecost (Acts 2:1-41) and also in the temple area following the healing of the lame beggar (Acts 3:1-26). But later, the believers were ordered to stop talking about Jesus. When they did not obey that order (Acts 4:1-31), persecution began.

Therefore, believers gradually began ministering in private homes rather than in public places (Acts 5:42). And many fled from Jerusalem. As they were scattered, they took the Gospel with them (Acts 8:4). Note that they were ordinary lay Christians, not the apostles (Acts 8:1). As a result of being scattered, they became missionaries, witnessing person-to-person without depending on an institutional church. Rather than persecution destroying the church, it caused it to expand.

It was at this time that Peter was led to go to Joppa to see Cornelius and, there in his home, speak to him and his relatives and friends (Acts 10). Also, about this time, Paul was converted and began his ministry of declaring Jesus to the Gentiles. He usually preached first in the synagogues, but when his message was rejected there, he began teaching wherever anyone would listen. In Corinth, he went to a private home (Acts 18:1-7). In Ephesus, he rented a hall (Acts 19:1-10). In Philippi, he taught on a riverbank. (Acts 16:12-13)

The early Christians witnessed to the saving power of Jesus whenever and wherever possible. As far as we know, they quoted Scripture from memory since copies of the Scriptures were scarce at that time. Those in the early church depended heavily on the Word of God. Christians under pressure today must do the same when they evangelize. All believers must present Christ, depending only on the Scriptures and the direction and power of the Holy Spirit.

2. Discipleship

In addition to evangelistic teaching about salvation in Jesus Christ, the early church was involved in teaching (discipling) new believers.

We are not told where they met to hold the training sessions, but we know that they were no longer welcome in the synagogues. So they probably met in private homes.

The account preserved for us in the book of Acts shows that after Christians presented Christ to people, they made an effort to follow up with a teaching ministry. The Jerusalem church sent Barnabas to Antioch for that purpose. (Acts 11:25-26)

Paul made a return trip to the cities he had successfully evangelized to strengthen and encourage the converts (Acts 14:21-23), and later he stopped again on his way to Jerusalem. (Acts 20:6-8)

One-on-one teaching is vital to a church in a hostile environment. It can be done at various places and at different times. Group meetings must usually be kept to a certain length of time, but one-on-one teaching can be any length of time. And it doesn't matter if the class is small—the "class" may include only one person. What is important is that the teaching be based on the Word of God to encourage and strengthen brothers and sisters in Christ in their Christian walk.

3. Ministry

Acts 6:1-4 shows one way the church in Jerusalem ministered to people in need: they had a *"daily distribution of food."* When the Grecian Jews in the church complained over how the distribution of food to their widows was being handled, the food distribution ministry was threatened. But after a church meeting was held and deacons were assigned to oversee the distribution, there was no longer a problem.

The Bible does not say that food was distributed only to the church people. We can assume that the church was also ministering to the community by serving food to them. Back in Acts 2:47, we read that they were *"praising God and enjoying the favor of all the people."*

On several occasions, churches outside of Jerusalem ministered to the Jerusalem church: they sent money to the poor in the church.

The modern practice of churches in one country paying the expenses for missionaries to go to another country or for providing Bibles and training materials follows this example.

Tithing—giving a percentage of one's earnings to the church—enables the church to carry on its ministry of helping and supporting people with needs. (Acts 4:34-35; Leviticus 27:30-32; Hebrews 7:4-5)

4. Fellowship

Examples of fellowship in the early church are more difficult to identify than examples of evangelism and teaching—because fellowship is basically a heart attitude toward one another.

Institutional churches today may have "fellowship meetings" in their weekly schedule, but whether or not real fellowship takes place depends on the heart attitude of those who attend those meetings. In the early church, fellowship was closely linked to gathering together for a "fellowship meal." An important part of that meal was the "breaking of bread" for the Lord's Supper. (Acts 2:42, 46)

We learn a negative lesson from the church at Corinth. The "fellowship" there was in sharp contrast to the loving fellowship in the Jerusalem church. Their "love feasts" (fellowship meals) were filled with strife instead of fellowship (1 Corinthians 11:17-30). In Corinth, even though the people met together, they had no fellowship. Paul writes that there were "divisions" among them. Today divisions in the church often cause church splits—church members become angry and a church becomes two churches, with the members not speaking to one another.

While the Jerusalem church had been able to settle their problems in love, the Corinthians were even taking their fellow believers before the pagan law courts (1 Corinthians 6:1-8). They had difficulty completing a project—gathering money to send a gift to the suffering Christians in Jerusalem (2 Corinthians 8:6, 10-11; 9:15). That isn't surprising. Since they didn't have real fellowship with each other and weren't concerned for one another, it is unlikely they would be concerned about strangers in Jerusalem (see 1 John 4:20). Paul's letters to Corinth deal at length with these problems.

The bond of fellowship among the New Testament Christians was based on a spirit of oneness, love and concern. Their relationship did not depend on meetings, organizations, programs and activities. They helped one another, bore one another's burdens and prayed for one another. This kind of fellowship thrived in spite of everything the Roman government could do.

The stronger the opposition, the more fellowship means to those in the Body of Christ. The Bible says the world will know we are Christians by our love (John 13:34). Love for one another can be one of the greatest outward expressions of faith for any church.

The fellowship meal offered an opportunity to those who had been blessed with material goods to minister to others by sharing their abundance. Sharing is an essential part of the love and concern that make up true fellowship. (see Acts 2:41-42; 44-47, 4:34-35)

5. Worship

Worship is recognizing and accepting God's glory, holiness and worth. An act of worship is an expression of this recognition.

Worship in the early church was simply believers "pouring out" their thanks from hearts that rejoiced in the Lord despite their circumstances. When early believers prayerfully together remembered Jesus and His sacrificial death on the cross for their sins, they were worshipping.

A group of Christians in hostile surroundings can celebrate the Lord's Supper without being limited to a certain building, a special time or a prescribed program. This type of worship *cannot be easily stopped* by enemies of the church.

The Jerusalem church met for *"the breaking of bread"* in various homes (Acts 2:41-47). The fellowship in Troas gathered in an upper room on the first day of the week *"to break bread"* (Acts 20:6-8). The large church at Corinth gathered occasionally to observe the *"Lord's Supper."* It was their abuse of this practice that caused Paul to write and give guidelines for such observances. (1 Corinthians 11:17-30)

In Luke 22:19, we read that Jesus *"took bread, gave thanks and broke it, and gave it to them* [the disciples], *saying, 'This is my body given for you; do this in remembrance of me.' "*

Jesus commanded the church to observe both "the breaking of bread" and baptism (Luke 22:19; Matthew 28:19). These are fundamental to the life of the church as members live out their obedience to Christ. Both should be consistently observed.

Both of these sacraments reveal all five functions of the church. They testify to our position in Christ (evangelism). They help others to understand the basis for our position in Christ (discipleship). They bring Christians together in a shared experience (fellowship). They focus our attention upon Christ (worship). And we go out from these sacraments to newness of life with a mandate to minister in and through the love of Jesus (ministry).

There are scriptural references to other times of worship such as Peter's prayer (Acts 4:23-28), and Paul and Silas' experience in prison (Acts 16:23-25). Worship was as frequent and spontaneous to the early church as it was to Moses and David in the Old Testament. But it was a simple expression of adoration and praise. There was no requirement of time, location, form, or even specific leaders.

D. FORMS: THE PRACTICES OF THE CHURCH

The Bible does not say much about the forms through which the five functions of the church may be expressed.

The places where churches meet and their activities may vary. Only churches in financially strong, unrestricted societies are able to have big buildings; video-cafés; complex programs; social activities; and huge budgets that provide for schools, hospitals, and orphanages. Although the Lord has blessed these activities in many places in the world, we must recognize that they are not essential to the existence of the church. In some countries, they are forbidden by the government. In other countries, the local economic situation makes it impossible.

The forms most widely used by institutional churches today have drifted far from the simplicity found in the New Testament.

A number of years ago, for example, some Vietnamese leaders thought that their lack of funds was the cause of the slow growth of Christianity there. On one occasion, the following conversation was overheard:

"Do you have communists in your part of the country?" the observer asked.

"Most assuredly. They are there," the Vietnamese leader replied.

"Are they growing in numbers and influence?" he then asked.

The leader hesitated momentarily, then admitted sadly, "Yes, they are growing very fast."

"Can you show me their meeting places and schools or introduce me to their leaders?" the observer continued.

"Certainly not," the leader said in disgust. "If they are known, they will be arrested."

"You mean they are secret, without buildings or property and still they grow in number?" the observer asked in amazement.

"Yes, you could say that," the leader responded.

"Then it must be that their growing influence does not depend on such things. Since they are wrong in their beliefs and *still* grow without money and buildings, why do you think the church of Jesus Christ needs them?" the man concluded.[2]

The New Testament church had none of these things, but they turned their world upside down. (Acts 17:6)

The early Christians did not confuse the church's functions with the church's forms. If they had done so, the church would have died in the bondage of Jewish legalism. The early churches were not burdened with big buildings, nor were they hindered by the lack of them. When they were permitted to do so, they met in public places. But when they were not permitted to do so, they met together in different houses at different times.

The Apostle Paul taught in the synagogues as long as the synagogues were open to him. When he was stopped from teaching in the synagogues, he began to teach in private homes. Or sometimes he met with others at a riverbank or in the market place, and taught or evangelized here. There were no signs to point believers from other communities to a place of worship, but believers were able to find others to fellowship with. The importance of such simple structure is evident in Acts 13:1-4.

The church of Antioch did not acknowledge any organizational authority between it and God. When the Holy Spirit led Paul and Barnabas out as missionaries, the Antioch church did not have to ask permission of someone else. And they were not burdened by long-range programs. The church leaders just prayed with them and sent them out. In those days, there were no mission boards, but there *was* great missionary activity.

Evangelists and missionaries had very little money, but as they ministered, local congregations met their needs. There were no seminaries and Bible schools, but the truth was committed to faithful people who knew the teachings of Christ, and they taught others (2 Timothy 2:2). Church leadership was valuable in selecting and sending out missionaries under the authority of the church. God has established the church and its leaders for our protection and spiritual covering.

The church can exist and carry on its functions of evangelism, discipleship, ministry, fellowship and worship without depending on physical forms and traditional methods. This vitally important truth tells us that any group of believers established by God is able to survive victoriously in hostile environments. When forms are confused with the functions of the church, these forms can become obstacles.

In many places in the world today, the forms most common to Christians living in free societies are forbidden. Some think that this means the church cannot exist in those places. Not so! Since the time of the Roman Empire, many governments have successfully suppressed outward forms and methods, but none have been able to destroy the church. When we commit ourselves to the biblical essence of the spiritual church, carrying out its functions in simple forms, we and our fellow believers will be a church that can survive victoriously under any circumstances.

Church growth may often bring persecution, but persecution does not always guarantee church growth.

E. THE HOUSE CHURCH CELL STRUCTURE

We have mentioned that the five functions of the church, especially discipleship, fellowship and worship—were frequently carried out in private homes. But the early church was not limited just to meeting in homes. At various times, different believers also used the temple, synagogues, lecture halls, open forums, riverbanks, ships and other places, especially to evangelize. It is encouraging to realize that all five functions of a church can be accomplished in a small house or apartment. In many restricted countries, this is the only available place. The New Testament specifically refers to five "house churches," and there were probably more. (Romans 16:3-5, 23; 1 Corinthians 16:19; Colossians 4:15; Philemon 2)

A house church has many advantages. No rent money has to be paid or no money spent to buy an additional building. Meeting as a house church encourages fellowship and friendliness. It does not attract unwanted attention from authorities and the meeting can easily be moved from one house to another.

The biggest problem is that space is limited. But this forces the church to meet in small groups, which provides opportunity for closer friendship, better accountability and more meaningful ministry. If a group becomes too large to meet in a home, it divides into two homes and the multiplication continues.

A disadvantage of house churches is the lack of fellowship among the different cell groups. In a highly restrictive society, this can also be an advantage. If the authorities find out about any one house church, this doesn't put the other house churches in danger. In some less restricted societies, the house churches can sometimes fellowship with believers of different groups in joint meetings. And occasionally, they are even able to join and celebrate in large, city-wide meetings.

In one country, for example, during a major festival, several house churches agreed to picnic in a particular part of a public park at the same time. Though they did not worship openly, the Christians were encouraged to see many other secret believers all together.

As we look again at the experience of the early church, we see that following the first few days of public ministry, persecution began. The Jerusalem church soon became too large to meet in one place. When the authorities ordered the apostles to stop preaching, Peter and John reported their threats to their own group or *"to their own people.... When they heard this, they raised their voices together in prayer to God."* (Acts 4:23-24)

After the death of Stephen, the church became more careful. For example, when Paul came to Jerusalem, Scripture says *"he tried to join the disciples, but they were all afraid of him, not believing that he really was a disciple."* (Acts 9:26)

However, in spite of their precautions, James (the brother of John) was arrested and killed. Then Peter was seized and put in prison. The church prayed earnestly for Peter's release, but they did not all meet in one place to pray for him.

When an angel miraculously released him, Peter went to the home of John Mark, where he apparently thought that believers would have gathered to pray. When Peter arrived there, he found that the door was locked, and believers were inside praying. He knocked but they were cautious about opening the door. He too was careful. After telling the group how God had sent an angel to bring him out of jail, Peter left and went to another place (Acts 12). It seems evident that those who are cautious are not cowardly or weak in faith.

Later, when Paul and Barnabas met with the Jerusalem church, elders were present as well as apostles (Acts 15:4, 22; 21:17-19). Perhaps these men were the leaders of the many house churches scattered throughout Jerusalem.

The church may be able to have a public witness through those leaders known to the government. At the same time, the leaders may be able to quietly encourage small house churches scattered throughout the area, where the five functions of the church are effectively working. In this way, the public witness of the church is merely a small part of the larger picture.

F. CELL (SMALL GROUP) CHURCHES

In 1982, the communists overthrew the government of Ethiopia and persecution of the church began. The buildings and property of one Christian denomination were confiscated. Many church leaders were imprisoned and their members were forbidden to meet. Christians went underground without leaders, without buildings, without the opportunity to meet together publicly or continue any of their public programs. In their secret meetings, they could not even sing out loud for fear of someone reporting them to the authorities.

Ten years later, the communist government was removed, and this allowed the Christians to come out of hiding. They were amazed to find their denomination's pre-persecution membership of 5,000 members had grown to more than 50,000 members in that ten-year period.

As in China, the Ethiopia house-church model reveals a great strength in small groups or "cells"—especially in evangelism. And this model is not just for restricted areas of the world. The largest church in the world, pastored by Rev. Dr. David Cho in Seoul, Korea—with more than 800,000 members—is also a cell-based church. It has a strong focus on all five functions, especially evangelism. Dr. Cho believes that cell groups are the best setting for introducing people to Jesus Christ. His church believes that new Christians, "new babes in Christ," should become spiritual "fathers" within six months. And they believe that cell groups offer the best training environment. Cell churches allow for not only church growth by addition, but also for church growth by multiplication.

A healthy church is the best church in good times and in bad times. Thus we need to realize that a church is healthy when it truly fulfills all the five functions as seen in the early church. (Acts 2:42-47)

When members only attend a weekly public congregation or a worship meeting, the church usually does not grow. Thus cell groups are vital to having a balanced church or, as one person calls it, a "two-winged" church. By that he meant that without small groups or "cells," a church is incomplete—as a bird trying to fly on one wing would be.

The ideal number for a cell group is ten to twelve people. When the group grows to over twelve people, it is ready to divide and grow again. Someone recommended that the group always have an empty chair in their meeting. That chair is for the next person who has just passed from being an unbeliever to being a believer. The empty chair is a continual reminder to the cell group members of the function of evangelism. It often directs focus of the praying at the meeting.

A church functions well when church responsibilities are shared. *Shared responsibility* means that the pastor is not seen as the *only* capable leader. If a church is to grow both in difficult times and in good times, lay people must be trained. Our Lord never intended His church to depend completely on just one person.

Adopting a cell group system aids the persecuted church. But it appears that the fastest growing churches today, even in free societies, adopt some form of cell group system.

Evangelizing our community is impossible without the whole church becoming involved. Leaders and pastors must take time to train the members. They must learn to delegate responsibilities to others.

One way to prepare for difficult times is to make every member of the church realize that each has a unique role and purpose in the Kingdom of God.

A pastor in Vietnam prepared for his arrest—which he was sure would happen—by carefully training the thirty members in his church to take roles as leaders. The day came when he was arrested and sent away to a remote prison camp. While there, he was encouraged to hear that his church had grown to more than three hundred members.

Our God is able to meet your needs and bless in many ways. Begin now to look for new and simpler ways to express your faith. Trust the Holy Spirit to guide you.

STUDY GUIDE/DISCUSSION QUESTIONS

PASTOR FOCUS

1. **Evangelism:** When the church is restricted, new and creative ways of evangelism and worship are used. In one restricted country, church members hired a bus, then invited relatives

and friends to go to the beach. On the bus, using a handheld loudspeaker, the pastor preached to the "captive audience." At the beach, everyone continued to talk and fellowship. And also those who received Christ while on the bus were baptized! As a pastor, how would you respond in your spirit to this method of evangelizing? Do you feel this pastor violated your principles of sensitivity?

2. Describe the differences between the Jerusalem church and the Corinthian church. (see 1 Corinthians 6:1-8; 2 Corinthians 8:6, 10-11; 9:15)

Jerusalem Church **Corinthian Church**

3. As we saw in previous chapters, churches in free societies usually express their faith through the institutional pattern. Therefore, that is the primary form familiar to most Christians. And it is easy for a repressive government to eliminate that form. Consider some of the options **you** would initiate under the rule of a repressive regime.

WOMEN'S FOCUS

What is the role and responsibility of the institutional church in a free society?

YOUTH FOCUS

What is "the church" according to the following passages of Scripture? What does each illustration mean to **you** today?

- 1 Corinthians 3:9

- 1 Corinthians 12:13, 27

- Hebrews 3:6

- Revelation 19:7-9

- Revelation 21:2, 9

- Ephesians 5:22-33

- Matthew 16:13-18

MEN'S FOCUS

1. Describe the Essence, Function and Form(s) of **your** church.

2. Who may belong to "the church" according to these verses?

   - 1 Peter 2:5, 9

   - Hebrews 4:16

3. What are the three minimum requirements for a church?
   - John 3:1-17; 2 Corinthians 5:17
     ______________ __________ "in Christ."

   - 1 Peter 2:5; 2 Corinthians 12:12; Matthew 18:20
     At least two _____________ ______________.

   - Ephesians 2:22; 1 Corinthians 12:25-26
     Committed to __________ and to __________ ___________.

4. What commitment should Christians make to each other?

5. One church leader defines evangelism as "presenting the Gospel in such a clear way that the hearer must either accept or reject Christ." Do you agree? Explain why or how **your** family has/has not been evangelized.

6. What is the best way to stimulate fellow Christians to do the work of evangelism?

7. How do you evangelize in a community where it is forbidden? How do you evangelize when you have no spiritual materials?

8. How can *small groups* help a *cell church* do the following things?
   - Serve one another — Galatians 5:13
   - Accept one another — Romans 15:7
   - Forgive one another — Colossians 3:13
   - Greet one another — Romans 16:16
   - Bear one another's burdens — Galatians 6:2
   - Be devoted to one another — Romans 12:10
   - Honor one another — Romans 12:10

• Teach one another	Romans 15:14
• Submit to one another	Ephesians 5:21
• Encourage one another	1 Thessalonians 5:11

17

THE CHURCH IN OPERATION

Flexible, Unstoppable and Growing

To Philemon our dear friend and fellow worker, to Apphia our sister, to Archippus our fellow soldier and to the church that meets in your home.
PHILEMON 1:2

While having lunch in (then) famine-stricken Marxist Ethiopia, a visiting pastor from the West said, "It must be terrible for you and your churches to live under communism."

The local leader looked around carefully, and then spoke softly about the severe hardships and unjust imprisonment of Christians. "These sufferings have refined the faith of our people. In our history, more people have come to faith in hard times than in easy times."

He continued, "I have been to your country, and I know your churches also have serious problems and temptations. I know that many Christians in your country are consumed by materialism and have little concern for the poor. Many Christian families are breaking up. Some churches try to attract people with entertainment.... I felt sorrow in what I saw and heard."

The Ethiopian church leader concluded, "I really am not sure whose church is better off, yours or ours!"[1]

A. FLEXIBILITY WITHIN THE CHURCH

The disciples complained to the Lord Jesus that a man who was not of their group was ministering in His name. The disciples had forbidden him to continue, but Jesus said, *"Do not stop him...for whoever is not against you is for you."* (Luke 9:50) Peter found this a very hard lesson to learn. The Lord had to deal with Peter very specifically through a vision and a dramatic experience before he could say, *"I now realize how true it is that God does not show favoritism but accepts men from every nation who fear him and do what is right."* (Acts 10:34-35)

The Apostle Paul had more to say about this idea. He summarized his teaching when he said, *"Who are you to judge someone else's servant?"* (Romans 14:4) And, *"You then, why do you judge your brother?...for we will all stand before God's judgment seat."* (Romans 14:10) He even approved of the preaching of some others who were preaching the Gospel with wrong motives (Philippians 1:12-18). Scripture clearly teaches that we should not cause divisions in the body because other leaders lead differently than we or our leaders do. (1 Corinthians 1:11-17)

We must be very careful about rejecting someone just because they do not serve the Lord the same way we do.

If we quietly go about the work the Lord has given us, we need not be overly concerned about how others feel led to serve Him.

People in the Bible responded to oppression in different ways.

- **Samuel:** When the Lord told him to anoint the future king, Samuel was afraid. So the Lord showed him how to cover what he was doing without telling a lie. (1 Samuel 16:1-5)
- **Elijah:** On one occasion, Elijah boldly defied the king (1 Kings 17:1). On another he was led of the Lord to run and hide. (1 Kings 17:3)
- **Esther:** In this beautiful Old Testament account, Esther became the queen, and did not even tell anyone that she was Jewish. But at the proper time, she did a very important service to her people, even risking her life. (Esther 7:1-4)
- **Daniel:** In the book of Daniel, Daniel and his three friends boldly faced death in defying the king, but God protected them. (Daniel 3 and 6)
- **Jesus:** In John's Gospel account, Jesus avoided the Jewish rulers and even hid Himself on one occasion. (John 8:59; 11:54)
- **Peter and John:** The authorities ordered Peter and John not to preach, but they refused to obey. (Acts 4:18-20)
- **Paul:** In the face of opposition, Paul was especially flexible. Sometimes he fled (Acts 9:23-30); sometimes he went to prison (Acts 16:22-24); sometimes he called upon God for miracles (Acts 13:10-11). But at all times, he allowed the Holy Spirit to show him what to do. He was guided by this principle: *"I have become all things to all men so that by all possible means I might save some."* (1 Corinthians 9:22)
- **Faithful saints:** In Hebrews 11, some faithful saints were delivered, and others were not. Just becaue a church or individual follows the Lord's leading, deliverance in not automatically guaranteed. The key seems to be *obedience* and *flexibility* under the leading of the Holy Spirit.

The extreme flexibility of the church and individual Christians in these biblical examples is seen in their responses to persecution. For example, compare the church at Jerusalem and the church at Antioch.

The church at Jerusalem was made up primarily of Jewish converts. They continued to express their faith in traditional Jewish ways, when these traditions did not contradict the Gospel.

The church at Antioch was made up of Gentile converts who did not have the background of Jewish traditions. Therefore, their fellowship meetings were less formal than those of the church in Jerusalem.

A conference was called in Jerusalem to determine whether the Antioch church should be required to follow the Jewish traditions. After a lengthy discussion, the apostles and elders decided that Gentile Christians should be free to express their faith as the Lord led, while in Jerusalem they continued in their Jewish traditions. They only asked that they do some things and not do others in order to not offend Jewish Christians. (Acts 15:1-35; 21:17-26)

- **The Early Church:** The church of New Testament times was a church in a hostile environment. The Roman government encouraged persecution throughout the whole Roman Empire. Yet Christianity triumphed and outlived its persecutors.

B. EXPRESSING FAITH IN THE CHURCH

We can learn from the experiences in the past century of many of our brothers and sisters in Christ living in restricted or repressed societies. For almost three decades—from the 1950s through the 1970s—believers in China were not able to express their faith in an institutional way. They had to discover new ways to worship and maintain their walk with the Lord. How did they do this?

During the Cultural Revolution (1965–1976), most abandoned the old institutional expressions and began to operate differently.

Although the new patterns of expression they used had to be very secret, they were effective.

Others struggled to maintain their public forms of worship as long as possible and they suffered greatly for it. Many were imprisoned and some were killed. God highly honors their bravery. They can be sure, as Paul testified, that their sufferings served *"to advance the gospel."* (Philippians 1:12)

But the government finally eliminated all public expression of faith. Many Christians around the world were deeply shaken by this turn of events and didn't know what to do. They wondered if God had abandoned China and if His church there had indeed died. Gradually, however, under the leadership of the Holy Spirit, faithful believers found valid ways to express their faith quietly, but dynamically, on a person-to-person basis.

In contrast to China, Saudi Arabia is a country that has not had an institutional church for over 1,400 years. Any local citizen who professes faith in Christ faces an automatic death sentence. Yet, despite the danger, hundreds of local Christians and Christians from other countries living in Saudi Arabia faithfully continue to meet in secret. And they survive and grow in one of the most hostile environments in our world today.

Creativity and flexibility under the leading of the Holy Spirit helps keep persecuted Christians going.

Christians in Saudi Arabia have unusual ways of communicating with fellow believers. One Saudi believer shared that even rest periods are turned into times of worship and sharing—done discreetly so as not to attract attention. Even in public, groups of three or four are able to casually meet together to share, worship and encourage one another.

In order for fellowship groups to survive, sometimes they are forced to shift from one meeting place to another. God honors their courage: new believers are added to the Kingdom of God. The creative ways they use to meet together and the methods they employ for fellowship are amazing. For security reasons, we cannot write about their specific strategies.

C. OUTWARD EXPRESSIONS OF FAITH

As we consider some of the common outward expressions of faith in Christ, we should include weddings, baptisms and funerals. Some governments have continued to permit religious weddings and funerals, even after they banned all other religious expressions. And Christians have taken advantage of this. For example, in the former Soviet Union, Christians have had a public witness at such events long after public witnessing was forbidden. The authorities find funerals especially difficult to control. In the most anti-Christian societies, a Christian's radiance at the time of the death of a loved one can have a deep influence on unbelievers at the funeral. It may even draw some to Christ.

Baptism is a church ordinance that is important to church life. It is a sign that a new believer has identified with the death, burial and resurrection of Christ. In many cultures, baptism is seen as the evidence that a person has become a Christian.

By being baptized, believers testify of their own "death to the old life" and "resurrection to live a new life." Throughout the history of the church, baptismal services have been an expression of worship, both for the baptized one and for believers observing the ordinance. (Romans 6:3-9)

The early Christians baptized new believers whenever and wherever the opportunity arose. Baptisms were often done publicly, as when John baptized Jesus in the Jordan River (Matthew 3:13-15). They were also done when two men were alone in the wilderness (Acts 8:36-39). Note that baptisms were not just performed by church leaders, but also by lay Christians. (John 4:2-3; Acts 8:36-39; 1 Corinthians 1:11-17)

In free societies, there may be justification for institutional church leaders to limit the ordinance of baptism to a particular method or to a service performed by someone authorized by the church. This was not what happened in New Testament times. And today, in societies where Christians are persecuted it doesn't happen either. It is often necessary to plan a baptismal service in extreme secrecy and perform it by whatever means available. Christians who have secretly participated in such a service testify of how greatly they were blessed.

Recently, in Nepal a new convert from Hinduism faced a seven-year term in prison after he was baptized. Another time, more than ten young converts were baptized at a meeting where a known government agent had come. When the group went out into the water to be baptized, he was in the "cook tent" enjoying a snack that had been prepared—just for him!

People who are bold enough to be baptized *in spite of government opposition* will likely be obedient witnesses for Christ in their society. That is proving to be so in Nepal. Since the 1990s, there has been exceptional growth of the church there.

D. THE VICTORIOUS CHURCH

Asian church leaders give the following points for a victorious church:

- **A church that experiences the power of the Holy Spirit daily**

Its members walk with the Lord. They are converted. They know and experience personal fellowship with God and show the fruit of the Spirit in their lives.

- **A church that experiences the fellowship of the Body of Christ**

This is very important. It includes not only fellowship but also loyalty—a loyalty that is willing to die for brothers and sisters. (see Matthew 25:40)

- **A church that knows the Bible and is able to use it**

This includes Bible memorization that helps believers resist false teaching.

- **A church that is serious about evangelism**

Its members know the reasons for evangelism. They are certain there is no other way of salvation but through Jesus Christ.

- **A church that is committed to serving the needs of society**

The church must know its responsibilities and exercise appropriate opportunities for helping others.

- **A church that is self-supporting and free from outside power and control**

The church must be not only free from outside power and control, but also it must be free from influential people who seek to control the church inside the country.

- **A church that knows the strengths and weaknesses of the opposition**

This includes all external as well as internal tactics of Satan.

- **A church that is bold and ready to witness even in the face of persecution**
- **A church that is committed to shared responsibility**

Laity and clergy share the load of leadership and ministry.

- **A church that is a praying church!**

STUDY GUIDE/DISCUSSION QUESTIONS

PASTOR FOCUS

1. There are many examples of the ways that forces opposed to Christianity have attacked the institutional church. Consider the following actual scenarios and decide how you would deal with them. Do you think a small informal church would have been able to deal more effectively with these situations?

- Two months after South Vietnam was taken over by the communists, a Christian wrote a friend, "Many new faces appear in our worship services and they lead us to discuss many things. In reality, we no longer worship but have political discussion meetings. Normally we would rejoice when new people join us in a worship service, but in this case it is obviously infiltration." What would **you** do?
- In China, the government initially allowed worship services to continue, but began to seize all church buildings not used for worship. They "took responsibility" for hospitals, clinics, orphanages and schools. What do **you** think should have been the attitude of Christians working in these places?
- In Cuba, the government of Fidel Castro allowed some churches to exist, but in many areas, the number of Christians was far more than the buildings could hold. They were not allowed to build larger church buildings and ministers were not allowed to conduct other meetings in other places—especially in homes. Even when everyone stands up during the service (in order to conserve space), many who would like to worship are turned away. How would **you** respond?
- In some Muslim countries, Christians from another country living there are merely tolerated, and national believers must remain completely unknown. Can such "secret" believers be real Christians? Can they carry on the functions of the church? How should they determine with whom to fellowship?

2. Hostile governments often want to scatter Christian groups to reduce their influence. In countries such as Kampuchea, whole populations have been forcefully resettled. In Vietnam, the government would increase taxes until a family could not survive in a particular place. Then the authorities would resettle

that family somewhere else. In the former Soviet Union, many Christians were exiled to Siberia. Because of that, Siberia is now one of the areas in Russia with the strongest Christian testimony. What if you and your family, for economic reasons, were forced to move to an area where you didn't know any other believers?

WOMEN'S FOCUS

1. Review the following "Asian Criteria for a Victorious Church." Rank them from #1 through to #10 as they describe **your** current church.

[#1] "Our Strongest Area" to
[#10] "Needs the Most Improvement"

[___] Our church experiences the power of the Holy Spirit daily—Repentance.
[___] Our church experiences the fellowship of the Body of Christ—Humility.
[___] Our church knows the Bible and is able to use it—Equipped.
[___] Our church is serious about evangelism—Outreach.
[___] Our church is committed to serving the needs of society—Ministering.
[___] Our church is self-supporting and free from outside power and control—Giving.
[___] Our church knows the strengths and weaknesses of the opposition—Discernment.

[___] Our church is bold and ready to witness even in the face of persecution—Faith.

[___] Our church is committed to shared responsibility—Biblical Leadership.

[___] Our church is a praying church—Intercession—Worship—Fasting.

Discuss the 10 points church leaders in Asia gave for what constitutes a victorious church. Do you agree? Are there points missing? Where does your group have its greatest strengths and weaknesses?

YOUTH FOCUS

1. Identify with a house church in China by doing the things below.

   • **Sing Songs Softly**

   Most house churches meet illegally and do not want neighbors to know of their presence. But they love to sing hymns. So they lean in together and sing the songs in hushed tones.

   • **Copy Scripture Passages**

   Some Chinese house churches like to copy passages of Scripture, not because Bibles are scarce, but because they believe it is a good discipline for getting the Word deep into the soul. Each member of the group copies out by hand five or ten verses and commits them to memory. Then all the writing paper is glued together to form a kind of scroll.

   • **Share Experiences of Suffering**

   In a Chinese house church, if you say, "I'm fine," then

something is regarded as spiritually wrong. If you are having a witness for Christ, there *must* be suffering to report, otherwise how do you know you are Christ's? Ask all members to tell the group how they have suffered for Jesus since the last time the group met. Reflect on how this exercise challenged **you** to be different from the surrounding world.

• **Live Through a Verse for a Whole Week**

House church Christians will often ask God for a Scripture verse, and then live every activity that week in the light of that verse. The following week, they report to the group all they have learned from "the school of life" in that verse.

• **Pray "Prison Style"**

Conditions in prison are harsh—overcrowding is common; the food is poor; the water is unsanitary.... Some house church Christians in Wenzhou do the following to identify with their brothers and sisters who are in jail: They first mark out a small area about twelve feet long. Then, packed like sardines, they all lie side by side in that area and pray for those in prison. This reminds them of the conditions their beloved leaders are in.

• **Target the Unreached Parts of Your Country in Prayer**

Chinese house churches spend long periods of time in prayer for outlying, unreached people in their country—people who have not heard the Gospel, such as the Muslims in Xinjiang, and the Tibetans of Tibet. Identify and target the unreached parts of your own country in prayer.

MEN'S FOCUS

1. Did communism destroy the church in China and Ethiopia or change it? Discuss the reasons together.

2. Have you thought of "Christian fellowship" in the way this lesson presents it? Have you experienced this kind of fellowship?

3. What can a group do if they become too large to meet in a home?

4. What does Satan hope to gain by having Christians sent away to other areas? Can this tactic work against him? If so, explain how.

5. Have you made any "adjustments" in typical institutional church practice to meet the local situation? Discuss.

6. GROUP ACTIVITY: Have each member of the group complete a SWOT chart for their own church group. Compare strengths and weaknesses and how they relate to the comparison of opportunities and threats.

Strengths	**Weaknesses (internal)**
Opportunities	**Threats (external)**

18

THE CHRISTIAN FAMILY

Facing the Future Together

All your sons will be taught by the LORD, and great will be your children's peace.

ISAIAH 54:13

Parable: A frail old man went to live with his son, daughter-in-law, and four-year-old grandson. The old man's hands trembled, his eyesight was blurred, and his step faltered. The family ate together at the table. But the elderly grandfather's shaky hands and failing sight made eating difficult. Peas rolled off his spoon onto the floor. When he grasped the glass, milk spilled on the tablecloth.

The son and daughter-in-law became irritated with the mess. "We must do something about Grandfather," said the son. "I've had enough of his spilled milk, noisy eating, and food on the floor." So the husband and wife set a small table in the corner. There, Grandfather ate alone while the rest of the family enjoyed dinner.

Since Grandfather had broken a dish or two, his food was served in a wooden bowl. When the family glanced in Grandfather's direction, sometimes he had a tear in his eye as he sat alone. Still, the only words the couple had for him were sharp admonitions when he dropped a fork or spilled food.

The four-year-old watched it all in silence. One evening before supper, the father noticed his son playing with wood scraps on the floor. He asked the child sweetly, "What are you making?"

Just as sweetly, the boy responded, "Oh, I am making a little bowl for you and Mama to eat your food in when I grow up." The four-year-old smiled and went back to work.

The words so struck the parents that they were speechless. Then tears started to stream down their cheeks. Though no word was spoken, both knew what must be done.

That evening, the husband took Grandfather's hand and gently led him back to the family table. For the remainder of his days he ate every meal with the family. And for some reason, neither husband nor wife seemed to care any longer when a fork was dropped, milk spilled, or the tablecloth soiled.

Children are remarkably perceptive. Their eyes ever observe, their ears ever listen, and their minds ever process the messages they absorb. If they see us patiently provide a happy, godly home atmosphere, they will imitate that attitude for the rest of their lives.

The wise parent realizes that every day the building blocks are being laid for their children's future.[1]

A. BIBLICAL EMPHASIS ON THE FAMILY

The family has been the basic unit of God's creation from the beginning. After He had created the world, plants and animals, God completed His creation by making man in His own image. Then from man He created woman. God could have chosen to create many human beings as He had created many plants and animals, and then set up a human government as His basic unit. But He did not do so. Rather He chose to create the family as the basic social unit, and the family unit became the basis for His relationship with mankind.

This is most clearly evident in the example of the Jewish family, although we see it in the Old Testament even before God called out the children of Israel to be a separate people. God spoke to Adam's family through Adam and He spoke to each succeeding generation through the head of the family. That is why these men are still known as the Patriarchs.

We see how God spoke to Noah, and through Noah saved Noah's whole family. When He called Abraham, however, the line of family relationship became especially evident. God made a covenant with Abraham that applied to his family and their descendants. God even began to refer to Himself as the God of Abraham, Isaac and Jacob, identifying Himself with this growing family. Then as God blessed Jacob with twelve sons and changed Jacob's name to Israel, God's people became known as the "Children of Israel."

By the time Moses was born four hundred years later, the closeness of the Hebrew family was evident in the risks his parents took to preserve his life. When Moses answered God's call to lead His people out of Egypt, his brother Aaron, sister Miriam, and even his father-in-law, Jethro, were used of God to assist him.

In the wilderness God gave Moses the law, one section of which the Jews call the *Shemah* (Deuteronomy 6:3-9; 11:18-21). This section speaks specifically of the family and its responsibilities. It includes a declaration of who God is; the commandment to love the Lord with all one's heart, rather than just superficially; the command to teach these truths diligently to the children and to reinforce the teaching with continual reminders. The family was to talk of these matters frequently, post reminders of them upon the walls and wear them on their bodies. The Word of the Lord was to be continually in their midst.

The Jewish feasts were also intended to strengthen the family and draw them to God as a worshipping unit. The Passover particularly held up the father as the spiritual head of the family. Each father was strictly commanded to pass on this observance to the eldest son. Throughout the long history of Israel, from the tabernacle to the temple to the synagogue, the family has survived as the basic unit of worship and loyalty. In many communities around the world where there were not enough Jews to build a synagogue, or where anti-Semitism was too strong for them to worship publicly, the Jewish family survived and Judaism survived.

The New Testament teaching regarding the family absorbs the Old Testament teaching and adds further details. The husband and wife become one, with the husband the spiritual head of the family as Christ is of the church (Ephesians 5:21-23). But both spouses are to submit to each other. Children are to be brought up *"in the training and instruction of the Lord."* (Ephesians 6:1-4; Colossians 3:20-21)

B. GOD'S PROTECTION OF THE FAMILY

God not only has established the family, but He has given His laws to protect it. Of the Ten Commandments, there are six that deal with interpersonal relationships. Of these six, three are intended to protect the family:

- *Honor your father and your mother*
- *You shall not commit adultery*
- *You shall not covet your neighbor's wife* (Exodus 20:7-17)

First, God established His plan for the family's organization, then He protected it from being undermined from within, and then protected it from attacks from without. Jesus extended this protection by enlarging upon the understanding of adultery (Matthew 5:27-28) and forbidding divorce except in the case of adultery. (Matthew 5:32)

Jesus plainly taught that a strong family unit is God's best for mankind. This is why Paul gives extensive teaching on marriage and the family in his letters. He makes a very strong statement in his first letter to Timothy that a man who does not take care of his own family is worse than an unbeliever. (1 Timothy 5:8)

C. CHALLENGES TO THE CHRISTIAN FAMILY

This high standard of family loyalty puts the Christian family on a collision course with many modern political systems. These political systems undermine the family unit by setting the state over parental authority. They do this by removing children from their parents' care with only minor justification, attempting to usurp family responsibilities in the teaching of moral values, providing government "day-care centers" to replace parental upbringing, and generally downgrading the importance of the home.

1. Time

In some totalitarian countries, the attack upon the family is even more aggressive. The authorities in such countries cut to a minimum the amount of time the family can be together. Both parents are required to work long hours outside the home, while the children are "cared for" by the state. What little time the parents might spend with the children is often consumed by attendance at required political meetings or waiting in long lines to buy scarce basic commodities.

2. Teaching

During the time that the children are in the care of the state, they are being intensively indoctrinated. Teachings are often specifically anti-Christian and subtly designed to destroy the family unit.

One well-known aspect of their teaching is often referred to as "children spying on their families." This is a poor term, because it implies that the children are aware that they are doing something against their parents. Generally, this is not the case. They are supposedly being taught to be "observant" and are rewarded for having noticed anything "unusual." For most children it is just a game, but it is an important source of information to the authorities in many countries.

Following the fall of Vietnam, for example, many attempting to escape were killed or captured because of tips turned in by children under twelve years of age! Christians inside the People's Republic of China tell us that one of the most serious problems a family faces is the question of when to let a small child know about Christ. If children are told when too young and they share their faith with the wrong people, the family may suffer.

In fact, it is not unusual for the Chinese government to take small children away from their parents and place them in government orphanages, if they learn that the parents are teaching them about Christianity. On the other hand, if the parents wait too long to share Christ with their children, they have already been indoctrinated with anti-Christian ideology.

3. Attractions

Christians often foolishly think that their children could never fall for the government "line." This is a serious mistake. Repressive governments do not hesitate to make promises they cannot keep, but they also make very basic, practical promises that they can and do keep. Idealistic young people are frequently attracted to these programs of social justice. Many of these Christians live in areas where there is little possibility of knowing economic security. The unfairness of a situation in which there are a few very wealthy people while the masses can barely exist is obvious.

When governments begin to make some real improvements, as they have done in China, these idealistic young people are attracted to their cause. Another factor that puts great pressure on young people is their natural patriotism. When repressive governments take over, they try to make everyone that does not enthusiastically support them look like an "enemy of the people." Pressure like this is hard for young people to resist.

Young people with Christian training should be more sensitive to injustice and corruption than others. When governments promise social equality and justice for all, it is very appealing. The point is that the lure of some political systems may put a real strain on the unity of the family. Those who have observed repressive governments over the years are aware that their promises are impossible to keep, and the popular slogans later have to be enforced with guns and barbed wire. But the young idealist may not be aware of this.

The communists took full advantage of these young people and did everything they could to discredit the church. They even quoted "liberal" church leaders who deny the authority of Scripture and the divinity of Christ. Only a Christian family that is firmly grounded in the Word of God will be able to resist the enemy's attempt to draw away children and young people.

4. Future: Education and Employment

If the children do successfully hold on to their faith, they may pay a big price. Advanced education may be denied them. Promotions in the menial jobs they are allowed to hold will be rare. The whole family may even be faced with open persecution, including physical violence. But if Christian families begin to realize the vitally important part they play in the victorious survival of the church, they will see that the family must stand.

There is much that families can do to be assured of victory in this battle the enemy is waging against them.

Being a Christian doesn't mean one is not concerned for political change and social justice. But change must be built on biblical principles that are not at the cost of the family or church.

D. THE FAMILY MODELING THE CHURCH

The Christian family is essentially a cell unit and thus a microcosm of the church itself.

1. Study the Bible together.

First, the family should study the Word of God together and become familiar with its teaching concerning the family. Serious effort must be exerted to establish relationships in the family that follow the teaching of Scripture. It is always a vital first step to accept the biblical standard as your personal standard. A solid Christian family cannot be built on knowledge alone. It takes active commitment to the biblical standard.

2. Dedicate children to the Lord.

Second, parents should consciously set each child apart to the Lord. This may be done in a "dedication service" in a church building, or a simple act of commitment in the privacy of the home. The Lord honors such commitment. If we knew the percentage of those who were committed to the Lord as children and are now actively serving Him, we would be amazed. Just a casual review of the stories of Christian leaders substantiates this point. Of course, such commitment is just the beginning of the spiritual influence that parents should have upon the child.

3. Carry out five functions of the church.

Third, the Christian family should actively be carrying out the five basic functions of the church within the family group: Evangelism, Discipleship, Ministry, Fellowship and Worship. The family can begin by worshipping together. This worship can be done in a variety of ways: reading and praying, listening to soul-stirring Christian music together and then having a time of praise, following the early church example of worshipping around the Lord's Supper, or any combination of these and other activities.

In many ways, the family worship time, especially when the Lord's Supper is observed, can be like the Jewish observance of Passover. It will have great spiritual impact on the family and draw it together. Bible teaching and the study of Bible doctrine should be going on in the family as well. Sometimes a casual family discussion of a difficult point of doctrine will have more lasting influence than many sermons.

Christian education should be based in the homes, and occasional family devotions are not enough. The family should strive to have a daily devotional time together, but regular planned study sessions are also needed. This is the best way for a father to reinforce his biblical position as spiritual head of the home.

The functions of fellowship and ministry are needed in many families today. The members of a Christian family can learn to enjoy each other and actively care for each other. Members who have become sensitive to the needs of other members learn to put love into action.

As the concept of family members sharing each other's burden becomes a part of family life, the family will soon be reaching out to others: relatives at first, perhaps, then friends and neighbors. Many of these may not yet know Christ. A caring, sharing family will present a living Gospel message that is hard to deny. Many Christians claim that their relatives and friends are the hardest to win to Christ. If families live a testimony for Christ in the home, this can change the heart of other family members. And as well, the home will be a witness to the community.

Sister Biral is a former Muslim who is able to recite Arabic prayers. Because of this she has gained the admiration and respect of her neighbors on a tiny island in the southern Philippines. Sister Biral is now a Christian. Despite persecution she continues faithfully to labor for the Lord. She and her husband look after a church comprised mostly of former Muslims.

Because love permeates their home, children of her neighbors have come to enjoy playing with the Biral children. They like to come to their home where they experience something different. There they are treated with much love. Constantly having other children in their home provides an opportunity for Sister Biral to share God's love with those little ones. Such a home draws people to Christ.

As other families are touched by the saving power of Christ, they should be taught to function as a church, too.

4. Set an example in prayer.

Fourth, the parents set an example in believing, fervent prayer. This includes their personal prayer life as well as leading the family as a praying unit. One important part of a developing prayer life is learning to recognize God's answers. The parents can help the children in this matter, so that they can be encouraged that God both hears and answers their prayers.

Children sometimes get the mistaken idea that God will give them whatever they ask. Some who oppose the church try to destroy children's faith in prayer by challenging them to pray for something specific like candy. When the Christian children pray to the Lord, they don't get any candy. But when the others pray to the *"opposer,"* they are immediately supplied. Children that have been raised in a praying family will not be so easily confused.

A Christian family that has followed these four steps will be strong in the faith and able to help their local institutional church as long as the Lord permits it to operate. If the time should ever come when public church meetings are no longer permitted, such a family can continue to stand for Christ from within their home.

E. THE CHURCH SUPPORTING THE FAMILY

What can the church be doing today to build strong Christian families? It is obvious that any steps the church would like to take to strengthen the family must be taken now. The following are some of the suggestions for strengthening the Christian family that have come to us from various countries of the world. You might consider them for your church.

1. Present sound biblical teaching on the family to every believer.

This includes taking a strong stand against the aspects of modern living that are breaking down family life. Satan is already subtly using the same attacks in "free" societies that he uses openly in restricted societies. Christians and churches should be involved in trying to prevent divorces from taking place by strengthening marriages. The rising divorce rate is a worldwide problem, but the increasing number of divorces among Christians makes us weep.

Help families understand the standards provided in the Bible on everything from sex to finances. Reinforce these standards as being relevant for today and provide guidance for young people in preparation for marriage. This helps strengthen marriages so Christian families can "stand strong through the storm."

2. Provide special guidance for people who become Christians to stay in relationship with their family.

Young people should be encouraged to honor their parents and attempt to draw them to Christ by their radiant lives. Too often young people have been encouraged to withdraw from active participation in their families because their parents were not Christian. This can be a serious mistake. Christian young people should stay in their own families if at all possible. This is even true in cases where they have been raised in homes that are anti-Christian, atheist or Muslim. Sometimes this is not possible, but as a matter of general policy they should be encouraged to remain in the family.

Spouses of non-believers have clear scriptural guidance as to the course they must follow. The Bible makes it clear that a Christian should not marry a non-Christian. But it also teaches that if one spouse is a believer and the other is not, the Christian should stay in the union and try to love the other one to faith in Jesus. (1 Corinthians 7:10-17)

3. Provide a Christian family relationship for individual believers within your fellowship who do not have families with which they can identify.

One way to do this is for a Christian family in the fellowship to "adopt" such an individual. The church can encourage such relationships so that each member has the opportunity to share in a family. Another way to do this, if the church is small enough, is for the church itself to provide family-quality relationships.

A way to check up on yourself is to see if any individual member spent the last holiday alone. Would you leave anyone of your family out of your celebration if it were possible for them to be present? Of course not. Paul made this kind of relationship so clear when he wrote to Timothy telling him to treat the other believers as members of his own family. (1 Timothy 5:1-2)

4. Center the Christian education efforts of the church on the family unit.

As an option, instead of dividing the family into various classes, encourage families to study together with some assistance and guidance from the church staff and elders. All families do not need to be studying the same subject; a variety of subjects and teaching materials could be made available. It is hard to estimate how much an approach so radically different from the standard Sunday school class method could strengthen the families. It might even revitalize the church.

5. Support and encourage the family in their efforts to see the five functions of the church active in their midst.

A church ought not to consider families who employ the five functions of the church in their family as a "threat" to their authority. A child could be truly baptized by his or her father rather than by the clergy. A family could observe the Lord's Supper in their home. A father can teach Scripture to his family. Strengthening the Christian family can only strengthen the family and the church.

STUDY GUIDE/DISCUSSION QUESTIONS

PASTOR FOCUS

1. In your fellowship group a Christian family is reportedly having a tough time. The father has not been a spiritual leader and this has caused problems for the wife and children. All relationships seem sour. There are rumors of an impending divorce if things do not improve. What can you and your fellowship do to help this family? What strengthening can external relationships do to help this situation?

2. How might the following suggestions for strengthening the family be activated in **your** church?
   - Provide sound biblical teaching on the family to every believer.

   - Give special guidance to young people or wives who respond to the Lord to prevent their decision from breaking up their family.

- Provide a Christian family relationship for individual believers within your fellowship who do not have families with which they can identify.

- Center the Christian education efforts of the church on the family unit.

- Support and encourage the family in their efforts to see the five functions of the church active in their midst.

WOMEN'S FOCUS

1. One of the ways that Satan often attacks a Christian group is by trying to win away the loyalty of their children. The enemy is aware that few of us give our children the attention and training they need and therefore, they are especially vulnerable. Many anti-Christian forces today are trying to entice children to support their causes. The communists often reward children for reporting on their parents. This is a very difficult matter to deal with and doubly so if the children are too young to understand what is happening. One Chinese family carefully hid their Christian beliefs from their own children because they feared that they would be reported! How strong are your children in the faith?

2. In some countries, the head of the family dictates the religious beliefs of the other members. What should a wife or child who becomes a believer do in regard to honoring their family and yet remaining true to the faith?

3. If the Christian family is essentially a cell unit, how are the following like a microcosm of the church itself?
   - Studying the Bible together
   - Dedicating children to the Lord
   - Carrying out the five functions of the church
   - Setting an example in prayer

YOUTH FOCUS

1. One way the enemy works against families in general, and children in particular, is through the selective offering of educational opportunities. If children do not show enthusiastic support for the authorities' point of view, they are denied further education. In many authoritarian societies this approach has effectively forced many young people to deny the religion

of their parents. In one African state, where the authorities are trying to revive the pagan traditions to strengthen their own political power, young people are pressured to join in ceremonies to evil spirits. If they refuse, they suffer severe persecution. If they submit, they fear that they have lost their Christianity. Could your friends face this kind of pressure? Could **you**?

2. Discuss methods of families protecting Christian children and enabling them to remain strong in their faith when required to attend non-Christian schools that give strong false indoctrination.

MEN'S FOCUS

1. Why is the family unit so important to God?

2. Of the Ten Commandments, six deal with inter-personal relationships. Of these six, three are intended to protect the family:
   - *Honor your father and your mother*
   - *You shall not commit adultery*
   - *You shall not covet your neighbor's wife* (Exodus 20:7-17)

What can individuals do to help strengthen families?

3. Identify how the following challenges affect families in a "free society" and in a "totalitarian country":
   - Time
   - Teaching
   - Attractions
   - Future: education and employment
   - Materialism

4. The hymn writer has said, "This world is no friend of God." What pressures do you feel the modern world brings against your family and its stand for God?

5. Has your fellowship seen its young people drawn away? What seems to be the attraction to them?

6. What do you think your fellowship could do to help strengthen your family?

Conclusion

STANDING STRONG THROUGH THE STORM

But thanks be to God! He gives us the victory through our Lord Jesus Christ.
1 CORINTHIANS 15:57

THE SECRETS OF STANDING STRONG

1. The secret of "Standing Strong" is always the cross.

The cross is God's way. The Lamb is placed upon the throne as we see in Revelation 17:14; 19:7-10; 5:6. In the same way, the mark of the cross upon our lives is our true victory.

In 2 Corinthians 1:9, Paul speaks of *the sentence of death* in himself as his way of overcoming death. Only as we are able to give God our future, our loved ones, even our own life, are we free to be more than conquerors.

2. The secret of "Standing Strong" is to live in the context of the Resurrection.

Paul writes in 1 Corinthians 15:19 that if the Resurrection never happened, we are of all people the most to be pitied. We alone have renounced this life's prospects and resisted this life's temptations for

Christ. This is our ultimate freedom: to deny ourselves, pick up our cross and follow Christ. Thus, we are to live our whole life in the context of the Resurrection.

In restricted countries, authorities seek to intimidate believers by probing for their weak spots and striking those weak spots. Anything they discover which has not been *crucified with Christ* becomes a potential point of vulnerability.

3. The secret of "Standing Strong" is the acceptance of and response to persecution.

"Those who hope in the LORD will renew their strength. They will soar on wings like eagles." (Isaiah 40:31)

An eagle knows when a storm is approaching long before it breaks. The eagle flies to some high spot and waits for the winds to come. When the storm hits, it sets its wings so that the wind will pick it up and lift it above the storm. While the storm rages below, the eagle soars above it. The eagle escapes the storm by using the storm to lift it higher. It rises on the winds that bring the storm.

When the storms of life come upon us—and all of us will experience them—we can rise above them by setting our minds on God and believing Him. The storms do not have to overcome us. We can allow God's power to lift us above them. God enables us to ride the winds of the storm that bring sickness, tragedy, failure and disappointment in our lives. We can soar above the storm. Remember, it is not the burdens of life that weigh us down; it is how we handle them.

4. The secret of "Standing Strong" is not in affluence and prosperity nor the absence of trouble, but obedience in the midst of trials and trouble.

"If you are insulted because of the name of Christ, you are blessed, for the Spirit of glory and of God rests on you." (1 Peter 4:14)

Though we don't usually think of our Lord Jesus as being rich, we read in 2 Corinthians 8:9 that before coming into the world He *"was rich."* And yet for our sakes, He left those riches—the riches and glory of heaven—to *"become poor."* Here on earth, Jesus had *"no place to lay his head"* (Matthew 8:20; Luke 9:58). And He suffered rejection, first, from His own people (John 1:11). Then as He suffered on the cross bearing the sins of the whole world, even His Father left Him. (Matthew 27:46)

Although we could consider Matthew rich before he left his tax collecting to follow Jesus, probably none of the other disciples were ever rich (Matthew 9:9). Like their Master, they too suffered. At one time, the apostles were whipped and when they were released, they left *"rejoicing because they had been counted worthy of suffering"* for Jesus (Acts 5:40-41), yet Acts 5:42 says, *"they never stopped teaching."*

The Apostle Paul was an influential religious leader and probably also wealthy, but he *"lost all things"* for the sake of Jesus (Philippians 3:8-9). The New Testament gives numerous examples of Paul suffering. He tells us that he was imprisoned, beaten, whipped, stoned; in shipwrecks; at times, thirsty and hungry, cold and without enough clothes. (2 Corinthians 11:23-27)

Therefore, from the example and teaching of the New Testament, we do not preach a Gospel of riches, prosperity and freedom from pain. *"In fact, everyone who wants to live a godly life in Christ Jesus will be persecuted."* (2 Timothy 3:12)

We preach a message of a God who suffered when He sent His beloved Son to earth knowing He too would suffer rejection and pain. But we also preach a message of a God who won through His conquering Son, who said, *"No servant is greater than his master. If they persecuted me, they will persecute you also.... In this world you will have trouble. But take heart! I have overcome the world."* (John 15:20; 16:33)

5. The secret of "Standing Strong" is being a servant of Jesus Christ.

Paul tells us that when Jesus came to earth He *"made himself nothing, taking the very nature of a servant"* (Philippians 2:7). The one who has obeyed the command in Mark 8:34 to *"deny himself and take up his cross and follow me"* is a servant of Jesus Christ. And His servants model the expected character of the believer as depicted in the Sermon on the Mount. (Matthew 5–7)

The qualities Jesus speaks of in the Sermon on the Mount contrast with the world's standard of *natural* behavior, especially in a battle. Mercy, purity, peace, forgiveness and grace have no place in the *natural* soldier fighting a *real* battle. But when we Christians are in a battle—a *spiritual* battle—Jesus recommends that we treat our enemies in a way that no one would expect us to. Unlike the *natural* soldier fighting in a physical battle, we are servant-soldiers in a *spiritual* battle and we win using weapons that are not *"weapons of the world."* The weapons we use have *"divine power."* (2 Corinthians 10:4)

We said at the beginning that this volume has been written out of the conviction that Christians all over the world will face increasing hostility. We believe this is shown in Matthew 24 and Mark 13.

We also said that we want to be prepared intellectually, spiritually and practically:

- *Intellectual preparation:* because the church must understand what the Bible teaches, especially about persecution and suffering.
- *Spiritual preparation:* because the church can pray and fast and engage in other activities that stress the importance of fighting the spiritual battle.
- *Practical preparation:* because the church can ensure that small groups can meet for prayer and fellowship without feeling they are compromising their faith. And the home can be looked at as the center of Christian work, witness and worship.

We also need to know how to respond to hostility. Our way is Christ's, who humbled himself, took up the cross, died for us all, but was exalted and given a name above every name; that at the name of Jesus, every knee should bow and every tongue confess Him as Lord. (see Philippians 2:8-11)

We are called to follow, knowing that Jesus Christ was the pioneer not only of servanthood, but also of eternal and resurrected life. No other people on earth can afford to live this way. Persecuted Church members have learned to accept this lifestyle. They challenge us to catch up to them, to get into step, to be more than conquerors, to be victorious overcomers through Him who loved us.

Thousands of Christians have stood for the Lord in spite of persecution, but thousands more failed to stand for their faith. Even in the days of great Roman persecutions only a fraction of those who had professed Christ stood true to the end. More Christians have suffered for their faith in the twentieth century than in any other time in church history. Why are some able to stand? *They have learned how to be victorious servant-soldiers and stand strong through the storm.*

Christine Mallouhi, in her excellent book *Waging Peace on Islam,* makes this significant conclusion:

> The victorious and triumphant Christian life does not conjure up pictures of suffering and death and feelings of abandonment. But this was all part of God's victory in Christ. If this was the path the Master trod why should it be any different for the servants? Jesus cried out "why?" and "where are you?" to God when circumstances were crushing him. God is always greater than our understanding of him and there will always be mystery about him that causes us to fall down in awe and worship. This mystery, which we want to tidily categorize, keeps causing struggles in our life. Every time we get God tidied up like a ball of rubber bands, another end bursts out and the struggle begins over again, until we learn to live in faith with untidy ends. If everything is clear then faith is irrelevant. We are not called to solve the mystery, but enter it.[1]

CLOSING THOUGHTS

Christians who "Stand Strong" are like nails:
The harder you hit them, the deeper they go.

Christians who "Stand Strong" are like rubber balls:
The harder you throw them down onto the floor,
the higher they rebound.

Christians who "Stand Strong"' are like flowers:
The more you crush them, the stronger the fragrance.

Christians who "Stand Strong" are like tea leaves,
You have to put them in hot water to know how strong they are.

Christians who "Stand Strong" are like bamboo:
The more you cut them down, the stronger they grow back.

You can—by God's grace and your obedience—
be a victorious Christian.

And you can STAND STRONG THROUGH THE STORM.

Appendix A

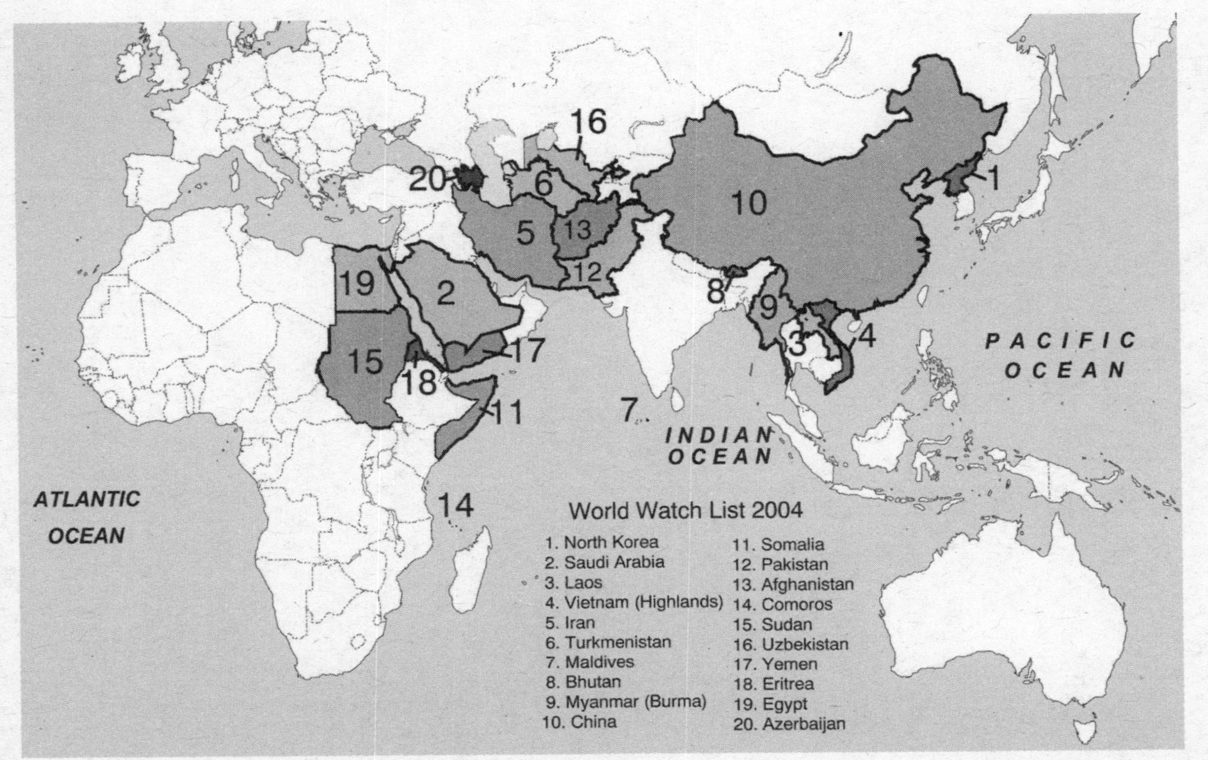

ATLANTIC OCEAN
INDIAN OCEAN
PACIFIC OCEAN
World Watch List 2004
1. North Korea
2. Saudi Arabia
3. Laos
4. Vietnam (Highlands)
5. Iran
6. Turkmenistan
7. Maldives
8. Bhutan
9. Myanmar (Burma)
10. China
11. Somalia
12. Pakistan
13. Afghanistan
14. Comoros
15. Sudan
16. Uzbekistan
17. Yemen
18. Eritrea
19. Egypt
20. Azerbaijan

Recommended Reading

INTRODUCTION—The Coming Storms

Hattaway, Paul. *Back to Jerusalem.* Carlisle, UK: Piquant Publishers, 2003.

CHAPTER ONE—Knowing Our Enemy

Lewis, C. S. *The Screwtape Letters.* Denver, CO: Mentor Books, 1988.

Alcorn, Randy. *Lord Foulgrin's Letters.* Sisters, OR: Multnomah Publishers Inc., 2000.

CHAPTER THREE—The Battle Around Us

Anderson, Neil T. and Rich Miller. *Freedom From Fear.* Eugene, OR: Harvest House Publishers, 1999.

CHAPTER FOUR—Spiritual Warfare

Arnold, Clinton. *Three Crucial Questions About Spiritual Warfare.* Grand Rapids, MI: Baker Book House, 1997.

Sherman, Dean. *Spiritual Warfare for Every Christian.* Seattle, WA: Frontline Communications, 1990.

Smith, Alice. *Dispelling the Darkness.* Houston: SpiriTruth Publishing, US Prayer Center, 1999.

Wagner, C. Peter. *Warfare Prayer.* Ventura, CA: Regal Books, 1997.

CHAPTER FIVE—God's Provision: Full Armor

Anderson, Neil T. *The Bondage Breaker.* Eugene, OR: Harvest House Publishers, 1990.

CHAPTER SEVEN—God's Provision: Prayer

Smith, Eddie and Alice Smith. *The Advocates: How to Plead the Case of Others in Prayer.* Lake Mary, FL: Charisma House, 2001.

CHAPTER NINE—Training in Righteousness

Lucado, Max. *The Applause of Heaven.* Dallas: Word Publishing, 1990.

Mallouhi, Christine A. *Waging Peace on Islam.* Downers Grove, IL: InterVarsity Press, 2000.

CHAPTER ELEVEN—Perseverance and Encouragement

Estabrooks, Paul. *Secrets to Spiritual Success.* Tonbridge, Kent, UK: Sovereign World, Ltd., 1996.

Beeson, Ray and Ranelda Mack Hunsicker. *The Hidden Price of Greatness.* Wheaton, IL: Tyndale House Publishers, 1991.

CHAPTER TWELVE—Forgiveness and Grace

Swindoll, Charles R. *The Grace Awakening.* Dallas: Word Publishing, 1990.

Yancey, Philip. *What's So Amazing About Grace?* Grand Rapids, MI: Zondervan Publishing House, 1997.

CHAPTER THIRTEEN—Our Unique Savior

Lutzer, Erwin W. *Christ Among Other gods: A Defense of Christ in an Age of Tolerance.* Chicago: Moody Press, 1994.

Strobel, Lee. *The Case for Christ.* Grand Rapids, MI: Zondervan Publishing House, 1998.

Zacharius, Ravi. *Jesus Among Other Gods.* Nashville, TN: Thomas Nelson/Word, 1999.

CHAPTER FOURTEEN—Our Unique Calling

Foxe, John. Rewritten and updated by Harold J. Chadwick. *The New Foxe's Book of Martyrs.* North Brunswick, NJ: Bridge-Logos Publishers, 1997.

MacArthur, John Jr., *The Power of Suffering.* Wheaton, IL: Victor Books, 1995.

Rhodes, Tricia McCary. *Taking Up Your Cross: The Incredible Gain of the Crucified Life.* Minneapolis: Bethany House Publishers, 2000.

Schirrmacher, Thomas. *The Persecution of Christians Concerns Us All: Toward a Theology of Martyrdom.* Bonn, Germany: Studies in Religious Freedom, 2001.

CHAPTER FIFTEEN—Responding to Persecution

McDowell, Josh and Bob Hostetler. *The New Tolerance.* Wheaton, IL: Tyndale House Publishers, 1998.

Retief, Frank. *Tragedy to Triumph.* Milton Keynes, UK: Nelson Word Ltd., 1994.

Brackin, Ron. *Sweet Persecution.* Minneapolis: Bethany House Publishers, 1999.

CHAPTER SIXTEEN—The Simplicity of the Church

Warren, Rick. *The Purpose-Driven Church.* Grand Rapids, MI: Zondervan Publishing House, 1995.

Johnstone, Patrick. *The Church Is Bigger Than You Think.* Great Britain: Christian Focus Publications, 1998.

Colson, Chuck. *The Body.* Dallas: Word Publishing, 1992.

CHAPTER SEVENTEEN—The Church in Operation

Atkerson, Steve (ed). *Toward a House Church Theology.* Atlanta: New Testament Restoration Foundation, 1998.

Beckham, William A. *The Second Reformation: Reshaping The Church for the 21st Century.* Houston: TOUCH Publications, 1995.

Finnell, David L. *Cell Group Basic Training.* Mississauga, Ontario, Canada: Worldteam Canada, 1994.

Neighbour, Ralph Jr. *Where Do We Go From Here?* Houston: Touch Outreach Ministries, 1990.

Simson, Wolfgang. *Houses That Change the World: Return of the House Churches.* Self-published, March 6, 2001.

Endnotes

CHAPTER TWO

1. Author unknown.
2. C. S. Lewis, *The Four Loves* (New York: Harcourt, Brace, 1960), p. 87.
3. Charles Stanley, "The Problem of Pride," Internet: http://www.oneplace.com/Ministries/In_Touch/Article .asp?article_id=762
4. Michelle Metzger, "How to Give a Speech Without the PowerPoint Training Wheels," http://www.mccom.com/ technique/archives/June2004/article_2.htm , June 15, 2004.
5. Charles Colson, "Salad-Bar Christianity," *Christianity Today* (August 7, 2000), p. 80.
6. Josh McDowell and Bob Hostetler, *The New Tolerance* (Wheaton, IL: Tyndale House Publishers, 1998), p. 42.
7. *Daily Bread* (Grand Rapids, MI: Radio Bible Class).
8. T. Sher Singh, "Glimmer of Hope at the Closing of Inter-faith Meeting," *The Toronto Star* (November 29, 1999), p. A21.
9. Personal Interview.

CHAPTER THREE

1. Brother David with Lela Gilbert, *Walking the Hard Road* (London: Marshall Pickering, 1989), p. 39.
2. Paul Marshall, "Nationalism,", *World Perspectives,* World Evangelical Fellowship, 1996, p. 9.
3. Ibid.

4. Charles W. Colson and Ellen Santilli Vaughn, *Against the Night: Living in the New Dark Ages* (Ann Arbor, MI: Servant/Vine, 1989), p. 33.
5. John Alexander, *The Secular Squeeze* (Downers Grove, IL: InterVarsity Press, 1993).
6. Keith Peters, Family News in Focus, June 24 2004, http://www.family.org/cforum/fnif/news/A0032641.cfm
7. Mark Albrecht, World Evangelism Fellowship Religious Liberty E-mail Conference, October 17, 2001.
8. C.S. Lewis, *Mere Christianity* (New York: Harper Collins Publishers, 2001), p. 35.

CHAPTER FOUR

1. Dr. Cho, message given in Mississauga, ON, 1998.
2. Alice Smith, *Dispelling the Darkness* (Houston: US Prayer Track, 1999), pp. 19-20.
3. Verbal report from Dr. David Wong, Asian Outreach, Hong Kong.
4. Clinton Arnold, *Powers of Darkness: Principalities and Powers in Paul's Letters* (Downers Grove, IL: InterVarsity Press, 1992), p. 99.

CHAPTER FIVE

1. Chart from the Internet: http://www.crossroads.to/text/articles/armorofgod.html/ Artwork by Louise Bass, bassL3 @juno.com
2. Source unknown.

CHAPTER SIX

1. Ivan Antonov, "Survival 101: How to Prepare for Imprisonment," *Prison Bulletin* (1989), p. 13.
2. Georgi Vins, *Let the Waters Roar: Evangelists in the Gulag* (Grand Rapids, MI: Baker Book House, 1989), p. 102.

CHAPTER SEVEN

1. Bill Bright, *The Coming Revival: America's Call to Fast, Pray, and "Seek God's Face"* (Orlando, FL: NewLife Publications, 1995), p. 65.
2. Ibid., p. 192.

CHAPTER EIGHT

1. Ross Patterson, *Heart Cry for China* (Tonbridge, Kent, UK: Sovereign World, 1989), p. 193.

CHAPTER NINE

1. Author unknown.

CHAPTER TEN

1. Author unknown.
2. Greg Laurie, *The Upside Down Church* (Wheaton, IL: Tyndale Publishers, 1999), p. 46.
3. Terry Brand, "God's Love Overcomes," *Open Doors Newsbrief* (July/August 1990), p 3.

CHAPTER ELEVEN

1. Personal Interview with Alice Yuan in Beijing, China, May 1993.
2. Swindoll, "Strengthening Your Grip on Encouragement," *New Wine* (May 1984), p. 24.
3. Charles R. Swindoll, *Strengthening Your Grip* (Waco, TX: Word Books, 1982), p. 48.
4. Georgi Vins, *Let the Waters Roar* (Grand Rapids, MI: Baker Book House, 1989), p. 42.
5. Brian Ross, "Toward an Intimate Fellowship," *Faith Alive*, p. 70.
6. Author unknown.

CHAPTER TWELVE

1. Philip Yancey, *What's So Amazing About Grace?* (Grand Rapids, MI: Zondervan Publishing House, 1997), p. 83.
2. Ed Loving, Bible translator and mission administrator, USA, 2004.
3. Yancey, pp. 88-94.
4. Charles R. Swindoll, *The Grace Awakening* (Dallas: Word Publishing, 1990), pp. 5-14.
5. Ibid., p. 13.
6. Yancey, pp. 219-227.
7. Swindoll, pp. 298-299.

CHAPTER THIRTEEN

1. Author unknown.
2. Author unknown.
3. Brother Andrew, *Is Life So Dear?* (Nashville: Thomas Nelson Publishers, 1985), pp. 14-15.
4. Mel Middleton, Sudan report—newsletter.
5. Thomas C. Oden, "The Church Castro Couldn't Kill," *Christianity Today* (April 25, 1994), p. 19.
6. Author unknown.
7. Patrick Johnstone, *The Church Is Bigger Than You Think* (Great Britain: Christian Focus Publications, 1998), p. 37.

CHAPTER FOURTEEN

1. Author unknown for preceding five points
2. Open Doors World Watch, January 2004, http://www.opendoors.org/content/wwlist.htm

CHAPTER FIFTEEN

1. Author unknown.

CHAPTER SIXTEEN

1. Anne Horton's Women's Group Evaluation of SSTS, Australia, 2004.
2. Personal story from missionary serving in Vietnam.

CHAPTER SEVENTEEN

1. Reg Reimer, "The Church in Adversity,", *Christian Week* (April 23, 1996), p. 10.

CHAPTER EIGHTEEN

1. Author unknown.

CONCLUSION

1. Christine Mallouhi, *Waging Peace on Islam* (Downers Grove, IL: Intervarsity Press, 2000), p. 52.

Index

For More Information on Open Doors

For updated prayer points, or to learn about additional resources and involvement opportunities with the Persecuted Church, please contact your national Open Doors office.

Open Doors
PO Box 53
Seaforth
New South Wales 2092
AUSTRALIA
www.opendoors.org.au

Missao Portas Abertas
Rua do Estilo Barroco, 633
Chacara Santo Antonio
04709-011 - Sao Paulo, SP
BRAZIL
www.portasabertas.org.br

Open Doors
30-5155 Spectrum Way
Mississauga, ON
L4W 5A1
CANADA
www.opendoorsca.org

Åbne Døre
PO Box 1062
DK-7500 Holstebro
DENMARK
www.forfulgt.dk

Portes Ouvertes
BP 139
F-67833 Tanneries
Cedex (Strasbourg)
FRANCE
www.portesouvertes.fr

Open Doors Deutschland
Postfach 1142
DE-65761 Kelkheim
GERMANY
www.opendoors-de.org

Porte Aperte
CP45
37063 Isola Della Scala, VR
ITALY
www.porteaperteitalia.org

Open Doors
Hyerim Presbyterian Church
Street No. 403
Sungne 3-dong
Kandong-gu #134-033
Seoul
KOREA
www.opendoors.or.kr

Open Doors
PO Box 47
3850 AA Ermelo
THE NETHERLANDS
www.opendoors.nl

Open Doors
PO Box 27-630
Mt Roskill
Auckland 1030
NEW ZEALAND
www.opendoors.org.nz

Åpne Dører
Barstolveien 50 F
4636 Kristiansand
NORWAY
www.opendoors.no

Open Doors
PO Box 1573-1155
QCCPO Main
1100 Quezon City
PHILIPPINES

Open Doors
Raffles City Post Office
PO Box 150
Singapore 911705
REPUBLIC OF SINGAPORE
www.opendoors.org/ODS/index.htm

Open Doors
Box 990099
Kibler Park 2053
Johannesburg
SOUTH AFRICA
www.opendoors.org.za

Puertas Abiertas
Apartado 578
28850 Torrejon de Ardoz
Madrid
SPAIN
www.puertasabiertas.org

Portes Ouvertes
Case Postale 267
CH-1008 Prilly
Lausanne
SWITZERLAND
www.portesouvertes.ch/en

Open Doors
PO Box 6
Witney
Oxon 0X29 6WG
UNITED KINGDOM
www.opendoorsuk.org

Open Doors
PO Box 27001
Santa Ana, CA 92799
USA
www.opendoorsusa.org